Guide to Safety at Sports Grounds

Fifth edition

department for
culture, media
and sport

www.tso.co.uk

Published with the permission of the Department for Culture, Media and Sport on
behalf of the Controller of Her Majesty's Stationery Office.

© Crown Copyright 2008
© Football Licensing Authority 2008

Fifth edition: First published 2008

ISBN 978 0 11 702074 0

Printed in the United Kingdom for The Stationery Office.

Contents

Section headings

Diagrams and tables

Preface

This new edition of the *Guide to Safety at Sports Grounds* updates the fourth edition which was published in 1997 following a detailed review that went back to first principles.

That document has generally stood the test of time. Indeed it is regarded as authoritative in many other countries.

However, the past few years have seen a growing emphasis on the use of risk assessment by sports ground management to enable it to identify and implement the measures necessary to ensure the reasonable safety of spectators. This is reflected in the new edition.

While there have been no significant safety failures resulting in the deaths of spectators at any ground in the United Kingdom since the publication of the previous edition, the potential for disaster remains. Tragedies continue to occur in other parts of the world. As many sports become ever more commercially driven, it is timely to remind ground management and its advisors of the danger of complacency and of the need for continual vigilance.

1: How to use this Guide

1.1   Status

The *Guide to Safety at Sports Grounds* is an advisory document for use by competent persons.

It is the distillation of many years of research and experience of the safety management and design of sports grounds.

The *Guide* has no statutory force but many of its recommendations will be made statutory at individual grounds by their inclusion in safety certificates issued under the Safety of Sports Grounds Act 1975 or the Fire Safety and Safety of Places of Sport Act 1987. For guidance on safety certification see the Bibliography.

The advice given in this *Guide* is without prejudice to the application of the appropriate Building Regulations, the Health and Safety at Work etc. Act 1974, and any other relevant legislation.

The information in this *Guide* is intended to provide useful guidance, but it is not a definitive statement applicable in all circumstances. Independent professional advice should be obtained before taking any action or refraining from taking any action on the basis of this information.

1.2   Scope

The Safety of Sports Grounds Act 1975 defines a sports ground as:

'A place where sports or other competitive activities take place in the open air, and where accommodation has been provided for spectators, consisting of artificial structures or of natural structures artificially modified for the purpose.'

The *Guide* applies to the safety of spectators at all sports grounds which meet the above definition, whether or not a safety certificate is in force.

The management of these grounds has a primary responsibility for the safety of spectators, and should therefore apply the recommendations in the *Guide* in order to achieve safe conditions.

Grounds to which the *Guide* applies are likely to include those which stage the following sports. This list is not intended to be comprehensive:

American Football	Horse Racing
Athletics	Lacrosse
Cricket	Motor Racing
Equestrian events	Polo
Football	Rugby (Union & League)
Golf	Speedway Racing
Greyhound Racing	Tennis
Hockey	

1.3   Objective and realistic aims

The objective of the Guide is to provide guidance to ground management, technical specialists such as architects and engineers, and representatives of all relevant authorities, in order to assist them in the assessment of how many spectators can be safely accommodated within a sports ground.

The document also provides guidance on measures intended to improve safety at existing grounds, in terms both of their design and safety management, while taking into account the constraints and difficulties which may exist at these grounds.

In addition, as explained in Section 1.6 below, the *Guide* offers guidance on how to apply good practice in the design and management of new grounds or newly constructed sections of grounds.

When applying the guidance and recommendations in the *Guide*, it should be remembered that the principal objective is "to secure reasonable safety at the sports ground when it is in use for the specified activity" (as stated in section 2(1) of the Safety of Sports Ground Act 1975).

Furthermore, in all assessments, a flexible approach should be maintained to take account of the individual type, function and layout of grounds. The requirements of spectators at horse or greyhound racing tracks, for example, are in many instances fundamentally different from those attending grounds used for football or rugby.

Whatever the sport, it should also be recognised that safety concerns are often directly related to the nature of specific events and the number of spectators attending.

It should also be remembered that the greatest risk to safety is complacency.

1.4   Management responsibility

Responsibility for the safety of spectators lies at all times with the ground management. The management will normally be either the owner or lessee of the ground, who may not necessarily be the promoter of the event.

In discharging its responsibility, the management needs to recognise that safety should not be seen as a set of rules or conditions imposed by others, but rather as standards set from within which reflect a safety culture at the sports ground. A positive attitude demonstrated by the management is therefore crucial in ensuring that safety policies are carried out effectively and willingly.

These policies should take into consideration the safety of all spectators, including, for example, those with disabilities, the elderly, families and children.

Representatives of management cannot, however, be reasonably expected to possess all the technical knowledge and skills required to assess and apply every recommendation in the *Guide*. Management should therefore, whenever required, seek guidance from competent persons who have the relevant qualifications, skills and experience. (For a definition of competent see Glossary.)

Representatives of the local authority with the relevant training and experience, together with police, fire and ambulance officers, will advise management on how to discharge its responsibility, and, in certain circumstances, may require measures to be taken in order to achieve reasonable safety standards. This does not, however, exonerate the ground management from its responsibility for the safety of spectators.

Although the *Guide* is not specifically aimed at risks to spectators from the sport itself, management also has a responsibility to take all necessary precautions to safeguard spectators against the effects of accidents in, or originating from, the activity on the pitch, track, or area of activity. Particular care is needed when the sport entails the use and storage of flammable fuels.

1.5 Achieving a balance

Safety at sports grounds is achieved by establishing a balance between good management and good design.

In this respect, safety at sports grounds cannot be achieved simply by ensuring that individual components of a ground – such as stairways, gangways, seated areas or terraces – are satisfactory in themselves. The inter-relation of these and other components is critical. None can be treated in isolation without consideration of the effect its design and management has upon the other components. They should all be compatible and combine to form a balanced unit.

Good management will not necessarily compensate for poor design and vice versa.

Designers should involve the people who will manage the sports ground to ensure that designs are fit for purpose.

For this reason it is recommended that readers of the *Guide* familiarise themselves with all sections of the document, including those which may strictly be beyond their personal remit.

1.6 New construction

Although not a definitive design guide, it will be noted that this document offers guidance on how to apply good practice in the design and management of new grounds or newly constructed sections of grounds.

Such guidance is highlighted throughout the *Guide* under the following heading:

For new construction:

The guidance is intended to ensure that new construction leads to a higher standard of safety and amenity than can be achieved at grounds already built.

In addition, unless the *Guide* recommends a higher standard, new construction should conform to the current, appropriate Building Regulations.

New construction should also, whenever possible and wherever specified, take into account current British Standards and the recommendations of other relevant advisory documents; for example, the series of Sports Grounds and Stadia Guides. These and other relevant documents are referred to in the appropriate sections, and are further listed in the Bibliography.

Although it is also recommended that, wherever possible, the refurbishment of existing structures should also seek to meet higher standards, it is recognised that this may not always be achievable. However, all refurbishment work should at least meet the standards set in the *Guide*.

1.7 Deviating from the Guide

The Guide seeks to encourage the meeting of achievable standards, particularly for new construction, but does not attempt to provide a universal minimum standard for existing sports grounds.

It may therefore be possible to deviate from individual guidelines without detracting from the overall safety of a sports ground.

However, it is stressed that the recommendations within the *Guide* are based upon research and experience. Deviations from the *Guide* should therefore only be acceptable when considered to be necessary and reasonable. An accumulation of deviations which result in the application of lower standards in relation to any part of the ground or any aspect of its management should be regarded as unacceptable.

It is the responsibility of ground management to ensure that any decision to deviate from the Guide should be recorded, with supporting written evidence, including the details of a risk assessment. If the deviation is then approved (by management and, where a safety certificate is in force, by the local authority), the action taken should strictly adhere to the contents of the written evidence.

It is further stressed that, unless it can be demonstrated that the alternative measures to be taken are able to achieve an equal or greater degree of safety than those recommended in the *Guide*, a capacity lower than the one which would otherwise be permitted will be required. The extent of such a reduction may be severe.

1.8 Revisions to the Guide

Annex D contains a brief summary of the key amendments and new guidance since the Fourth (1997) Edition.

2: Calculating the safe capacity of a sports ground

2.1 The importance of calculating a safe capacity

As stated in Chapter 1, the principal objective of the *Guide* is to provide guidance on the assessment of how many spectators can be safely accommodated within the viewing accommodation of a sports ground used for a sporting event.

This assessment is the most important step towards the achievement of reasonable safety.

The purpose of this chapter is to outline the main factors which must be considered in making an assessment, leading to a calculation of the final safe capacity of each section of the ground.

Clearly the assessments made will differ according to the individual ground and to the type of spectator accommodation being assessed; primarily whether it is for seated or standing accommodation. But the factors to be applied in each case are the same for every ground, regardless of the sport being staged.

Diagrams 2.1 and 2.2 summarise the factors to be assessed for both seated and standing accommodation.

To further illustrate the methods of assessment and calculation, worked examples are also provided in Annex A. However, the details of each step can only be fully understood by a thorough reading of the whole *Guide*.

The assessment and calculation process will require properly detailed plans of the ground, where practical drawn to a scale of 1:200. Wherever possible the physical dimensions should be verified on site.

At the majority of sports grounds, the capacities of each section will be added to establish the final capacity of the ground as a whole. However, as explained in Section 2.12, there are certain grounds – including, for example, those staging horse racing or golfing events – where it may be difficult to calculate the overall capacity of the whole ground. In such cases, however, the final capacities of individual sections of viewing accommodation must still be calculated and occupation levels of all areas determined so that, where necessary, numbers are controlled to ensure they do not exceed a safe occupancy level.

Management must undertake a series of risk assessments (see Sections 3.3e, 3.6, 15.3 and 18.2). These must be taken into account when assessing the (P) and (S) factors (see Section 2.4).

2.2 Applying the capacity calculation

Once the final capacity of a section or of the whole ground is determined (as explained in Section 2.3), under no circumstances should a larger number of spectators be admitted.

If the final capacity is lower than the level management ideally requires, it can only be raised after the necessary remedial work has been completed, and/or the quality of safety management improved, and the area in question then re-assessed.

Similarly, if part of the ground is required to be closed, this must be done. It must not be re-opened for spectator viewing for any reason until the necessary remedial work has been completed to remove the deficiencies which led to its closure, and not before these measures have been approved by the relevant authority.

2.3 Factors to be considered

The common factors which apply to both seated and standing accommodation can be summarised as follows.

a. The entry capacity of the section

The entry capacity is the number of people who can pass through all the turnstiles and other entry points serving the section, within a period of one hour.

b. The holding capacity of the section

This is the number of people that can be safely accommodated in each section.

In the case of seats, this will be determined by the actual number of seats, less any that cannot be used safely owing to seriously restricted views (see Section 12.6) or their inadequate condition (see Chapter 5), and an assessment of the (P) and (S) factors.

(P) and (S) factors are explained in Section 2.4.

In the case of a standing area, this will be determined by a number of features, including crush barrier strengths and layouts (see Chapter 11), areas which offer restricted views, and a further assessment of both the (P) and (S) factors.

c. The exit capacity of the section

This is the number of people that can safely exit from the viewing area of the section under normal conditions (see Chapter 10).

d. The emergency evacuation capacity

This is determined by the emergency evacuation time, which is based largely on the level of risk of the section and its associated emergency evacuation routes (see Chapter 15).

The emergency evacuation capacity is the number of people that can safely negotiate the emergency evacuation routes and reach a place of safety within that set time (see Chapter 10).

e. The final capacity

Having established all the above figures, the final capacity of the section, and thence of the whole ground, will be determined by whichever is the *lowest* figure arrived at for (a), (b), (c) or (d).

Diagrams 2.1 and 2.2 summarise the main steps outlined above.

2.4   The (P) and (S) factors

In order to calculate the holding capacity (as defined in Section 2.3), each part of the ground's viewing accommodation should be assessed according to its physical condition. This assessment is known as the (P) factor.

Similarly, each part of the ground's viewing accommodation should be assessed according to the quality of the safety management of that area. This assessment is known as the (S) factor.

To help in the assessment of the (P) and (S) factors, it is recommended that each should be given a numerical value. This value should be quantified as a factor of between 0.0 and 1.0, as the following examples indicate:

a.   Where the physical condition of the accommodation is of a high standard, a (P) factor of 1.0 should be applied.

b.   Where the physical condition is extremely poor, a factor of 0.0 should be applied. As explained below, this would have the effect of imposing a zero capacity on the area assessed.

c.   An intermediate assessment might result in, for example, a (P) factor of 0.6, or perhaps an (S) factor of 0.8.

While recognising that it is difficult to place specific numerical values on such assessments, it is nevertheless essential and inevitable that some form of quantified assessment be made. It may also be noted that this form of assessment is now widely used in other safety related fields.

Owing to the wide variation of conditions and facilities to be found at sports grounds, the *Guide* does not seek to place specific values on any of the elements that are likely to be considered when assessing (P) and (S) factors. This is because the assessments should not aim to create a cumulative scoring system in which values for individual elements are simply added together.

Instead, the assessment should reflect a considered and reasonable overall judgement of the physical condition or safety management of the area in question, taking full account of all circumstances and the wider guidance in this document.

For example, Sections 12.19 and 12.20 explain the assessment of (P) and (S) factors for seated accommodation. Sections 13.23 and 13.24 provide similar guidance for the assessment of standing accommodation. Worked examples of capacity calculations in Annex A also show how (P) and (S) factors are applied.

The (P) and (S) factors should be reassessed annually and when there is a physical alteration to the sports ground or a change in the nature of the event, safety management structure or personnel. Where a safety certificate is in force the reassessment should be agreed with the local authority.

2.5   Carrying out (P) and (S) factor assessments

It is the responsibility of ground management to ensure that (P) and (S) factors are assessed and, where a safety certificate is in force, that those assessments are agreed in consultation with the local authority.

It is recommended that (P) and (S) factors should be assessed by competent persons with knowledge and understanding of the ground concerned, its operation and the general principles of safety.

It is further recommended that written records of all assessments be kept. Where a safety certificate is in force the assessments should be held with the safety certificate.

Written records of the assessment should identify any deficiencies found, so that these can be acted upon by the ground management, thereby leading to a potential increase of the (P) or (S) factors (which in turn may lead to an increase in the holding capacity).

Similarly, the records will enable any other deficiencies to be monitored, which may in turn require a reduction of the (P) or (S) factors.

2.6 Seated accommodation – calculating the holding capacity

As stated in Section 2.3, one of the figures needed in order to calculate the final capacity is the holding capacity. It should be noted that the holding capacity of a seated area will not automatically correspond with the number of seats provided. The following factors must also be considered:

a. Seats that offer a seriously restricted view (as defined in Section 12.6) should be discounted from the holding capacity.

b. Seats that exceed the numbers permitted between radial gangways in each row (see Section 12.16) may be discounted from the holding capacity.

c. Seats that are damaged, unavailable for use or whose dimensions fall below the specified minimums for seating row depths, seat widths and/or clearways (see Sections 12.13 and 12.14) should be discounted from the holding capacity.

Having established the number of useable seats, (P) and (S) factors must then be applied (see Sections 12.19 and 12.20).

Having established values for both the (P) and (S) factors, the holding capacity of the seated area can thus be calculated as follows:

**holding capacity = the number of useable seats
x (P) or (S), whichever is lower**

It is stressed that the (P) and (S) factors should not be multiplied by each other, but that the lower of the two factors should be applied to the calculation.

2.7 Standing accommodation – calculation process

The calculation of the holding capacity for standing areas is considerably more complicated than for seated areas. As shown in *Diagram 2.2*, three steps are involved:

Step 1: To establish the **available viewing area** (A)

Step 2: To establish the **appropriate density** (D)

Step 3: Using both the above figures, to establish the **holding capacity.**

The three steps are explained in the following sections.

Reference should also be made to the worked examples in Annex A.

2.8 Step 1 – calculating the available viewing area

The available viewing area (A) is not the entire area available for standing spectators. Rather, it consists only of the areas immediately behind crush barriers, less those areas from which only seriously restricted views are possible (see Section 13.12).

The extent of the areas behind crush barriers depends on the strength of those crush barriers, and how far the crush barriers are spaced apart in relation to the angle of slope. For further guidance on the inter-relation of these factors, see *Table 11.2*.

Once the crush barriers have been tested, and the spacings between barriers and the angle of slope measured, the available viewing area can then be calculated, as follows:

a. If, as recommended, the crush barriers are provided continuously between radial gangways, and are designed for the correct loads and spacings according to *Table 11.2*, all areas behind the crush barriers will be considered as the available viewing area (see *Diagram 11.3* and Worked Example 1 in Annex A).

b. If the crush barriers are not continuous between radial gangways, only the areas behind individual crush barriers should be counted, according to the strength of each individual barrier. All other areas must be discounted, even though in practice they will be occupied by standing spectators (see Worked Example 2).

c. The available viewing area must be limited if there is excessive spacing between barriers (see *Table 11.2* and Worked Example 3).

d. Areas immediately behind those crush barriers which have failed the testing procedures outlined in Chapter 11 must also be discounted from the available viewing area.

e. If the crush barriers are not continuous and there are no clearly marked gangways, further areas must be discounted, calculated on the basis of how much space – measured at 1.2m wide – the required number of gangways would take up if provided (see Worked Example 2).

f. Standing areas without crush barriers cannot be considered as safe unless the capacity is set at such a level that the risks are minimised.

    If the standing area has no crush barriers, but has a front barrier (be it a barrier, rail, wall or fence) which meets the horizontal imposed load requirements of a crush barrier, the available viewing area will be limited to the space immediately behind the front barrier, depending on the strength of the barrier (see *Table 11.2*, and Worked Example 4).

g. Where there are no crush barriers, and the front barrier (be it a barrier, rail, wall or fence) does not meet the horizontal imposed load requirements of a crush barrier, it is recommended that the available viewing area does not exceed a depth of 1.5m behind the front barrier. In practical terms this is the equivalent of approximately four persons deep.

    A similar depth limitation should apply to areas of level standing, regardless of the loading of any front barrier. This is because the view of spectator standing beyond this depth is likely to be too seriously restricted (see Worked Example 5).

h. It is recognised that there are standing areas and enclosures at certain sports grounds – such as lawns in front of stands at race courses – which are used for both general circulation and viewing, and where the recommendations provided in paragraphs (f) and (g) above may not be appropriate. These areas might not have any crush barriers or even a front barrier which meets the loading requirement of a crush barrier. However, because the nature of the sport requires that spectators are able to move freely, it is likely that crowds will be spread throughout the area, rather than being concentrated behind the front rails.

In such circumstances, the available viewing area may extend beyond 1.5m behind the front rail, and may cover those parts of the enclosure from which viewing is possible, provided that in order to allow for circulation a significantly reduced (P) factor is applied (as explained in Section 13.20 and Worked Example 6).

If this approach is taken, it must be demonstrated through risk assessment, effective monitoring and appropriate safety management procedures that there is no forward movement or exerted pressure concentrated on the front rails (see Section 11.15). Even if all these measures are implemented a careful assessment should be made of the (P) and (S) factors for each individual division or separate area of viewing accommodation.

It is also stressed that the calculation of capacities for such enclosures should be separate from the calculation of capacities for any seated or standing accommodation adjoining them. Where there is a free-movement of spectators between, for example, a lawn area and a standing terrace, ground management must ensure that neither area is filled beyond its capacity.

It should be noted that in all cases any areas affected by seriously restricted views must still be discounted from the available viewing area.

2.9 Step 2 – calculating the appropriate density

Having established the available viewing area (A) in square metres, this must then be considered in conjunction with the appropriate density (D). The appropriate density is expressed in terms of a number of spectators per 10 square metres.

For the purposes of calculating the capacity of standing areas at sports grounds, the maximum number that can be applied is 47 persons per 10 square metres.

This maximum figure will then be subject to the assessment of the physical condition of the area (P), and the quality of the safety management of the area (S).

As stated in Section 2.4 it is recommended that (P) and (S) factors be quantified as a factor of between 0.0 and 1.0. Guidance on the assessment of (P) factors can be found in Section 13.23, and on (S) factor in Chapters 3 and 4, and Section 13.24.

Having established both the (P) and (S) factors, the appropriate density (D) of the standing area is then calculated using the following formula:

appropriate density (D) = (P) or (S) factor (whichever is lower) x 47

Thus, if both the (P) and (S) factors are 1.0, the appropriate density will be 47 persons per 10 square metres.

If the (P) factor is 0.6 and the (S) factor is 0.9, the appropriate density will be 28.2 persons per 10 square metres; that is, the lower of the two factors (0.6) x 47.

Further examples of the application of (P) and (S) factors are provided in the worked examples in Annex A.

2.10 Step 3 – calculating the holding capacity

Having established the available viewing area (A) and the appropriate density (D), the holding capacity of the standing area can then be calculated using the following formula:

$$\text{holding capacity} = \frac{A}{10} \times D$$

It should be noted that at grounds staging different types of sport, the holding capacity may vary for each sport. For example, the free movement of standing spectators between different areas of viewing accommodation may be permitted at one sporting event but not at another, resulting in a different appropriate density being applied to the calculation (see Section 13.16).

2.11 Establishing the final capacity

As stated in Section 2.3, whether for seated or standing areas, having established the holding capacity of the area, a comparison must then be made between:

a.   the holding capacity

b.   the entry capacity

c.   the exit capacity

d.   the emergency evacuation capacity.

The final capacity of the section or whole ground will be determined by whichever is the lowest figure of the four criteria.

As stated in Section 2.2, once the final capacity of a section, and thence of the whole ground, is determined, in no circumstances should a larger number of spectators be admitted without remedial work and the approval of the relevant authorities.

2.12 Overall capacities

As stated in Section 2.1 , there are certain sports grounds – including, for example, those staging horse racing or golfing events – where it may be difficult to calculate the overall capacity of the whole ground.

Such grounds may contain large areas of open land to which entry by members of the public is not controlled, and where spectators may view the event from areas not strictly designed as viewing accommodation.

In such cases, the capacities of individual, enclosed sections of viewing accommodation must still be calculated, and a risk assessment undertaken to identify the effective monitoring and appropriate safety management procedures necessary to ensure the number entering each section is strictly controlled (see Chapter 7).

Furthermore, ground management is responsible for the safety of spectators in all parts of the ground at all times during the event. It is therefore recommended that it should determine the expected occupation levels of all areas, including open land. Ground management should then ensure that the physical condition and safety management systems and the ingress, egress and emergency evacuation capacity are sufficient for these numbers of spectators. Failing that, management will need to control the number of spectators admitted so as to ensure that this does not exceed a safe occupancy level.

Diagram 2.1 Calculating the capacity of seated accommodation

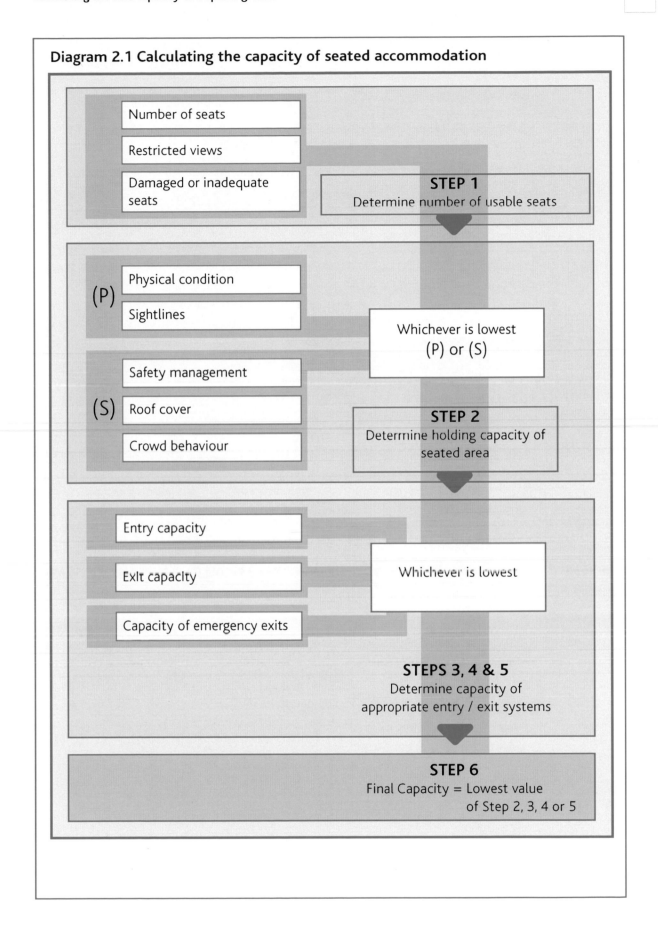

Diagram 2.2 Calculating the capacity of standing accomodation

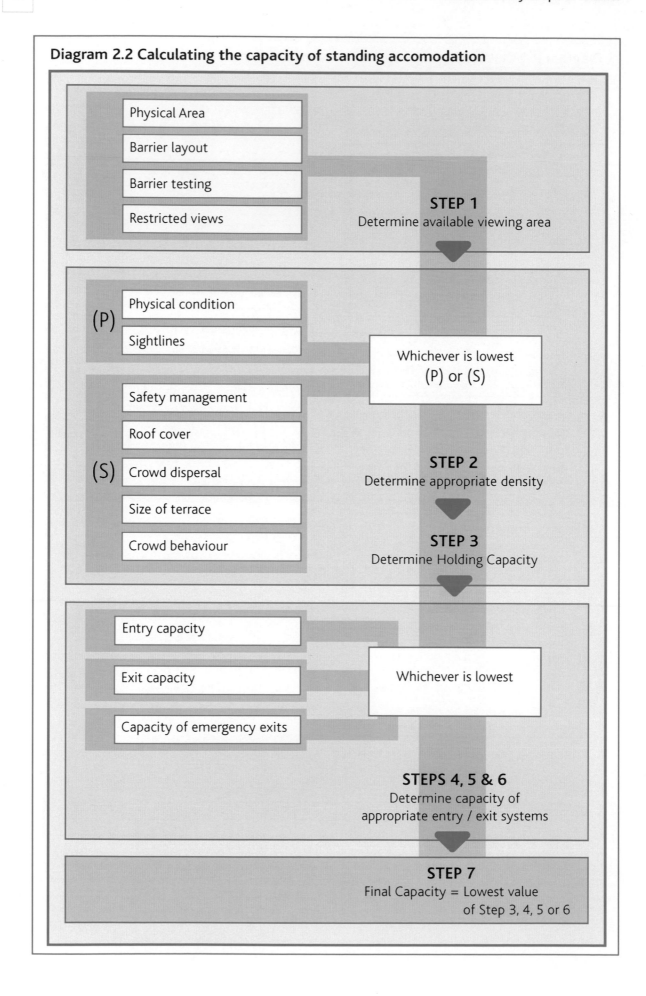

Physical Area

Barrier layout

Barrier testing

Restricted views

STEP 1
Determine available viewing area

(P)

Physical condition

Sightlines

Whichever is lowest
(P) or (S)

Safety management

Roof cover

(S) Crowd dispersal

Size of terrace

Crowd behaviour

STEP 2
Determine appropriate density

STEP 3
Determine Holding Capacity

Entry capacity

Exit capacity

Capacity of emergency exits

Whichever is lowest

STEPS 4, 5 & 6
Determine capacity of
appropriate entry / exit systems

STEP 7
Final Capacity = Lowest value
of Step 3, 4, 5 or 6

3: Management – responsibility and planning for safety

3.1 Management responsibility for safety

As emphasised in Chapter 1, responsibility for the safety of spectators at sports grounds lies at all times with the ground management.

The management will normally be either the owner or lessee of the ground, who may not necessarily be the promoter of the event.

Representatives of the local authority, together with police, fire and ambulance officers, should – preferably through a co-ordinated approach – advise management on how to discharge this responsibility and, in certain circumstances, may require measures to be taken in order to achieve reasonable safety standards. This does not, however, exonerate the ground management from its responsibility for the safety of spectators.

3.2 Demonstrating that responsibility

Safety should not be seen as a set of rules or conditions imposed by others, but rather as standards set from within that reflect a safety culture at the ground.

A positive attitude demonstrated by the ground management is therefore crucial in ensuring that safety policies are carried out effectively and willingly.

3.3 Meeting that responsibility

The detailed management responsibilities described in this chapter and referred to in later chapters fall into the following basic categories, each of which management should address in establishing a safety management structure:

a. Legislation:

Management should be aware of

    i.   the requirements of the safety certificate (if applicable)

    ii.   safety of sports grounds legislation (additional guidance on safety certification is available from the Football Licensing Authority – see Bibliography)

    iii. fire safety legislation (see Section 3.6 and Chapter 15)

    iv. health and safety at work legislation (see Section 3.5)

    v   legislation relating to people with disabilities (see Section 3.7)

    vi   civil contingencies legislation (see Bibliography)

    vii. any other specific pieces of legislation that may have relevant safety implications.

b. Staffing

Management should:

i.   identify those to whom it intends to allocate safety duties

ii.   draw up and keep under review job descriptions for all posts holding safety duties and resource such posts

iii. appoint an occupationally competent (see Section 3.11) safety officer and deputy

iv.   ensure all operational safety related posts are held by appropriately trained and competent persons.

c. Planning

Management should:

i.   draw up a written safety policy for spectators (see Section 3.5.a)

ii   draw up an operations manual (see Glossary)

iii. draw up contingency plans (see Section 3.17)

iv.   agree an emergency procedure plan (see Section 3.20)

v.   agree a statement of intent (see Section 3.24)

vi.   agree procedures for accommodating all spectators, including those with disabilities, the elderly, families and children and, where appropriate, supporters of visiting clubs.

d. Monitoring and records

Management should:

i.   using standard forms, record all incidents and circumstances which have the potential to cause accidents, prioritise and monitor subsequent remedial actions and maintain an audit trail

ii.   conduct periodic safety audits and reviews, in particular after any major event, and draw up any consequent action list

iii. ensure that no other management decisions or policies compromise safety at the sports ground

iv.   maintain records of each event in respect of the event itself, stewarding, the fabric of the ground and first aid and medical provision.

e. Risk assessment

Throughout the *Guide* reference is made to the need for management to conduct risk assessments (see for example Sections 15.3 and 16.18).

Management must carry out site-specific risk assessments for all events including any ancillary activities. Risk assessment should not impose a burden but should encourage the formulation of practical and systematic action plans to reduce the level of risk to spectators.

It is recommended that the assessments should be undertaken by competent persons with the appropriate skills and experience. Specialist advice may need to be sought, but members of the management's safety team should contribute their own experience and knowledge of the ground being assessed, including its operation during events.

Risk assessment should consist of the following steps all of which should be documented:

i.   identify hazards to which spectators may be exposed

ii.   determine which spectators may be harmed and how

iii.   evaluate the risks and decide on the precautions to be taken

iv.   record the findings and implement preventative and/or protective measures

v.   assess and review the adequacy and effectiveness of such measures and revise them where necessary.

Experience has shown that hazardous situations may develop immediately before and during events. These may not have been identified in the pre-event risk assessments. It is therefore recommended that management should implement a system of ongoing risk assessment during the event. This will assist and inform its safety decisions as the event proceeds. Such risk assessments should be documented.

It is recommended that when conducting risk assessments, management should consult with the relevant authorities. Further guidance is available from the Health and Safety Executive and, for fire risk assessments, from the Department for Communities and Local Government (DCLG) and the Scottish Executive (see Bibliography).

3.4   Safety management and the (S) factor

As explained in Section 2.4, the assessment of a ground's capacity should take into account the quality of safety management – that is the (S) factor. An important indicator to be used when determining the (S) factor is the standard to which the safety management structure, as outlined in this chapter, is implemented.

For example, it is not enough to have a written safety policy for spectators. That policy must be fully implemented and understood by all staff. Similarly, a safety officer may have a detailed job description, but may fail to meet its requirements on event days. Contingency plans may have been drawn up, but never tested.

If all the management's safety-related responsibilities are fully met, and the stewarding is of a high standard (see Chapter 4), an (S) factor of 1.0 should be applied.

Where there are deficiencies in any aspect of the safety management, the (S) factor should be reduced accordingly. If appropriate, the (S) factor could be set as low as 0.0, and therefore the capacity of the area in question will be zero.

Management should therefore be aware, that where a safety certificate is in force, its own performance in safety-related matters will have a direct effect on the calculation of the sports ground's capacity.

3.5   Health and safety at work legislation

The safety management of a sports ground and its spectators should not be viewed in isolation, but as part of a total, integrated system for managing health and safety within the organisation as a whole (see Bibliography).

In particular, ground management should be aware of two complementary requirements under health and safety at work legislation:

a. **Written statement of policy**

Organisations with five or more employees must prepare a written statement of their general policy, organisation and arrangements for health and safety at work. While the legislation and its accompanying guidance concentrate on employees, there is an added clause requiring provision for 'other persons resorting to the premises'. This may include contracted staff and media personnel (see Chapters 4 and 19).

b. **Risk assessment**

All employers are required to assess the risk to workers and any others who may be affected by their undertakings. In carrying out such a risk assessment ground management may find it helpful to utilise the recommendations of this *Guide* (see also Section 2.3.e).

3.6   Fire safety legislation

Management should be aware of the requirements of the Regulatory Reform (Fire Safety) Order 2005 (see Bibliography). In particular, it must plan, organise, control, monitor and review the necessary preventive and protective measures and record these arrangements in writing. The Fire (Scotland) Act 2005, as amended, and the Fire Safety (Scotland) Regulations 2006 (see Bibliography), introduced similar requirements in Scotland.

In carrying out fire risk assessments, ground management should refer to Chapter 15 and the DCLG publication *Fire Safety Risk Assessment – Large Places of Assembly* (see Bibliography). For guidance in respect of fire safety in sports grounds in Scotland, reference should be made to the Scottish Executive publication *Practical Fire Safety Guidance for Places of Entertainment and Assembly* (see Bibliography).

3.7   Disability Discrimination Act

Management should be familiar with the Disability Discrimination Act 2005, which requires all providers of goods, facilities and services to take reasonable measures to ensure that they are not discriminating against disabled people (see Bibliography).

Management has a continuing and evolving duty to meet the requirements of the Act. It must also be aware that this duty applies to everyone, whether paid or voluntary, providing services on its behalf.

3.8   Written spectator safety policy

Every ground management should have in place a written spectator safety policy. (In effect, this policy will be an extension of that drawn up in respect of employees under the health and safety at work legislation referred to in Section 3.5 above.)

Such a policy demonstrates that management has devoted thought and effort towards the safety and welfare of spectators. Having to write down the policy helps concentrate the mind. It also shows whether the policy has been fully thought out in practical terms.

The safety policy should:

a. explain management's safety objectives and the means of achieving them

b. be agreed by management and disseminated and explained to all members of staff, contract staff, part-time and voluntary workers

c. demonstrate that from the highest level of management downwards there is a positive attitude to public safety

d. be reviewed by management on an annual basis and revised as necessary.

It is important that the spectator safety policy does not conflict with any conditions of the sports ground's safety certificate (where applicable). For this reason, consultation with the local authority is recommended in the formulation of a spectator safety policy.

3.9 Drawing up a spectator safety policy document

The spectator safety policy document should clearly indicate:

a. the ground management's philosophy on safety

b. with whom lies ultimate responsibility for safety at the ground

c. to whom responsibility is delegated

d. the chain of command

e. how the safety policy is to be implemented and communicated

f. how the safety policy is to be audited, by internal or external means, and reviewed.

The policy document and any subsequent revisions should be signed and dated by the person identified with ultimate responsibility on behalf of ground management.

Advice on how a safety policy document can be drawn up is available from the Football Licensing Authority and the Health and Safety Executive (see Bibliography).

3.10 Chain of command

Management must keep the safety officer informed in good time of all proposals and material works taking place at the sports ground and not make unqualified assumptions about the impact on safety requirements.

In order for the ground management's safety policy to be implemented, it is essential that the policy outlines a personnel structure, or chain of command. This is to ensure that:

a. those having to implement the policy recognise their role within the chain of command and have a clear understanding of the decision making process in safety matters

b. ground management is able to control and supervise the safety management operation

c. spectator safety at the event can be quickly and accurately monitored

d. liaison with other agencies follows agreed procedures

e. follow-up action on structural or safety management issues can be co-ordinated efficiently.

3.11 Appointing a safety officer

Ground management is responsible for appointing an occupationally competent safety officer. This person must be given a detailed job description, clearly identifying the functions of his or her post. It is essential that a safety officer is not given any additional duties on an event day which might reduce his or her effectiveness in the principal role. Nor should the safety officer take on such duties during an event.

Where a safety certificate is in force, the local authority should be informed of the appointment. If the safety officer cannot effectively carry out his or her duties in full the (S) factor should be reduced.

Although the appointment of a safety officer may be on a part-time basis, experience has shown that employment on event days only can result in too onerous a workload. Safety officers must not be assigned on the day to events where they have had no input into the safety management planning.

3.12   Requirements of a safety officer

In order to discharge properly his or her responsibilities, a safety officer should meet the following requirements:

a.   Competence

A person will be regarded as occupationally competent (see Glossary) for the role of safety officer when he or she has sufficient training, experience and knowledge, to be able to implement the functions detailed in the job description.

It is recommended that a safety officer should as a minimum have, or be working towards, a level 4 spectator safety qualification on the relevant qualification framework.

b.   Status

The safety officer should be recognised as being in overall control of operational safety management issues on an event day. On non-event days, the safety officer should be regarded as a principal adviser to the ground management on all spectator-related safety issues.

c.   Authority

On event days, a safety officer must have the authority to make safety-related decisions without having to refer to senior management or board members.

d.   Accountability and access to management

A safety officer should be directly accountable to the person with ultimate responsibility to safety, to whom the right of direct access is essential.

e.   Identification and communication

On event days it is essential that the safety officer is easily identifiable, and can be contacted immediately at all times. If it is necessary during an event for the safety officer to leave the control point (see Chapter 16), a competent person should be left on duty in the control point. The safety officer should also remain in direct contact with that person, either by radio or telephone.

3.13   Deputising

Because of the key role played by a safety officer, it is essential that he or she has a deputy with sufficient training, experience, and knowledge to serve in the safety officer's absence and to share duties on event days.

It is recommended that the deputy should have, or be working towards, a level 4 spectator safety qualification on the relevant qualification framework.

Deputies should also be appointed for other key supervisory roles in the chain of command.

3.14   Staffing – risk assessment

While members of the public are inside the sports ground, it is the responsibility of management to ensure that sufficient safety staff are on duty.

A detailed risk assessment should be undertaken for each event before determining the final number, location and duties of safety staff (stewards). The risk assessment should include consideration of the following factors:

a. audience profile

b. any perceived increase or decrease in risk

c. duration of the event

d. changes to the sports ground, for example the erection of temporary structures.

3.15 Stewarding plan

Staffing numbers will vary considerably at each ground, according to its size and configuration, and the nature of the event. However, experience has shown that by ensuring the availability of staff for the following categories, management should meet the needs of most sports grounds, matches or events:

a. supervisory staff: for example, the deputy safety officer, chief steward(s) and supervisors

b. static posts: for example, crowd monitoring points, exits, activity area perimeter gates, escalators and other strategic points or areas

c. mobile posts; typically a ratio of one steward per 250 of the anticipated attendance

 This ratio should be increased to up to one per 100 of the anticipated attendance where the risk assessment shows a need for a higher level of safety management, for example at a high profile event or where there are large numbers of children or where there is a likelihood that large numbers of spectators will not comply with safety instructions.

d. specialist stewards: for example, for areas used by children or spectators with disabilities

e. additional stewards: if needed for deployment in particular circumstances or for particular events.

Other staff, such as car park attendants and turnstile operators, may also be deployed for stewarding and other safety duties, provided that the conditions set out in Section 4.3 are met.

However, unless they form a recognised part of the safety management structure, individuals such as members of groundstaff, security guards, hospitality staff and commissionaires should not be counted among the safety staff.

The number of stewards occupying static posts and the location of these posts together with the number of mobile posts should be clearly recorded in writing in a stewarding plan. The number of stewards provided should not fall below the minimum number identified in this plan.

Further information on stewarding is provided in Chapter 4.

3.16 Responsibility for training and competence

Ground management has the responsibility for ensuring that all safety personnel whether in-house or provided under contract are competent and, where not already qualified, have received sufficient training (see Section 4.8) to carry out the duties and responsibilities assigned to them.

3.17 Contingency plans

Ground management should assess the risk of any incident occurring at the sports ground which might prejudice public safety or disrupt normal operations; for example, fire, power cuts, bomb threats, delayed starts or crowd disorder. (For a suggested list of headings, see Section 3.18).

Such incidents often arise with little or no warning and may not be capable of being dealt with by the management operating under normal conditions. Management should therefore prepare contingency plans to determine specific actions and/or the mobilisation of specialist resources.

The contingency plans should be reviewed both annually and after any incident, significant near miss or exercise. Following the review the contingency plans should be presented to the board of directors (or equivalent body) for ratification.

Contingency plans should lay down a structured and graduated response with clear guidelines on the measures to be adopted in particular circumstances, bearing in mind both internal and external factors specific to the individual sports ground.

Exercises to test contingency plans must be staged at least once a year in consultation with the relevant authorities and emergency services.

It is essential that the safety officer, deputy and appropriate stewards have a full working knowledge of all of the contingency plans. The procedures set out within contingency plans should also be made familiar to all staff at the sports ground, not only to those with specific safety-related duties.

Guidance on contingency planning is available from the Football Licensing Authority (see Bibliography).

3.18 Suggested headings for contingency plans

The contents of contingency plans will vary according to the type of sports ground, its location and the nature of matches or events being staged. However, experience has shown that the following headings can be adopted to suit most situations:

a. Fire

b. Bomb threat, suspect package, terrorist attack (including chemical, biological, radiological or nuclear)

c. Buildings and services

    i. damage to structures

    ii. power cut or failure

    iii. passenger lift or escalator failure

    iv. gas leak or chemical incident

d. Safety equipment failure

    i. turnstile counting mechanism

    ii. closed circuit television

    iii. public address system

    iv. electronic information boards

      v.   stewards' radio system

      vi. internal telephone systems

      vii. fire warning and other fire safety systems

   e. Crowd control

      i.   surging or crushing

      ii. pitch incursion

      iii. late arrivals or delayed start

      iv. lock outs including progressive turnstile closure

      v.   disorder inside the ground

      vi. large scale ticket forgery

   f. Emergency evacuation

   g. Severe adverse weather

   h. Ticketing strategy in the event of an abandoned fixture

   i.   Features/considerations specific to the location

3.19 Counter-terrorism

Terrorism can come in many forms. These may include not merely physical attacks but attacks on vital information or communication systems, causing disruption and economic damage, and threats or hoaxes designed to frighten and intimidate.

If there is an increased risk of terrorist activity at a particular venue, because of either a specific threat to the event or general threats or incidents elsewhere, it may be necessary to search spectators more thoroughly prior to entry. This may require extra temporary arrangements and the deployment of additional resources on the approaches to the turnstiles or entry points, which in turn may reduce the rate at which spectators can enter. Spectators likely to be affected should be warned in advance of the potential delays.

Measures designed to counter terrorism should be integrated wherever possible with existing contingency and emergency plans.

For detailed guidance refer to *Counter Terrorism Protective Security Advice for Stadia and Arenas* produced by the National Counter Terrorism Security Office (see Bibliography).

Specific advice relating to a particular sports ground can be sought from specialist advisers through the local police service.

It should be emphasised that security measures must never compromise spectator safety.

3.20 Emergency plan

An emergency plan (also known as an emergency procedure plan or major incident plan) is prepared and owned by the emergency services for dealing with a major incident occurring at the sports ground or in the vicinity (for example, an explosion, toxic release or large fire).

Although contingency plans are prepared by the ground management and the emergency plan is prepared by the emergency services, the two plans must be compatible.

Consultation must therefore take place between ground management, the police, fire and ambulance services, the local health authority and local authority, in order to produce an agreed plan of action, including access for emergency vehicles, for all foreseeable incidents (see also Section 18.13).

3.21   Safety audit

In addition to the inspections and tests recommended in Chapter 5 and the routine monitoring of safety performance through inspection and surveillance, it is the responsibility of management to ensure that a safety audit is carried out at least once a year. The intention of an audit is to make a deeper and more critical appraisal of all elements of the safety management systems.

Such audits should be conducted by persons who are, preferably, independent of the systems being audited, but who may be from within the organisation.

When assessing the (S) factor of a sports ground, the relevant authority may wish to be aware of the content of the safety audit report.

3.22   Keeping records for each event

Management is responsible for keeping records of each event, including:

a. details of all pre-event inspections (as listed in Section 5.9 and 5.10)

b. details of the pre-event briefing (see Section 4.14) and, where appropriate, any training given to stewards

c. the number of spectators admitted to the ground, and, where appropriate, to each section of the ground (see Chapter 7)

d. the numbers and posts of all first aiders and doctor(s) in attendance (see Chapter 18)

e. incident forms recording any accident or incident which might have led to an accident (see Section 4.16 and 18.14)

f. details of all first aid or medical treatment provided, while preserving medical confidentiality regarding the identity of those treated (see Section 18.14)

g. details of all emergency drills or evacuation exercises plus any incident which tested the contingency plans

h. details of any non-routine opening of an exit door or gate

i. details of any assumption of control by the police

j. details of any defects relating to the safety of the ground arising from the event, plus details of any remedial action taken

k. reports of any significant motion of the structure (see Section 5.5)

l. details of all fires and fire alarm activations

m. details of all emergency systems failures

The above list is for guidance only and is not intended to be comprehensive in all circumstances.

3.23 Policing

While responsibility for the safety of spectators lies at all times with ground management, at certain sports grounds and for certain matches or events the presence of the police may be required to maintain public order and prevent the commission of offences.

Management should give all possible assistance to the police and provide reasonable facilities for the police within the control point.

Dependent upon the event taking place at the sports ground, it may be beneficial to provide other additional facilities, such as a detention room and an area for briefing.

Police officers are not present to overcome inadequacies in safety management. Their presence should not in itself be a justification for raising a ground's capacity.

Whether there is a police presence or not, responsibility for the enforcement of ground regulations remains with the management.

3.24 Statement of intent

If there is to be a police presence in or at the sports ground, management should discuss with the police the division of responsibilities and functions between the two parties; for example, whether particular posts are to be staffed by stewards or by police officers, and who will assume responsibility in particular circumstances.

The outcome of these discussions should be recorded in a statement of intent.

It is emphasised that the statement of intent is a management statement and not a legal document. It does not constitute a conscious or implied request for police services.

3.25 Accommodating visiting supporters

At sports grounds where supporters of visiting clubs or teams attend, advance planning between the ground management, the visiting club or team and the police is essential to ensure that such supporters are:

a.   directed and welcomed to the ground

b.   directed to the appropriate entrances

c.   accommodated safely

d.   always kept clearly informed of any special arrangements made for them inside the ground and on their departure.

Liaison between the management and police may be necessary to ensure that the likely numbers of visiting supporters is known. In consultation with the police, management should also determine clear policies on the accommodation of home and visiting groups of supporters, and on appropriate ticketing arrangements. There should be debriefing meetings to evaluate these arrangements and, if necessary, formulate changes for future events.

When a large number of spectators are expected from a non-English speaking country, management should provide verbal or written information in the language of the visiting supporters.

3.26 Segregation

If ground management adopts a policy of segregating groups of supporters, the arrangements for admitting spectators should be drawn up in consultation with the local authority and police, and be carefully controlled to ensure as far as possible that segregation is effective.

Each segregated area must have its own independent means of egress or evacuation (see Chapter 10).

Where considered necessary, a neutral or sterile zone may be provided between groups of supporters. However, in all cases it is recommended that the method of segregation used should be flexible (see Section 12.20).

Management should ensure that each segregated area offers full access to sufficient toilet and catering facilities. It should not be necessary for spectators in segregated areas to have to cross barriers or seek special permission to use such facilities (see also Chapter 9). Management should also ensure that wherever possible sufficient viewing accommodation and facilities are provided in each segregated area for disabled spectators.

3.27 Ejection and detention

Ground management should, in consultation with the police, draw up clearly defined procedures for the ejection and/or detention of persons who commit offences within the sports ground.

In drawing up this policy particular regard should be paid to the treatment and care of those under 18 and vulnerable adults.

3.28 Safety in the wider management context

As stated in Section 3.2, safety should not be seen as a set of rules or conditions imposed by others, but as standards set from within which reflect a safety culture at the ground. In addition, the safety management of a ground and its spectators should not be viewed in isolation.

By a process of consultation therefore, all branches of the ground management and event day personnel should be aware, or be made aware, of the safety implications arising from their own actions and policies.

The main areas of policy are outlined in the following four sections.

3.29 Ticketing

Admission policies adopted by the ground management can have a direct effect on the safe management of spectators.

a. Where a capacity or near capacity attendance is expected for an event, admission should normally be by ticket or electronic entry card only.

b. Tickets for seats which offer restricted views or are uncovered should be marked accordingly, and the buyer forewarned (see Sections 12.6, 12.8, 13.12 and 13.14).

c. Tickets for seats with severely restricted views should not be sold.

d. The entry card or that part of the ticket retained by the spectator after passing through a ticket control point or turnstile should clearly identify the location of the accommodation for which it has been issued.

e.   A simplified, understandable ground plan should be shown on the reverse side of the ticket or, where admission is by entry card, shall be provided at the time of purchase (see also Section 7.9.f).

f.   Colour coding of tickets or entry cards, corresponding to different sections of the ground, should be considered (see also Section 7.9).

g.   Stewards should be familiar with the ground plan and able to direct spectators to any other section of the ground (see Chapter 4).

h.   Management should ensure that all sections of the ground, all aisles, rows and individual seats, are clearly marked or numbered, as per the ground plan and ticketing information.

For further details of ticket-related matters, see Sections 7.10 and 12.20.

3.30   Sale of refreshments

In order to ensure that circulation areas are kept clear of trip hazards, and to minimise the risk of fire, adequate receptacles should be available for the disposal and collection of all waste and litter resulting from the sale of refreshments.

All refreshments sold in general spectator areas should be served in soft containers. Hard containers such as glasses, bottles or cans can constitute a danger in congested areas, and may even be used as missiles.

Hot drinks should be dispensed in suitable containers preferably with appropriate lids, so as to minimise the risk of scalding or burns to spectators.

3.31   Alcohol

The possession and consumption of alcohol is controlled by current legislation in England and Wales (see Bibliography) at the following sporting events:

a.   any association football matches in which one or both of the participating teams represents a club which is for the time being a member (whether a full or associate member) of the Football League, the Football Association Premier League, the Football Conference National Division, the Scottish Football League or Welsh Premier League, or represents a country or territory; or

b.   any association football matches in the competition for the Football Association Cup (other than in a preliminary or qualifying round).

At these events it is an offence to:

c.   possess alcohol or to be drunk whilst entering, or trying to enter, the ground

d.   be drunk inside the ground

e.   in general spectator areas, to possess alcohol in any part of the ground that offers sight of the pitch during the period commencing two hours before the start of the match and finishing one hour after the end of the match

f.   in hospitality boxes and other rooms which overlook the pitch, to possess alcohol during the period commencing 15 minutes before the start of the match and finishing 15 minutes after the end of the match

g.   be in possession of bottles, cans or other portable containers which are for holding drink and which, when empty, are normally thrown away or returned to the supplier and which are capable of causing injury to a person struck by them. This applies to any spectator entering or trying to enter the ground, and any spectators in any area of the ground from which the event may be directly viewed.

There is also legislation in Scotland (see Bibliography) which prohibits the provision and consumption of alcohol within spectator areas inside Scottish football grounds and allows, in limited circumstances, the provision and consumption in hospitality areas provided the view of the pitch is obscured.

3.32   Commercial or non-sporting activities

Management has a direct responsibility to ensure that commercial or non-sporting activities do not in any way compromise safety at the ground, either by creating any physical obstructions, hindering the safety operation or endangering spectators.

Areas of concern include:

a.   advertising hoardings, loudspeakers, media installations or any other item, permanent or temporary, whose height, bulk or placement might obstruct sightlines and/or block emergency gates or openings

b.   high volume and lengthy musical presentations which interrupt normal communications between safety personnel at key moments

c.   firework and other pyrotechnic presentations

d.   excitation of a structure by the activities of spectators (see Section 5.5).

Guidance on the safety implications of media provision is provided in Chapter 19. The use of grounds for events other than sporting events is covered in Chapter 20.

3.33   Pre-event activities

All pre-event activities should be the subject of a site specific risk assessment.

For example, it has become common practice for players to go onto the field of play to warm up. As spectators may not be watching or paying attention to the activity, consideration should be given to the protection of spectators during this period. The provision of protective netting, notices and/or announcements over the public address system may reduce the possibility of spectators being injured by balls during the warm-ups.

At grounds such as certain racecourses, where spectators have access to or cross the area of activity, management will need to ensure that they are not doing so at times when they might be at risk, for example from horses cantering up to the start.

Management should ensure that the use and behaviour of mascots, whether children accompanying players onto the playing area or club mascots in fancy dress, do not adversely affect the safety of spectators.

3.34   Other management responsibilities

In addition to the responsibilities for safety outlined in this and the following two chapters on management, the attention of ground management is also drawn to the following:

a.   the requirements of fire safety (see Chapter 15)

b.   first aid and medical provision (see Chapter 18)

c.   site traffic management plan

Management should ensure that its site traffic plan co-ordinates with the local authority's overall traffic management plan for the adjoining areas. The traffic management plan should also cover staff training and personal protective equipment. Further guidance is available from the Health and Safety Executive.

d. the specific requirements and criteria of particular international and national sporting bodies and tournament organisers. Note, however, that the advice in the *Guide* should take precedence over such requirements and criteria.

3.35 Notifying the local authority

Where a safety certificate is in force in respect of the sports ground or stand(s) within the ground, the management should ensure that details of all consultations, arrangements and plans between them and the police, fire, ambulance services and with the local health authority, are notified to the local authority.

4: Management – stewarding

4.1   The need for stewards
Effective safety management requires the employment, hire or contracting of stewards in order to assist with the circulation of spectators, prevent overcrowding, reduce the likelihood and incidence of disorder, and provide the means to investigate, report and take early action in an emergency. In carrying out these duties, stewards should always be aware of, and ensure the care, comfort and well-being of all categories of spectators.

4.2   Agreement on responsibilities
Where an event requires the presence of police officers, the duties and responsibilities of stewards should be agreed between the ground management and the police. This agreement should form part of the written statement of intent (see Section 3.24).

4.3   Definition of a steward
A steward (also referred to at certain sports grounds as a marshal) is a person who has obtained a level 2 stewarding qualification within the relevant qualifications framework, or is undergoing training and assessment for such a qualification, and who is employed or contracted by management to act in accordance with the general recommendations of the *Guide*, and, where appropriate, the specific requirements of the safety certificate.

As stated in Section 3.15, other staff, such as car park attendants and turnstile operators may also be deployed for stewarding and safety duties, provided that:

a.   they have obtained a level 2 stewarding qualification within the relevant qualification framework, or are undergoing training and assessment for such a qualification (see Section 4.8)

b.   they are appropriately attired, equipped and briefed

c.   minimum stewarding numbers as identified in the safety certificate or the ground management's own stewarding plan are maintained at all times.

Individuals such as ground staff, security guards, hospitality staff and commissionaires should not be considered as stewards, unless suitably trained and qualified as such.

4.4   Security personnel
Stewards and CCTV operators who undertake licensable conduct, as defined in the Private Security Industry Act 2001, also require a licence from the Security Industry Authority, save in the following circumstances. The Violent Crime Reduction Act 2006 removes this requirement for in-house personnel at sports grounds in England and Wales where a safety certificate from the local authority is in force for all or part of the ground, provided that these personnel are engaged in conduct for which the safety certificate has effect.

In the case of visiting stewards (see Section 4.13) the sports ground at which they are employed in-house must also have a safety certificate from the local authority.

In Scotland any steward or CCTV operator undertaking licensable conduct requires a licence from the Security Industry Authority.

Further detailed guidance is available from the Security Industry Authority (see Bibliography).

4.5 Appointment of stewards

Stewards should be fit and active with the maturity, character and temperament to carry out the duties required of them. They should be able to understand and communicate verbal and written instructions in English.

Applicants should be interviewed and, where necessary, tested before appointment to ascertain that they meet these requirements.

4.6 Stewards' status and remuneration

Although stewards are appointed on a part-time basis, they are an integral part of the safety management team, a status which should be made known to them and reinforced by the positive attitude of ground management.

Experience shows that the standard and quality which management can expect from stewards is likely to be linked to the remuneration and general level of consideration they receive. This may affect not only the stewards' performance on event days but also their willingness to attend training sessions.

Stewards' responsibilities are considerable, and at times onerous. The level of payment should reflect this. In return, management can expect a higher standard of applicant and a greater level of commitment.

4.7 Duties of stewards

While these may vary, depending on the size and configuration of the ground and the nature of the event, the basic duties of stewards (whether in-house, hired or contracted) should be to enforce the management's safety policy, the requirements of the safety certificate, where applicable, and all ground regulations.

There are ten basic duties for stewards, summarised as follows:

a. to understand their general responsibilities towards the health and safety and welfare of all spectators, other stewards, ground staff and themselves

b. to carry out safety checks

c. to control or direct spectators who are entering or leaving the ground, to help achieve an even flow of people to and from the viewing areas

d. to assist in the safe operation of the ground, not to view the activity taking place

e. to staff entrances, exits and other strategic points; for example, segregation, perimeter and exit doors or gates which are not continuously secured in the open position while the ground is in use

f. to recognise crowd conditions so as to ensure the safe dispersal of spectators and the prevention of overcrowding, particularly on terraces or viewing slopes

g. to assist the emergency services as required

h. to provide basic emergency first aid

i.   to respond to emergencies (such as the early stages of a fire); to raise the alarm and take the necessary immediate action

j.   to undertake specific duties in an emergency or as directed by the safety officer or the appropriate emergency service officer.

This list is for guidance only and is not intended as a substitute for training leading to a nationally recognised qualification. For details of such training and further references for stewards' duties, see Bibliography.

4.8   Training

It is the responsibility of management to ensure that all safety personnel, whether employed in-house or under contract, are trained and competent to undertake both their normal duties and their roles under its emergency and contingency plans. The training should also cover the specific needs of vulnerable and juvenile spectators.

Training must be conducted by occupationally competent persons using suitable training resources and material that will provide the relevant underpinning knowledge to satisfy the requirements of the National Occupational Standards for those relevant vocational qualifications.

During the training programme, stewards should be assessed by occupationally competent assessors to demonstrate their competency against the National Occupational Standards and performance criteria of the relevant vocational qualification.

It is recognised that, at any given time, some stewards will probably not have had the opportunity to complete their training and assessment. However no steward should be deployed at the sports ground until they have undertaken all aspects of relevant familiarisation and induction training. Stewards should not work unaccompanied until they have satisfied the following criteria:

a.   they have received training to provide the underpinning knowledge for the following units in the National Occupational Standards for Spectator Safety:

  i.   C29 – Prepare for spectator events

  ii.   C35 – Deal with accidents and emergencies

  iii.   C210 – Control the entry, exit and movement of people at spectator events.

b.   they have attended four events as a steward.

All stewards should complete their training, assessment and qualification within 12 months thereafter.

Supervisors should receive additional training that develops their skills and competencies especially when responding to unplanned incidents. It is recommended that supervisors hold a level 3 spectator safety qualification on the relevant qualification framework.

All training and assessment records must be complete and fully maintained to ensure the training and assessments can be verified by the relevant awarding body and, where a safety certificate is in force, the local authority.

Where there are significant numbers of unqualified stewards undergoing training the (S) factor should be reduced.

4.9 Contract or agency stewards

Management should ensure that the contract or service level agreement with agencies or external bodies for the supply of stewards specifies:

a. the stewards' duties and responsibilities

b. their required training and qualifications

c. where appropriate, the number who must be fully qualified and the number who may still be undergoing training and assessment

d. the records to be maintained and supplied to management by the agency or external body.

4.10 Code of conduct for stewards

Stewards are representatives of the management, and during many events are the only point of contact between the management and the public. It is therefore recommended that management draw up a code of conduct for all stewards.

A code of conduct might include the following matters:

a. Stewards should at all times be polite, courteous and helpful to all spectators, regardless of their affiliations.

b. Stewards should at all times be smartly dressed. Their appearance should be clean and tidy.

c. Stewards are not employed, hired or contracted to watch the event. They should at all times concentrate on their duties and responsibilities.

d. Stewards should never:

    i. wear clothing that may appear partisan or may cause offence while on duty

    ii. celebrate or show extreme reaction to the event

    iii. eat, drink or smoke in view of the public

    iv. consume alcohol before or during the event

    v. use obscene, offensive or intimidatory language or gestures.

4.11 Control and communication

The stewarding operation should be co-ordinated from the ground's control point, which should maintain an efficient means of communication with the stewards and/or their supervisors (see Chapter 16).

4.12 Identification

Experience shows that spectators react more favourably towards stewards who are readily identifiable. It is also important that stewards are easily identifiable by fellow stewards and safety personnel. All stewards should therefore be provided with high-visibility, weather-proof jackets or tabards which meet current safety standards or some other clearly visible means of identification. Armbands alone are not acceptable.

The stewards' jackets or tabards should clearly indicate the duty performed by the steward; for example, safety officer, chief steward, supervisor, steward or car park steward.

The jacket or tabard should also carry a unique number, by which each supervisor or steward can be identified.

4.13   Visiting stewards

There are certain matches or events where it may be beneficial to invite suitably trained and qualified stewards from visiting clubs or organisations. Such stewards must arrive before the ground is open to the public and in time to be fully briefed as to the construction and configuration of the ground, the safety arrangements and their specific duties.

4.14   Briefing

The briefing of stewards forms a necessary component of effective safety management. Arrangements for this will vary according to the number of stewards involved. If the total number does not exceed 50 it may be possible for all stewards to be briefed together, by the safety officer or chief steward. Where there are more than 50 stewards on duty, experience shows that it may be more beneficial to use cascade briefings where the safety officer or chief steward brief supervisors, who then brief their individual sections.

An accurate record of briefings should be kept. For this reason it is recommended that they are scripted by the safety officer and retained with the post-event summary (see also Sections 3.3.d and 3.22).

4.15   De-briefing

A de-brief of stewards is also necessary, to ensure that any incidents or problems are referred to the safety officer for follow-up action. As with briefing, the arrangements for the de-briefing will vary according to the number of stewards involved.

As part of the de-briefing procedure, incident forms should be completed by stewards and handed to the supervisor, chief steward or safety officer.

4.16   Stewards' documentation – safety handbook

Every steward should be fully appraised in writing of his or her duties and responsibilities. This can be achieved by the issue of a safety handbook.

A suggested list of headings is as follows:

a.   introduction to the sports ground; its layout and management

b.   general requirements of stewards

c.   communication and radio call signs

d.   duties before event

e.   duties during event

f.   duties after event

g.   emergency procedures

h.   training

i.   contingency plans (see Section 3.18 for headings)

j.   ground regulations

k.   fire precautions and fire fighting

l.   specific responsibilities (according to role or duties)

m.   code of conduct

n.   plans of ground

o.   positioning of key point telephones and fire safety points

p.   notes.

4.17 Stewards' documentation – checklist

The duties and responsibilities of a steward may also be summarised on a simple checklist or 'aide-memoire' card, to be issued to all stewards for carrying during the event. The contents of this checklist should follow a standard format, as established in the safety handbook. All such stewards' documentation should be available for inspection by authorised persons.

4.18 Training exercises

Exercises should be carried out on a regular basis, and at least annually, to ensure that procedures laid out in the contingency plans operate smoothly. Records should be kept of the duration of the exercise, of the instruction provided and of the personnel involved. At least 14 days' notice of the intention to hold such exercises should be given to the local authority (where a safety certificate is in force), and the emergency services.

4.19 Keeping records

It is important to retain an accurate record of all training sessions, assessments and briefings. In addition, a records or profile form should be maintained of each steward. The type of information to be recorded should include:

a.   name, age, address, and contact numbers

b.   relevant professional and vocational qualifications (for example, fire-fighter or first aider)

c.   training sessions attended

d   matches or events attended

e.   duties or position in the ground for each event

f.   assessment of progress.

Such records should be readily available for inspection by authorised persons.

4.20 Stewarding and the (S) factor

As explained in Sections 2.4 and 3.4 the assessment of a sports ground's capacity should take into account the quality of safety management – that is, the (S) factor.

An important indicator to be used when determining the (S) factor is the standard of stewarding.

It is the responsibility of management to assess the stewarding, and, where a safety certificate is in force, agree that assessment with the local authority. The assessment should be based on the requirements outlined in this chapter.

Where the safety management structure meets the requirements set out in Chapter 3, and the stewarding is of a high standard, an (S) factor of 1.0 should be applied. Where the stewarding is poor – for example, there are insufficient numbers of stewards in attendance or stewards are not attending to their duties – the (S) factor should be reduced.

Records should be carefully kept so that:

a.   deficiencies which have been identified and recorded can be acted upon and the stewarding operation improved, thereby increasing the (S) factor

b.   further deficiencies can be identified and monitored, thereby possibly entailing a reduction in the (S) factor.

5: Management – structures, installations and components

5.1 Definitions

For the purpose of this *Guide* the term structures includes seated and standing accommodation, whether permanent or temporary, roofs, floodlight pylons, stairways, barriers, boundary walls and fences.

Examples of installations include mechanical and electrical systems, public address systems and fire detection systems

Examples of components include seats, signs, fixtures and fittings.

5.2 Maintenance and the (P) factor

It is the responsibility of management to assess the (P) factor for each section of viewing accommodation, and, where a safety certificate is in force, agree those assessments with the local authority. An important indicator to be used when determining the (P) factor is the standard of maintenance (see Sections 2.1 and 2.5).

If all structures, installations and safety-related components at the ground are maintained in good condition and working order, a (P) factor of 1.0 should be applied.

Where there are deficiencies, the (P) factor should be reduced accordingly.

If appropriate, the (P) factor could be set as low as 0.0, and therefore the capacity of the area in question will be zero.

It is imperative therefore that maintenance procedures for both new and existing structures are properly understood. It is further recommended that a system of planned maintenance be adopted. Where necessary, professional advice on this matter should be sought from competent persons.

It is also essential that maintenance is carried out in accordance with the written instructions provided by the designer or manufacturer.

For new construction: the provision of operating and maintenance manuals detailing the expected life cycles of components should be a necessary part of the completion of any new project. This is notwithstanding any separate tests and inspection periods which may be recommended below or form part of the annual inspection.

The maintenance of new structures may be equally, or even more onerous than that of existing structures. Management should be aware that the provision of a new structure does not reduce its responsibility for the maintenance of a safe structure.

A planned preventative maintenance schedule and its implementation demonstrate that the management is taking its responsibilities for maintenance seriously. They may also be relevant when assessing the overall (S) factor.

5.3   Good housekeeping

In addition to maintenance, several of the recommendations listed in this chapter might otherwise be described as elements of 'good housekeeping'.

As stated in Section 3.2, it is emphasised that safety should not be seen as a set of rules or conditions imposed by others, but rather as standards set from within which reflect a safety culture at the sports ground.

Good housekeeping is a fundamental part of fostering and maintaining a safety culture at the sports ground.

Management should therefore demonstrate a positive attitude in this respect, and in doing so, encourage a conscientious, co-operative and vigilant attitude among all members of staff.

In particular, all staff must identify and report to management at an early stage any problem which might compromise safety, be it relating to the structures at the ground, its systems, facilities or equipment.

Their efforts and, if appropriate, suggestions, should always be acknowledged, and they should be informed of any resultant remedial action.

A positive attitude towards good housekeeping should also be communicated to visiting personnel and outside contractors (see also Section 5.6).

5.4   Structures

All structures at sports grounds should be safe, serviceable and durable at all times during their use, and where necessary, fire-resistant. They should comply with statutory requirements, including those for health and safety at work. In this context management and designers should be familiar with their responsibilities under the Construction (Design and Management) Regulations 2007 Regulations (see Bibliography).

In order to be safe, a structure should be capable of resisting all loads in service (including sporting and non-sporting use) with an adequate reserve of strength and without motion that would cause alarm to people on or in the structure.

Specialist advice from chartered engineers with the appropriate skills and experience should be sought to assess the adequacy of all load-bearing elements in a sports ground.

Designers should pay particular attention both to minimising the risk of progressive or disproportionate collapse from unforeseen incidents, and to the dynamic response of structures (see also Sections 5.5 and 14.6). In doing so, designers should:

a.   systematically assess conceivable hazards to structures and design the structures to be stable and robust in the light of a risk assessment

b.   adopt structural forms which minimise the effects of the hazards identified

c.   provide ground management with manuals which define the key elements and components of the structure requiring regular inspection and maintenance.

5.5   Structural dynamics for permanent structures

In addition to the ability to resist static loading, structures at sports grounds may also need to resist dynamic loading. Permanent structures particularly sensitive to dynamic loading include those with long spanning or cantilevered seating decks.

In such cases, specialist advice from chartered engineers with the appropriate skills and experience should be sought to assess the dynamic behaviour of the structure.

Dynamic load effects may be caused by:

a. excitation by wind

b. excitation by the activities of spectators; if these activities are rhythmic the effects can be severe.

For further detailed guidance on all aspects of the dynamic performance requirements for permanent grandstands excited by the activities of spectators, see *Dynamic Performance Requirements for Permanent Grandstands Subject to Crowd Action – Interim guidance on assessment and design* published by the Institution of Structural Engineers (see Bibliography).

For guidance on the structural dynamics of temporary demountable structures, see *Temporary Demountable Structures – Guidance on Procurement, Design and Use*, published by the Institution of Structural Engineers.

5.6 Construction work at existing grounds

It is the responsibility of management to ensure that construction work taking place at an existing ground does not prejudice the safety of spectators occupying any part of the ground during an event.

Management should also ensure that any partly constructed structure, if brought into use before completion, complies with the recommendations of the *Guide*.

Where work is in progress that could affect the safety of spectators, management should ensure that the contractor has completed that part of the work in sufficient time prior to an event and has confirmed in writing that the construction area is safe, tidy and that spectators may safely be admitted.

An inspection should be undertaken in sufficient time to confirm that the arrangements are acceptable. In the event the arrangements are not suitable the affected part of the ground must not be used. The inspection records should be maintained during the construction and be available for inspection.

Further detailed guidance is available in the LDSA publication Safety of Sports Grounds No 6 – *Guide to Safety at Sports Grounds During Construction* (see Bibliography).

5.7 Anti-vandalism

Precautions should be taken to prevent people from climbing on to roofs, pylons, hoardings and other structures. Where possible such structures should be fitted with unclimbable devices; for example, stout barriers or close-boarded enclosures.

Where fitted, anti-vandal devices should preferably be at least 2.4m from the base of the structure.

Ground management should consult with the local planning authority and police on permissible security and anti-vandal solutions.

5.8 The importance of inspections and tests

Regular and detailed inspections and tests are a necessary and important function of safety management. Where applicable, they are also an essential part of the safety certification process.

Inspections, measurements and tests should seek to eliminate or minimise the potential risks to spectators and staff, and to ensure that all structures, installations and items of equipment are safe, performing to a sufficient standard and fit for the purpose for which they were intended.

As outlined in this chapter, it is the responsibility of management to:

a. ensure that proper maintenance is carried out

b. encourage attitudes and establish procedures which lead to good housekeeping

c. draw up and adhere to a programme of inspections and tests

d. ensure that such inspections, measurements and tests are carried out by suitably qualified persons

e. record the details of inspections, tests and any remedial work carried out, including the dates of completion

f. allocate adequate resources to carry out these tasks.

It should be noted that the guidance on inspections and tests which follows refers only to structures, installations and components. Inspections and tests concerning such matters as stewarding, fire safety, first aid and medical provision, are covered in the relevant chapters.

It should also be noted that the lists which follow are for guidance only and are not intended to be comprehensive or applicable to all sports grounds. Nor is any order of importance intended.

For further references relating to inspections and tests, see Bibliography.

5.9   Inspections and tests 24 hours before an event

Management should ensure that at least 24 hours before each event, the following structures, installations and components are inspected and tested by competent persons, and the test results recorded.

a. fire warning and other fire safety systems (see Sections 15.13 and 15.14)

b. stewards' radio systems (see Section 16.11)

c. emergency telephones (see Section 16.12)

d. public address system (including its intelligibility i.e. the ability to clearly hear and understand a message from the public address system over and above other sounds in the local area), hearing enhancement systems and back-up loud hailers (see Section 16.14)

e. closed circuit television system (see Section 16.16)

f. video or electronic information boards (see Section 16.23)

g. auxiliary power supplies (see Section 17.11)

h. emergency lighting systems (see Section 17.13)

i. temporary television camera platforms and gantries and other media installations (see Section 19.3)

j. carbon monoxide detection systems where fitted

k. methane detection system where fitted.

At some venues such systems may not be permanently in place. Where equipment is transported between venues it should be tested as soon as it is available and in place.

If any of the above systems are not operating properly and if the faults cannot be rectified before the event, contingency plans (see Sections 3.17 and 3.18) should provide for the use of acceptable substitute measures. Failing this the (P) and possibly (S) factors should be recalculated and agreed. This would lead to a reduction in the capacity or, if necessary, the closure of the relevant areas of spectator accommodation. If tickets have been sold in advance and the event is 'sold out' this could lead to the event being postponed or cancelled.

5.10 Inspections and tests before an event

Management should ensure that, before each event, structures, installations and components are inspected and tested by competent persons, to check that:

a. all structures are free from any damage, corrosion or deformation which might create a potential danger to the public

b. exit doors, emergency exit doors, gates and pitch perimeter gates, whether operated manually or electronically, are functioning (see Sections 10.16 and 10.17)

c. all entry and exit routes are clear of obstruction, free from trip hazards, and their surfaces are not slippery; and all such routes can be safely and effectively used (see Chapters 6 and 10)

d. turnstiles and metering or entry monitoring systems are functioning (see Chapter 7)

e. there are no accumulations of combustible waste or litter, particularly in voids and other areas vulnerable to fire; and all areas to which the public have access are generally clean

f. containers used to store combustible waste or litter are secure (see Section 15.10)

g. hazardous materials have been removed, or safely stored, well away from public areas (see Section 15.10)

h. fire fighting equipment is in position and in good order (see Section 15.15)

i. areas to which public access is prohibited are appropriately locked or sealed off

j. where appropriate, the ground does not contain any accessible items which could be used as missiles

k. directional signs are in place and, where appropriate, illuminated (see Section 16.28)

l. temporary signs and fittings are secure and in their appropriate positions

m. the means instantly to remove or breach any fence, advertising material or other obstruction that might impede the exit of spectators into the area of activity in an emergency are in place

n. any temporary equipment that has had to be installed on the day is working satisfactorily before the event commences.

In each case, if problems are identified, remedial action should be taken before the public is allowed access to the affected area.

5.11   Inspections during the event

During an event, management should ensure that:

a.   litter and waste is not allowed to accumulate, and is removed to secure containers whenever possible

b.   materials are not allowed to accumulate or be stored in circulation, exit or escape routes

c.   all gangways, exits, emergency exits and escape routes are kept clear.

5.12   Inspections after the event

Following each event, management should ensure that:

a.   a general visual inspection of the ground identifies any signs of damage or deformation which might create a potential danger to the public, with particular attention to the condition of seats, terraces, viewing slopes, barriers and stairways

b.   combustible waste and litter is cleared (particularly from voids) and either removed or stored in secure containers

c.   any outstanding matters of concern are recorded and arrangements made for remedial action before the next event.

5.13   Annual inspection

Management should arrange a detailed annual inspection of all structures, components and installations.

This inspection should:

a.   ensure that all standing surfaces, seats, stairs, ramps, doors, gates, boundary walls, fences, and claddings are fit for their intended purpose

b.   ensure that load-bearing elements are capable of withstanding the loads to which they are likely to be subjected and that they perform properly their required functions

c.   assess which barriers should be tested in accordance with the guidance found in Chapter 11

d.   ensure that all mechanical and electrical installations are in good order, and, if required, serviced (see Chapter 17).

The annual inspection should be carried out by competent persons with the appropriate qualifications and experience.

Other periodic tests, other than annual ones, may also be required; for example, under the terms of the designer or manufacturer's written instructions, or as specified by the local authority.

5.14   Structural appraisal

The extent to which a detailed structural appraisal is necessary for existing structures cannot be prescribed. Much will depend upon the type of structure, its size, condition, location, the materials used in its construction and the standard of maintenance. The Standing Committee on Structural Safety (SCOSS) (see Bibliography) advises that an interval between appraisals of 6-10 years is likely to be appropriate for most large structures at sports grounds.

Risk assessment should form an integral part of the appraisal process, with structures being categorised according to complexity and risk. The risk assessment should be used to supplement the criteria for the annual inspection (see Section 5.13) where appropriate. The more complex structures should be subjected to independent checking.

Structural appraisal criteria should be established taking account of:

a. load factors used in the original design

b. the degree of redundancy present

c. the risk of disproportionate collapse

d. the consequence of failure.

The acceptability of the current condition of the structure should be determined on the basis of inspection (and testing where necessary) and analysis. If the condition is found to be unacceptable that part of the sports ground should be taken out of use. Work to remedy the situation should be specified and undertaken and then inspected before the affected structure or part of the sports ground is brought back into use.

The appraisal methods described by the Institution of Structural Engineers in the publication *Appraisal of Existing Structures* are to be recommended (see Bibliography). The appraisal should be carried out by a competent chartered engineer.

5.15   Keeping records

Responsibility for the keeping of comprehensive and accurate records lies with management.

The quality of these records may also be regarded as a good indicator of the overall quality of the safety management structure.

Records should be kept in a specified place at the ground or in the management's office, for a period of six years, and should indicate:

a. the level of competence required of those carrying out inspections, measurements and tests

b. the qualifications and status of the persons responsible for carrying out inspections, measurements and tests

c. the results of inspections, measurements and tests, and any remedial action taken.

The documentation should be available for inspection by the relevant authority.

It is good practice to keep a back-up copy of these records securely off site to aid business continuity.

5.16   Plans and specifications

Management is advised to retain clear, up-to-date plans and specifications. Any symbols used should be shown on a key.

Plans and specifications may include the following:

a. a general plan of the sports ground

b. a general plan of approach roads and car parks

c. the general arrangements of each stand, by floor level

d. the principal means of ingress and egress

e. the names of each stand, terrace or section, its capacity and any relevant information regarding categories of spectators

f. the location of:

    i. the central control point

    ii. key point telephones

    iii. stewards' posts

    iv. fire points

    v. public address speakers and zoning

    vi. emergency exits and escape routes

    vii. first aid room

    viii. places of safety and of reasonable safety

    ix. high risk areas (such as plant or boiler rooms, or fuel stores)

    x. rendezvous and access points for the emergency services

    xi. fire warning panel and any repeater panels

    xii gas shut off and other isolating devices.

g. general constructional specifications.

Management is also advised to retain, or have accessible, plans and specifications relating to all recent constructions.

Where a safety certificate is in force, the plans and specifications should include any other details required by the local authority.

6: Circulation – general

6.1 Planning and management of circulation

Circulation routes provide the means for spectators to move in and out, and around the ground, under both normal and emergency conditions.

As a necessary function of a sports ground, circulation routes must be planned and managed safely. However, it should also be recognised that such routes, and circulation areas in general – their design, efficiency and related facilities – are closely allied to the comfort and enjoyment of spectators.

Safe circulation is achieved by:

a. physical means – primarily good design and construction, reinforced by technical aids and clear signposting

b. human resources – primarily good stewarding, reinforced by technical aids, communications, maintenance and good housekeeping.

Although conditions vary considerably at grounds, largely depending on the type of sport being staged, planning and management must also take into account the fact that circulation routes and circulation areas in general function differently according to the nature of the event, the numbers attending, and the categories of spectators attending. For example, certain events may attract higher numbers of children, family groups, elderly people or people unfamiliar with the general layout of the sports ground.

The dispersal of disabled spectators around the ground, and particularly on upper levels of stands, has considerable implications for the safe management of circulation areas, and for the design and management of exit and emergency evacuation routes.

Wherever possible, and in all cases of new construction, management and designers should take account of the current British Standard on means of escape for disabled people (see Bibliography). This provides guidance on suitable stairs, ramps and refuges (see also Section 10.12). Where, because of constraints posed by existing buildings, it is not possible or practicable to apply the British Standard fully, alternative ways of meeting its objectives should be sought.

Although entry points for wheelchair users may need to be kept separate (see Section 7.8), and vertical circulation routes clearly defined, designers should ensure that horizontal circulation routes can be shared without compromising safety for either disabled or non-disabled spectators.

Where appropriate, corridors and passageways need to be wide enough to allow wheelchair users to manoeuvre, where necessary to turn through 180° and to allow other wheelchair users to pass. For further guidance, reference may be made to the Sports Grounds and Stadia Guide No. 1 – *Accessible Stadia* (see Bibliography).

The DCLG publication *Fire Safety Risk Assessment – Means of Escape for Disabled People (Supplementary Guide)* (see Bibliography) provides additional information on accessibility and means of escape for disabled people.

6.2 Creating a balanced system

Circulation cannot be planned or managed simply by ensuring that individual sections of a ground, such as stairways, concourses or gangways, are satisfactory in themselves. The inter-relation of these and other components is critical.

All parts of the circulation system should be compatible and combine to form a balanced whole.

6.3 Multi-functional circulation areas

Circulation areas – that is, areas where spectators both gather and pass through – should perform properly all their intended and actual functions.

For example, concourse areas in stands may form part of the ingress and egress systems, but also provide access to catering outlets and toilets, together with holding areas where spectators can gather to eat and drink, and/or view television monitors (see Chapter 9). Detailed guidance on concourse design and management is provided in the Sports Grounds and Stadia Guide No. 3 – *Concourses* (see Bibliography).

6.4 Zoning of circulation routes

For new construction: wherever possible, new grounds should be planned so that there are continuous circulation routes around the spectator accommodation, linked to both ingress and egress routes. *Diagram 6.1* illustrates the basis for such planning.

6.5 Design of circulation routes and areas

Detailed guidance on specific areas of circulation follows in Chapters 7–10.

However, it is stressed that the following requirements apply to all circulation routes and areas. Where deficiencies exist, the (P) and/or (S) factors should be reduced accordingly.

a. Maintaining safe conditions

Circulation routes and areas should be kept unobstructed where there is a direct movement of spectators, be free of trip hazards, and have slip-resistant floor surfaces. Detailed guidance on slip resistance can be found in the CIRIA publication – *Safer surfaces to walk on* (see Bibliography).

b. Design

Circulation routes and areas should be designed to be free from obstructions and fire risk.

c. Width

For new construction: circulation routes (including stairways and gangways) should be a recommended minimum of 1.2m wide.

For existing construction: circulation routes (including stairways and gangways) should be a minimum of 1.1m wide.

(Where handrails are fitted, see Section 8.8.)

Diagram 6.1 New construction – zonal planning

When planning certain types of sports grounds or rebuilding existing ones (excluding those where spectators may be ambulatory during the event such as racecourses and golf courses), it may be helpful to plan the circulation areas in terms of five different but linked zones, as follows:

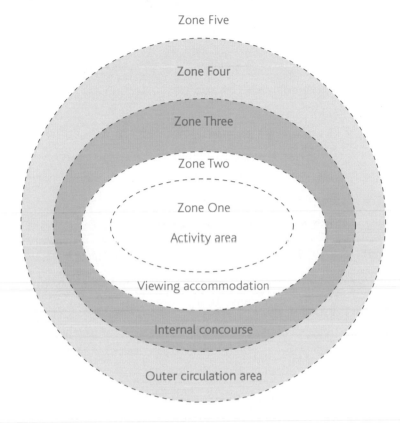

Zone Five

Zone Four

Zone Three

Zone Two

Zone One

Activity area

Viewing accommodation

Internal concourse

Outer circulation area

Outside the sports ground

Zone One: the pitch or area of activity. This may be considered a place of reasonable safety, to which spectators can be evacuated before using other emergency exits (but see Sections 9.13.b and 14.16). Even where this is protected from Zone Two, Zone One should still be accessible to spectators via any gates or openings in the pitch or area of activity perimeter barriers.

Zone Two: spectator viewing accommodation.

Zone Three: internal concourses and hospitality areas. If this area needs to be evacuated in an emergency, it should preferably be to Zone Four.

Zone Four: the outer circulation area. Zone Three and Four may, in certain situations, be considered a place of reasonable safety, to which spectators can be evacuated before exiting to Zone Five. In planning terms, Zone Four can serve as a vital access area for emergency and service vehicles, without disrupting circulation in Zone Two.

Zone Five: a buffer zone outside the sports ground perimeter, used for the public to gather before entry and for links to car parks and public transport. The public should be able to circumnavigate the perimeter in this zone, in order to find an appropriate point of entry. Zone Five should be the designated place of safety in the event of an emergency.

d. **Headroom**

All parts of the ground to which the public have access should have a minimum headroom of 2.0m. Wherever possible, this should be raised to 2.4m, especially in circulation routes and viewing areas (particularly the rear of covered seated stands).

e. **Signs**

Circulation routes and areas should be identified by clear signs, illuminated where necessary (see Section 16.28).

f. **Lighting**

Circulation routes and areas should be well lit, by natural and/or artificial light, under both normal and emergency conditions (see Sections 17.10 and 17.13).

6.6   Management of circulation routes

In order to maintain a free, unimpeded flow of people, management should ensure that circulation routes are kept as clear as possible of all non-essential items and personnel. This will require:

a. regular clearance of waste, litter and spillages

b. the monitoring of all circulation areas by stewards and/or CCTV

c. preventing non-essential personnel (such as off-duty staff) from gathering around key areas, such as stairways, gangways and vomitories.

Where there is a free movement of spectators between different viewing areas, further management controls may also be necessary, as detailed in Sections 13.16 and 13.20.

6.7   Management policies and circulation

Management should recognise that a number of apparently non-safety-related policies and practices can have both positive and negative effects on the efficiency of circulation systems. These might include:

a. ticketing or entry arrangements (see Section 7.9)

b. the distribution and positioning of vendors

c. the distribution and positioning of television monitors, scoreboards and other points of interest

d. commercial or media-related activities which involve placing vehicles, temporary structures, cables or extra personnel in key areas (see Chapter 19)

e. commercial activities or promotions which encourage spectators to gather in strategic areas or involve the distribution of handouts, refreshments or gifts

f. the opening or closing of catering or commercial outlets before, during or after an event, in such a pattern that the loading of circulation systems becomes either greater or lesser at key times

g. segregation arrangements which necessitate extra barriers, divided concourses, sealed-off areas or dead ends.

6.8 Access and egress for emergency vehicles

In addition to monitoring circulation areas for spectators, management should ensure that adequate access and egress is provided for emergency vehicles to all buildings within the sports ground. Wherever possible such routes should be separate from those used by spectators for ingress and egress or, alternatively, provide for the parking of emergency vehicles so that spectator routes are not obstructed.

The police, fire and ambulance authorities should be consulted about the suitability of access routes in order to produce an agreed plan of action, including access for emergency vehicles, for all foreseeable incidents (see Section 3.20).

7: Circulation – ingress

7.1 The need to count

Spectators entering all sections of the ground, including VIP and lounge areas, should be accurately counted at their time of entry, and their number controlled in order to ensure that overcrowding does not occur. This applies even if entry to the event is by ticket or electronic entry card only.

If the procedures for accurately counting spectators are deficient, or if the entry procedures themselves lead to congestion, delays, or any breakdown of the safety management of spectators, the (S) factor should be reduced accordingly when calculating the capacity (see Section 2.4).

7.2 Counting on entry

Each section of spectator accommodation should be served by metered turnstiles or other means of counting, in order to keep a tally of the number of spectators admitted to that section.

Where one section of a ground is served by a bank or banks of turnstiles, the metering system should be capable of recording an overall total for all the turnstiles. This total should be quickly available at any given time so that appropriate action can be taken once a pre-determined figure – for example, 90 per cent of the total capacity – has been reached.

This is important for two reasons:

a. Management will need to assess how long it will take for the remaining people outside the ground (if any) to be admitted before the start of the event. If the number queuing is greater than can be admitted at the prevailing rate of admission, wherever possible extra turnstiles should be opened to cope with the demand. If this is not possible, consideration should be given as to whether or not the start of the event should be delayed.

b. When entry is other than by ticket or entry card for reserved seats, management will need to know when the section is near capacity so that:

   i. the turnstiles can be closed before the capacity is exceeded

   ii. people queuing or approaching the turnstiles can be warned, and where appropriate, re-directed to entrances serving other sections of the ground.

As stated in Sections 3.17 and 3.18, contingency plans to cater for the above situations should be prepared. For further guidance on counting spectators on entry, see Section 16.21.

7.3 Computerised monitoring

In order for the ground's safety management to have instant access to the figures being metered or counted at each turnstile or entry point, and for rates of admission to be accurately assessed, it is recommended that a computerised monitoring system should be installed wherever practicable.

Where installed, however, management should also prepare contingency plans to deal with the system's failure (see Sections 3.17 and 3.18).

7.4 Entry capacity

As stated in Section 2.3, one of the calculations required to determine the capacity of a sports ground, or one section of the ground, is the entry capacity.

The entry capacity is the number of people who can pass through all the turnstiles or entry points serving either the whole ground or one section, within a period of one hour.

7.5 Factors affecting the entry capacity

The rate at which people can pass through each turnstile or entry point will vary according to a number of local factors. The rates of entry should therefore be measured at least once a year and recorded.

The main factors affecting the rate of entry are:

a. the number and dispersal of turnstiles/entry points

b. the adequacy of directional information and communications

c. the means of entry; for example, cash payment, ticket, entry card or voucher

d. the division of entry categories; for example, adults, concessions or groups

e. the design and condition of turnstiles/entry points

f. the capabilities of turnstile operators

g. the efficiency of the system and the ability of the spectator to understand the system of recognition where electronic entry cards are in use

h. the level of searching required, particularly at times of high security alert. The use of metal detectors, bag and body searching may significantly reduce the rate of passage.

7.6 Calculating the entry capacity

As stated in Section 7.4, the entry capacity is the number of people who can pass through all the turnstiles or entry points serving either the whole ground or one section, within a period of one hour.

However, for the purposes of the calculation, and in order to ensure that spectators are admitted at a rate which is compatible with dispersal arrangements for them inside the ground, an upper limit has been set on this number.

For the purposes of calculating the entry capacity, the upper limit is set at 660 persons per turnstile (or other entry point) per hour.

Where the recorded rate of entry proves to be less than 660 persons per turnstile per hour, that lower figure is the figure which should be used for the purposes of calculating the entry capacity. Where the recorded rate of admission proves to be greater than 660 persons per turnstile per hour, the upper limit of 660 should still apply when calculating the entry capacity.

It is acknowledged that in certain circumstances, for example where there are no turnstiles or there are electronic entry card systems, spectators may be able to enter more quickly. Experience has shown that, in the majority of circumstances, by using a maximum of 660 persons per hour sufficient turnstiles will be available to allow all spectators using entry cards to gain entry before the start of the event at a reasonably safe rate.

If the entry capacity is lower than the holding capacity of the section served by those turnstiles, the final capacity of that section should be reduced accordingly, as explained in Chapter 2.

7.7 Providing a sufficient number of turnstiles or entry points

Although the entry capacity is determined by the number of spectators who can be admitted within a period of one hour, in practice many grounds admit spectators well in advance of the start of a sporting event. However, for many events, large numbers of spectators arrive close to the starting time.

These variations should be recognised when determining the number of turnstiles or entry points to be provided, or staffed on particular event days.

For example, providing the exact number of turnstiles to serve one section purely on the basis that each one will theoretically admit 660 persons per hour may result in a build-up of queues outside the ground, as latecomers arrive shortly before the start.

It is also inevitable that certain turnstiles will operate more slowly than others; for example, those which admit large numbers of children.

For all spectators to be admitted in time for the start, therefore, a larger number of entry points may be required than might otherwise be the case if the number were based purely on the application of the 660 figure.

7.8 Design and management of entrances and entry routes

The design and management of entrances and entry routes should take into consideration the following:

a. Entrances to each part of the ground should, wherever practicable, be designed and located so as to allow for the even distribution of spectators and to prevent local pressure building up outside the ground.

b. Walls, fences and gates should not provide the opportunity for hand or foot-holds which might assist climbing. They should be regularly inspected.

c. The installation of closed circuit television should be considered in order to assist in the monitoring of crowd densities outside the ground and throughout the ingress/egress routes (see Sections 16.16–16.20).

d. The design of the turnstile and its housing should allow for the operator to see and communicate clearly with entrants.

e. Turnstiles are not suitable for use by wheelchair users, visually impaired spectators and people with assistance dogs. The most practical design solution is to provide level access via a gate or door, with an appropriate vision panel, which is staffed by a steward. Arrangements must be in place to ensure that all those entering by such routes are counted among the spectators attending the event.

f.   Entrances should be sited so that the flow of people from them to the spectator accommodation is, as far as possible, evenly distributed. Where this distribution is uneven and gives rise to congestion at an entrance, consideration should be given to changing the turnstile or entry point arrangements, and if possible, to directing more people to under-used entrances. Additional measures might include improved signposting and increased stewarding, both inside and outside the ground.

g.   Entry routes should not be obstructed. Amenities such as refreshment kiosks or toilets should be located away from the immediate area of the turnstiles and entry routes.

h.   Entry and exit routes are often common to each other and in such cases the considerations which apply to exit routes therefore apply also to entry routes (see Chapter 10).

7.9   Providing clear information

Spectators should be provided with clear, consistent information on all aspects of entry. Wherever practical, the following measures should be considered:

a.   All entrances and entry routes should be clearly signposted and, if used in non-daylight hours, adequately lit (see Section 17.10).

b.   All turnstiles and entry points should be numbered. These numbers should be identifiable, and should be recorded in all documentation relating to the ground, including ground plans and contingency plans.

c.   Clear ground plans showing all entrance points should be displayed at strategic points outside the ground, ideally so that people approaching the ground can decide which entrance to use as early as possible.

d.   Consideration should be given to the practice whereby colours (red, blue, green and yellow etc) are used to identify the different parts of the ground. Replicating the colours on tickets and signs will help spectators locate their seats. It will also avoid staff and the emergency services being confused by, for example, changes in sponsors' names.

e.   Tickets or entry cards, where issued, should satisfy the following requirements:

  i.   they should clearly identify the location of the accommodation for which they have been issued (including any colour coding as in (d) above)

  ii. they should have a ground plan reproduced on the back of that part of the ticket retained by the spectator or provided separately with the electronic entry card

  iii. information on the ticket or provided separately with the entry card should correlate with the information provided both inside and outside the ground.

For further guidance on ticketing and admission policies, see Sections 3.29 and 7.10.

f.   Event programmes or race cards, where issued, should include a clearly labelled plan of the ground, indicating the entry/exit routes to and from different parts of the ground, and details of emergency evacuation procedures (see Section 16.30).

g.   Spectators should be made aware of the ground regulations, and in particular of any articles which are prohibited from the ground. This can be achieved by the use of posters, and by repeating the information on ground plans and tickets, and in event programmes.

For further guidance on the communication of information, see Chapter 16.

7.10 Admission policies

As stated in Section 3.29, policies adopted by the ground management can have a direct effect on the rates of admission and the management of entrance areas and spectator accommodation in general.

Specific points to consider include:

a. Cash sales

To ensure a steady flow of spectators into the ground when entry is by cash, the admission price should ideally be set at a round figure which avoids the need for large amounts of small change to be handled.

The turnstile operators should also be provided with adequate amounts of change, topped up if necessary by staff assisting the operators.

b. Ticket or entry card only sales

The advantages of confining entry to tickets or entry cards are that the rate of admission should be higher than for cash sales, and the system allows different categories of spectator (for example, parent and child) to purchase adjacent seats and enter the ground together.

If tickets or entry cards are sold on the day of the event, wherever possible separate sales outlets should be provided. These outlets should be clearly signposted, and positioned so that queues do not conflict with queues for turnstiles or other entry points.

c. Reserved (or numbered) seat ticket or entry card sales

Selling tickets or entry cards for specific numbered seats has the advantage that the seats are more likely to be sold in blocks. This policy helps to avoid random gaps and ensures that in the key period preceding the start of the event there will be less need for stewards to have to direct latecomers to the remaining seats, or move spectators who have already settled.

Another advantage of this policy is that it makes it possible for management to sell the total seated capacity of the ground, or section of the ground (as opposed to a policy of unreserved seat sales, as explained below).

d. Unreserved seat sales

Selling unreserved seats, whether by cash or ticket, has the advantage of being easier to administer. However, spectators are prone to occupy seats in a random pattern, and, as stated above, it can be hard to fill unoccupied seats in the key period before the start of the event.

For this reason, when seats are sold unreserved, a reduction in the number of seats made available for sale is likely to be necessary. This reduction may be in the region of 5–10 per cent of the total capacity of the section, according to local circumstances.

e. No ticket or cash entry on the event day

If all tickets have sold out in advance, or if the management decides not to sell tickets or allow cash entry on the day of the event, every effort should be made to publicise this fact in the local press and media. In addition, signs advising the public of the situation should be placed along all approaches to the ground, in order to avoid an unnecessary build-up of crowds outside the ground and its entrances.

f.   Ticket design

The design of tickets can have a direct effect on the rate of admission. For example, clear, easy-to-read information will speed the ability of the turnstile or entry-point operator to process the ticket. Similarly, if anti-counterfeiting features are incorporated (as is recommended), simple procedures should be in place for the operator to check each ticket's validity.

g.   Electronic entry card design

In case of card systems, where no operator is immediately present, it is essential that the card user has clear instructions both with the card and on the card reader, at the point of entry, on how to:

i.   present the card for validation

ii.   seek assistance should the reader fail to recognise the card as valid and therefore prevent entry. (In the case of failure of the whole or part of the system an agreed contingency should be in place to ensure safe entry).

For more guidance on ticketing, see Sections 3.29, 7.9 and 12.20.

7.11   Crowd build-up

Dangerous overcrowding can be caused if spectators are able to force their way into a ground already full or nearly full, for example by scaling or breaking through boundary walls, fences, gates or turnstiles.

To avoid this danger boundary walls, fences and gates should be of the appropriate height and strength, should not provide the opportunity for climbing, and should, where possible, be monitored by CCTV. Turnstile areas should be stewarded wherever there is a potential threat of forced entry.

Contingency plans should be drawn up in order to deal with situations where unduly large crowds gather outside. Local knowledge of the ground and crowd patterns should be taken into account in drawing up such contingency plans.

It should be stressed that the opening of additional or under-used entrances could lead to both sudden uncontrolled movement and possible crushing. If management's contingency plans dealing with large crowds outside includes the opening of additional entrances the plan must also contain sufficient measures to prevent the uncontrolled movement of the crowd. It should also ensure that spectators who enter in such situations can still be accurately counted, and that adequate stewarding arrangements are in place for their dispersal once inside the ground.

Under no circumstances should there be uncontrolled admission into the ground.

8: Circulation – vertical circulation

8.1 Introduction

Management and designers should consider all aspects of vertical circulation.

The disposition, design and management of stairways, ramps, lifts and escalators at sports grounds should be such as to provide smooth and unimpeded circulation for spectators under all conditions.

This chapter should therefore be read in conjunction with Chapters 6, 7, 9 and 10 on circulation and Chapters 12-14 on spectator accommodation.

8.2 Stairways and gangways

It is emphasised that for the purposes of design and assessment, the criteria applying to stairways at sports grounds are, in part, different to those pertaining to radial gangways.

The following definitions should therefore be noted:

a. **Stairway**
   A stairway is that part of a structure which is not a radial gangway but which comprises of at least one flight of steps, including the landings at the head and foot of stairways and any landings in between flights.

b. **Radial gangway**
   A radial gangway is a stepped or sloping channel for the circulation of spectators through viewing accommodation, running between terrace steps or seat rows.

c. **Lateral gangway**
   A lateral gangway is a level channel for the circulation of spectators through viewing accommodation, running parallel with terrace steps or seat rows.

Further guidance on the provision and design of gangways can be found in Sections 12.9-12.11 (for seated accommodation) and Sections 13.4–13.6 (for standing accommodation).

8.3 Design of stairways

Movement on stairways, especially downward movement, poses a considerable potential risk to crowds both in normal circumstances, such as at the end of an event, or in an emergency. The effects of stumbling, pushing, jostling and congestion are potentially dangerous if, as a result, the crowd suddenly surges forward or if, for any reason, any individuals suddenly change direction.

For new construction: in order to minimise hazards the design of stairways should comply with all the relevant requirements of the current Building Regulations.

For new and existing construction: the specific needs of sports grounds require that stairways should meet the following basic specifications:

a.   the stairway width should be uniform (see Section 8.5)

b.   all goings and risers on each stairway should be uniform between floors

c.   open risers should not be used

d.   winders (that is, tapered treads) should not be used

e.   stair treads should be slip-resistant, have durable edgings, and, where appropriate, have adequate drainage. Detailed guidance on slip resistance can be found in the CIRIA publication – *Safer surfaces to walk on* (see Bibliography)

f.   all nosings should be clearly marked

> **In new construction**, and where possible in existing construction, this should be by means of a permanently contrasting material 55mm wide on both the tread and the riser, which should not constitute a trip hazard.

g.   adequate separation should be provided between channels so that there is no overspill from one channel to another

h.   stairways should be positioned to take advantage of natural light and ventilation, but where the natural lighting is deficient the stairway should be adequately illuminated by artificial light (see also Sections 17.10 and 17.13).

Further guidance on flights of stairways, and certain of the above requirements (including specific dimensional criteria), can be found in the following sections.

8.4   Flights of stairways

Flights of stairways should not provide long, uncontrolled paths down which crowd pressures and surges can be created. For this reason:

a.   Number of risers

> **For new construction:** Individual flights should consist of no more than 12 risers. However, where the stairway is a secondary stairway for escape only, this may be increased to 16 risers. Reference should also be made to the Building Regulations.

> **For existing construction:** Individual flights should consist of no more than 16 risers.

b.   If there are more than 36 risers in consecutive flights, the path of the stairway should change direction of travel by at least 30°.

8.5   Dimensions of stairways

The design of stairways (and stairway channels) at sports grounds should comply with the following dimensions:

a.   Widths

> **For new construction:**
> Recommended minimum width: 1.2m   Maximum width: 1.8m

For existing construction:

Minimum width:　　　　　　　1.1m　　　Maximum width: 1.8m

Existing stairways and stairway channels of between 1.8m and 2.2m wide should, wherever possible, be narrowed to no more than 1.8m by the installation or relocation of suitable barriers.

Existing stairways and stairway channels wider than 2.2m should be divided into channels in order to meet the width requirements above.

b.　**Goings**

Minimum depth:　　　　　　280mm　　　Preferred depth: 305mm

c.　**Risers**

For new construction:

Minimum height:　　　　　　　150mm (this is also the preferred height)

Maximum height:　　　　　　　170mm or 180mm where the stairway is a secondary stairway for escape only. Reference should also be made to the Building Regulations.

For existing construction:

Minimum height:　　　　　　　150mm (this is also the preferred height)

Maximum height:　　　　　　　190mm

d.　**Landings**

The going of each landing, at the head and foot of stairways, and between flights, should be not less than the width of the channel of the flight.

e.　**Headroom**

Minimum headroom dimensions are provided in Section 6.5.

8.6　Barriers and handrails – definitions

It is emphasised that in terms of their dimensions and design loadings, barriers are not handrails, even though in certain situations – see Section 8.7.b – in practice they might be used by people as handrails.

For the purpose of the Guide, a barrier is any element, whether permanent or temporary, intended to prevent people from falling, and to retain, stop or guide people (see Section 8.7).

A handrail is a rail normally grasped by hand for guidance or support (see Section 8.8).

Further guidance on barriers is provided in Chapter 11. Further guidance on handrails used in gangways in seated areas can be found in Section 12.11.

8.7　Barriers on stairways

As illustrated in *Diagram 8.1*, barriers are used for two different purposes on stairways.

a.　**Barriers to stop people falling**

Where stairways are situated next to, or in the middle of, open wells, or open spaces, barriers designed to prevent people from falling should be provided on the open side or sides. These barriers should be not less than 1.1m high.

At grounds where small children are likely to be in attendance, additional guarding which is non-climbable and has no openings through which a 100mm sphere can pass should be provided.

b. **Barriers to divide stairways into channels**
Stairways separated into channels must be divided by the provision of barriers. Such barriers may be designed to a height of 1.0m, in which case they can also function as a handrail.

If installed to a height of greater than 1.0m, however, separate provision for handrails should be made in the design, as specified in Section 8.8 and shown in *Diagram 8.1*.

In both the above situations, the barrier heights should be measured from the pitch line, or from the surface of the landing. The barriers should also be designed to resist a horizontal imposed load as specified in Table 11.1.

8.8 Handrails for stairways and ramps

As stated in Section 8.6, a handrail is provided for people to grasp, for guidance or support. If the handrails are to serve only as handrails for stairways or ramps – that is, they are not barriers as described in Section 8.7.b – the design should meet the following requirements:

a. Handrails of the same height should be provided on both sides of stairways, landings and ramps.

b. **For new construction:** handrails should be a minimum height of 900mm, and a maximum height of 1.0m, measured vertically from the pitch line or from the surface of the landing.

For existing construction: handrails should be a minimum height of 840mm, and a maximum height of 1.0m, measured vertically from the pitch line or from the surface of the landing.

c. Wherever possible, handrails should project no more than 100mm into the width of the stairway or ramp. If the projection is greater than 100mm the usable width of the stairway should be measured between the handrails, and should be at least 1.1m (1.2m recommended for new construction).

d. Handrails should extend by at least 300mm beyond the top and bottom of any stairway, measured from the vertical of the first and last risers, or from the start and finish of the ramp.

e. Handrails should be robust, securely fixed, and their fixings designed to be fit for purpose.

f. The surfaces of handrails should be smooth, with no sharp projections or edges.

Diagram 8.1 Barriers and handrails on stairways

This diagram illustrates a stairway with a wall on one side and an open space
(or well) on the other.

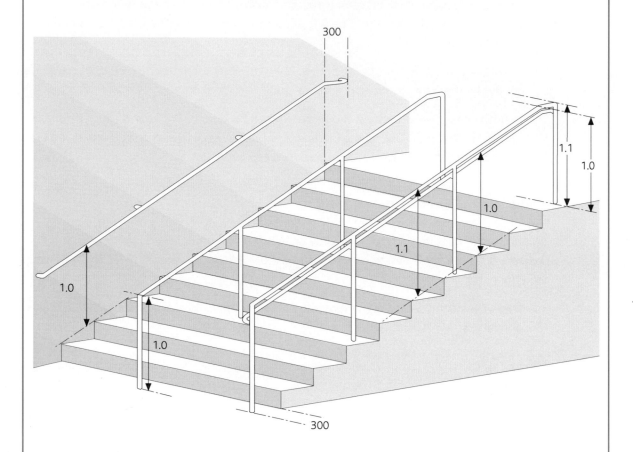

A barrier is installed to prevent people falling over the open side. Because this barrier has to
have a height of 1.1m, a handrail is attached at a lower level for guidance or support.
The handrail's height of between 0.9m and 1.0m measured from the datum (that is, from
the pitch line). Note that each end of the handrail bends around the ends of the barrier, and
that if small children are likely to use the stairway, additional guarding should be provided
(see Section 8.7.a).

Another handrail is fixed to the wall. This too is fixed at a height of between 0.9m and 1.0m
above the datum. Particular care has to be taken when fixing such a handrail, in order to
prevent it pulling away from the wall.

Finally, the central barrier, which divides the stairway into channels, is classed as a barrier,
and is therefore subject to the loading requirements of Table 11.1. As stated in Section 8.7.b,
a barrier in this location may be designed to a height of 1.0m, thus enabling it to be used
also as a handrail.

Whatever the design of the central barrier, the handrails on either side of any stairway
channel should be the same height.

8.9 Controlling the flow at the head of stairways

In order to ensure a free flow of people, and avoid crowd pressures building up, the head of each stairway should be designed so that flow onto the stairway is uniform across its width. Similarly, where a stairway is divided into channels, the approach should be designed to ensure a uniform flow down each channel.

The design of approaches to the head of each stairway should meet the following requirements:

a. The approach should be level.

b. It should be designed so that people can approach the stairway only by walking towards the direction of the stairs, and/or from its sides but not diagonally.

c. In areas of spectator accommodation, any approach from directly behind a stairway (that is, from higher up the seating deck or standing area) should be controlled using the same methods as recommended for vomitories; by the routing of gangways or, in standing areas with no gangways, by the positioning of barriers around the entrance to the stairway (see Section 9.9).

d. No part of the approach should be less than 1.2m in width (1.1m for existing construction).

e. Where the approach to the head of a stairway is greater than 3m in width, the flow of spectators should be strictly controlled by barriers, as illustrated in *Diagram 8.2*.

8.10 Discharge from exit stairways

The flow of spectators as they move away from the foot of exit stairways should be controlled so that the exit routes discharge either:

a. at ground level, and lead directly to a place of safety in the open air, or

b. onto walkways or concourses of adequate dimensions at any level, provided these also lead directly to a place of safety in the open air.

For the purposes of the *Guide*, a place of safety is a place where a person is no longer in danger from the effects of fire (see Section 15.16).

8.11 Ramps

Ramps can be a useful alternative to stairs, but there is concern about their suitability for negotiating small changes of level within sports grounds, because they may not be easily seen by spectators during an emergency evacuation.

Where substantial changes of level are involved, ramps generally occupy considerable amounts of space because of the low pitch and frequent landings required to make them suitable for wheelchair users.

The physical effort required of wheelchair users and carers to negotiate long ramps, means that a passenger lift or platform lift is generally the appropriate form of vertical circulation for transferring between storeys.

In addition, steep ramps can cause or exacerbate uncontrolled forward movement and lead to an accident.

Diagram 8.2 Approaches to the head of stairways

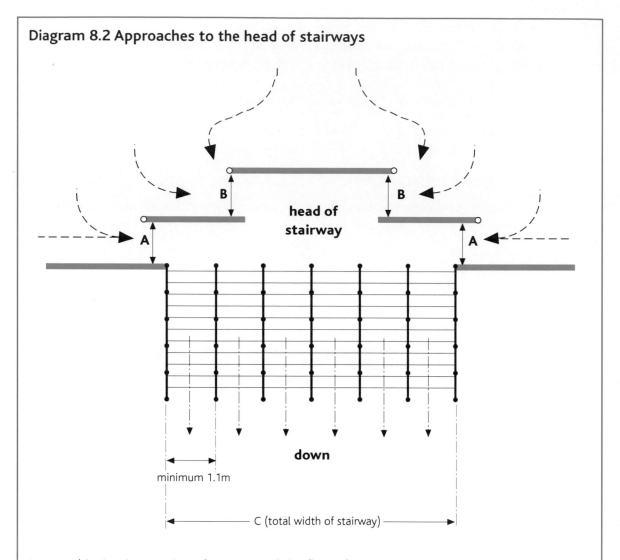

head of stairway

minimum 1.1m

down

C (total width of stairway)

As stated in Section 8.9, in order to control the flow of spectators as they approach the head of a stairway, it is necessary to position barriers as shown above. The barriers should be designed on the following basis:

The minimum width of A or B should be 1.1m (1.2m for new construction), but the aggregate width of A + B on one side of the stairway should be not more than 3m.

To establish the correct widths for A and B, the following calculation should be used, where C = the total width of the stairway:

$$2 (A + B) = \frac{2C}{3} \quad \text{or} \quad (A + B) = \frac{C}{3}$$

From this calculation, it can be seen that stairways wider than 9m would require the addition of more barriers at the head of the stairway.

To achieve visibility in crowded conditions, consideration should also be given to extending selected vertical posts (marked above with a black circle) to above head height.

(For guidance on the rates of passage to be applied to stairways see Section 10.5 and 10.6.)

Where provided, ramps should therefore meet the following requirements:

a. **For new construction:**
   The maximum gradient should not exceed

   1 in 20 for a going of up to 10m;
   1 in 15 for a going up to 5m; and
   1 in 12 for a going not exceeding 2m.

   For existing construction:
   The maximum gradient should not exceed 1 in 10.

b. The gradient of any ramp should preferably be constant and should not be broken by steps.

c. The surface should be uniform and slip-resistant (see Bibliography).

d. Handrails should be provided using the same criteria as those applying to stairways (see Section 8.7).

8.12 Passenger lifts

A passenger lift is the most suitable means of vertical access for disabled people and should be provided wherever possible. For further references and design considerations see the Bibliography.

Wheelchair users and other spectators with impaired mobility need sufficient time and space to manoeuvre into the lift and should be able to reach the controls on the landing, and also in the car itself.

Sufficient space should be provided in front of lifts so that people waiting for them will not obstruct crowd flows.

It is important to note that the design of a passenger lift may determine whether it may be used in the event of an emergency evacuation. For details of the design and usage of lifts for evacuation purposes see Section 10.12d. Consideration should be given to the size of lifts where the medical plan (see Section 18.3) provides for their use to transport injured spectators on stretchers.

In addition to passenger lifts, internal stairs should always be provided as an alternative means of vertical access, designed to suit ambulant disabled people and those with impaired vision.

8.13 Escalators

Escalators should conform to the relevant British Standard. Escalators are not a suitable means of vertical access for all disabled people. Therefore wherever an escalator is installed between floors, a clearly signposted alternative access by lift should be provided.

Although escalators may form an integral part of the entry and exit systems at certain sports grounds, they should not be used for the purposes of calculating the emergency evacuation capacity.

Escalators should discharge into a space sufficiently large and clear to avoid people being unable to step off the escalator in congested situations. Consideration should also be given to the possible consequences of any breakdowns, particularly of one flight within a series of multiple level escalators. It may be necessary to provide alternative exit routes leading from the escalators landings to staircases or large safe areas, in order to avoid crowd build up on landings in the case of breakdowns.

If an escalator fails, it becomes a static staircase. In most cases it will have more than 12 uneven risers. Stationary escalators present hazards that management should recognise particularly during emergency evacuation, because of:

a.   the variations in riser height at the top and bottom of the flight

b.   the probable increased riser height beyond that of a stairway

c.   the possibility of unsatisfactory barrier loadings to their side construction (see Section 11.2).

9: Circulation – concourses and vomitories

9.1   Concourses and vomitories

This chapter provides guidance on the safe circulation of spectators in those areas which do not exactly fit into categories outlined elsewhere in the *Guide*, but which may also serve as integral parts of ingress, egress and emergency evacuation routes. The chapter should therefore be read in conjunction with Chapters 6, 7, 8 and 10 on circulation, Chapters 12-14 on spectator accommodation and Chapter 15 on fire safety. Further detailed guidance on all aspects of the design and safety management of new and existing concourses is available in the Sports Grounds and Stadia Guide No. 3 – *Concourses* (see Bibliography).

For the purpose of the *Guide*, a concourse is defined as a circulation area that provides direct access to and from viewing accommodation to which it may be linked by vomitories, passageways, stairs or ramps. It serves as a milling area for spectators for access to refreshments, entertainment and toilets, and may also be part of the entry and exit routes.

A vomitory is an access route built into the gradient of a stand which directly links spectator accommodation to concourses, and/or routes for ingress, egress and emergency evacuation. Passage through a vomitory can be either level, or via stairways, and can flow either parallel or transverse to the rows of terraces or seats.

9.2   Concourses and safety

The safety management of many sports grounds tends to concentrate attention and resources on ingress and egress routes and viewing areas. However, it should be recognised that concourses are an integral part of the circulation system and must therefore be monitored and managed at all times when spectators are in the ground.

Increasingly, concourses also form an important access route to facilities provided for the comfort and enjoyment of spectators. As such, it is important that neither the design nor management of concourses adversely affects the safety of spectators. This is a particular concern at existing grounds where concourses, originally designed for general circulation only, have been fitted with additional facilities which considerably add to the concourses' usage during peak times.

Key concerns are the size of the concourse, the travel routes between the concourse and vomitories, and between the concourse and ingress, egress and emergency evacuation routes. In general, these routes should be as direct as possible.

9.3   Concourses and fire safety

The presence of commercial and catering facilities in concourses – particularly when these have been added to existing structures – also raises concerns about fire safety. For this reason, under no circumstances should any significant modifications be carried out, nor any commercial or catering outlet be installed, nor any changes to wall or floor surfaces be effected, without prior consultation with the authority responsible for enforcing fire safety legislation. This consultation should be recorded in written form.

9.4   Size of concourses

The ease of circulation and the comfort of spectators will be largely determined by the width and spatial arrangements of the concourse.

For new construction: The width should take into account the entry, exit and emergency evacuation capacities required, as for any circulation route. The width should then be increased to take into account the additional anticipated usage of related facilities. Experience shows that this usage may be greater than is often expected.

Whilst it is difficult to determine a precise occupancy level for a concourse it is recommended that the size of the concourse should be determined using a predicted occupancy level of between 30% and 50% of the capacity of the viewing area that the concourse serves.

It is recommended that all new sports ground concourses should be designed to allow at least $0.5m^2$ per person (a density of 20 persons/10 m^2) expected to occupy the concourse at peak times.

However, consideration should also be given to the potential usage of concourses by spectators at events other than the sport for which the ground is primarily designed. This usage can be considerable if the event spans several hours, if inclement weather conditions prevail, and if large numbers are in attendance (as, for example, at a concert, for which the pitch or area of activity is used for viewing).

For existing construction: where concourses have been upgraded with additional facilities, leading to greater usage at peak times, management should allocate extra stewarding, and where appropriate, extra CCTV coverage, in order to monitor the circulation and milling of spectators. Where necessary, the management's contingency plans (see Sections 3.17 and 3.18) should include a response to the problem of overcrowding in concourses.

If congestion in concourses is a regular occurrence, consideration should be given to resiting or providing additional facilities in other areas (see Section 9.8).

9.5   Circulation on concourses

Concourses should be designed to allow for the smooth, unimpeded passage of people through the ingress and egress routes. In addition, careful design should ensure that during periods of peak use circulation is not impeded.

In order to achieve this, the following requirements should be considered:

a.   The positioning of travel routes – for general ingress, egress or access to toilets or catering outlets – should be determined, and should not create cross flows; that is, people moving along the concourse should not be impeded by large numbers crossing their path.

b.   Similarly, the positioning of catering outlets and toilet entrances should be such that queues do not impede the circulation of people along the concourse, nor the entry of spectators into the concourse direct from turnstiles.

c. Catering outlets and toilet entrances should not create any unacceptable risk, or be positioned immediately next to the foot of vomitories or stairways leading from spectator accommodation. This is to avoid congestion in the vomitories owing to the potential build-up of queues.

d. To avoid congestion and discomfort, there should be an adequate number of toilets and catering outlets provided. These should be spaced sufficiently apart in concourses to avoid queues for each becoming disorderly, thereby creating additional potential congestion.

e. The siting of television monitors, or any other forms of display which might encourage large numbers of people to mill around, should be such that congestion is not created around key areas in the concourse; for example, close to the foot of vomitories, or close to toilet entrances.

9.6 Design of concourses and related facilities

The design of concourses should, wherever possible, take the following factors into consideration:

a. Signs should be provided at such a level and in positions which enable people to read them during periods of peak usage. The signs should also be placed facing both lateral and transverse directions to enable people entering the concourse from any ingress point or from a vomitory to make a quick decision as to which direction to take in order to reach their intended destination.

b. Where possible, natural lighting should be maximised in order to assist in the safe and efficient flow of people towards exits, and to create a more comfortable environment.

c. Contrasting colours, for example on floors, walls, fittings, handrails and furniture, are recommended as these will be of benefit to all spectators and greatly assist the safety of those who are visually impaired.

d. The flooring of concourses should be slip-resistant, in particular in areas where spillage is likely (for example, around catering outlets), and in areas where rainwater can be tracked in from vomitories and external areas (see Section 6.5.a).

e. Where concourses form part of an emergency evacuation route they should be designed as areas of very low fire risk, having at least a 30 minutes fire resistance from catering and other outlets which may contain a fire risk. Consideration may also need to be given to the provision of smoke containment and/or extraction measures (see also Section 10.10).

f. At grounds where areas of spectator accommodation are segregated, the design of concourse areas should ensure that any divisions do not exclude the provision of amenities in one part of the concourse.

g. The planning of concourses, whether new or for refurbishment, should take into account the service needs of all facilities, and other management details such as the location and type of litter bins and the provision of shelving for refreshments. These should not be sited in such a way as to impede passage through egress routes.

9.7 Management of concourses

Owing to their considerable use during peak periods, it is essential for management to allocate resources and staffing to the management of concourses, before and during events.

The following factors should be considered:

a. Management should ensure that concourses are competently stewarded and, where necessary, monitored by the use of CCTV cameras.

b. The siting of any temporary fittings or kiosks should not impede the circulation of spectators through the concourse.

c. The delivery of supplies and services to catering outlets or toilets should not impede spectator circulation.

d. Waste, litter and spillages should be collected and removed at regular intervals. Spillages are regarded as a contaminant and will adversely affect the slip resistance of floor surfaces. Detailed guidance on slip resistance can be found in the CIRIA publication – *Safer surfaces to walk on* (see Bibliography).

e. Management should consider the provision of a safety station on each concourse. This is an area containing emergency equipment such as fire extinguishers, a fire blanket and a loud hailer, along with an emergency or key point telephone and contact details for the first aid post. It can provide an effective communication point between the ground control point and stewards on the concourse. It can also serve as reporting point for staff in the event of an emergency. It is not suggested that a safety station should be staffed at all times. However, stewards should all be aware of its location.

9.8 Prevention of overcrowding

It is recognised that spectators will not be distributed evenly throughout a concourse. There may be greater concentrations immediately adjacent to refreshment outlets. However, where the overall occupancy level in a concourse is likely to reduce the floor space below $0.5m^2$ per person, management should assess whether it needs to put in place strategies to control the numbers entering it. These could include:

a. opening up a controlled capacity overflow area outside the concourse, for instance for catering and other facilities

b. extending the opening times of the catering and other facilities so that spectators do not all seek to enter the concourse at the same time

c. providing refreshment services at other points within the spectator viewing area

d. limiting the facilities on the concourse, for example by closing bars or turning off televisions, so that spectators are discouraged from entering

e. using stewards and the public address system to advise spectators that concourses are congested.

If the management's strategy for controlling the numbers entering the concourse fails to resolve the overcrowding, the (S) factor (see Section 2.4) for the viewing accommodation served by the concourse should be reduced.

9.9 Vomitories

Vomitories are a common means of reducing travel distances in stands. They are also an aid to safety management, allowing stewards and other personnel to gain direct and easy access to particular areas. There are several different designs and layout of vomitories but, in general, the following requirements should be met:

a. If passage through the vomitory is by steps, the design, dimensions, barriers and handrails should meet the requirement for stairways (see Chapter 8).

b. Whether passage through the vomitory is by steps or by level passage, its approaches should also be controlled as for any stairway at a sports ground; that is, people should be able to approach the vomitory only from the front and/or from its sides. The approach to the vomitory may only be from behind if it is controlled by the routing of gangways.

c. In standing areas where there are no gangways routed around the vomitory, it is recommended that such gangways be provided. If this is not practical, however, barriers should be positioned at each side of the vomitory's entrance. This is to ensure that spectators approaching from behind have to pass around the ends of the barriers and therefore approach the vomitory entrance from the sides.

These barriers should be protected (by infill or screening), to prevent spectators climbing through and approaching from behind.

d. In all areas of spectator accommodation, where appropriate, consideration should also be given to providing protection against objects being accidentally knocked onto spectators passing through the vomitory.

e. Management should ensure that no spectators or non-essential staff are allowed to stand in vomitories during an event. Similarly, during ingress and egress, stewards should position themselves to ensure the unimpeded passage of spectators. This is essential towards the end of an event (or significant part of an event) in order to prevent overcrowding and not to impede those spectators who wish to leave.

f. It is recommended that vomitories are clearly identified both internally and externally and on all site plans so that resources can be quickly directed to wherever they may be required.

10: Circulation – egress and emergency evacuation

10.1   Safety issues

It is generally recognised that a period of great risk to crowd safety is at the time of leaving the sports ground. It is important, therefore, to provide exit systems capable of accommodating safely the passage of people within an acceptable period of time, and to avoid congestion and psychological stress.

Exit systems may comprise gangways, stairways, passageways, ramps and other means of passage.

Management should ensure that exit routes are planned and managed safely, to provide for spectators a smooth, unimpeded passage through an exit system until they reach the boundary of the ground, or, in an emergency, a place of safety.

In order to achieve this, management should ensure that:

a.   there are sufficient numbers of exits in suitable locations

b.   all parts of exit routes are of adequate width and height

c.   people do not have to travel excessive distances in order to exit from the spectator accommodation

d.   provision is made for the control of spectators entering an exit system

e.   all exits are identifiable in both normal and emergency conditions.

This chapter offers guidance on the design and management of exit systems both under normal conditions and for emergency evacuation. However, it is stressed that congestion and accidents can occur under normal conditions, and that people react and respond in diverse ways according to their perceptions of risk.

Furthermore, pressures that can arise during the time of exit must be contained and controlled by attention to the detailed design of elements which form part of the exit systems, such as stairways (see Chapter 8), barriers (see Chapter 11) and gangways (see Chapters 12 and 13).

10.2   Basic design principles

Smooth, unimpeded flow through an exit route is best achieved by ensuring that the exit system does not narrow along its length.

If, at any point along the route, there are elements narrower than those preceding, constriction can occur, causing people to converge in the narrower points.

In addition, controlling the crowd flow at the beginning of the route – that is, within the viewing accommodation – is vital to ensure that people enter the exit system at an acceptable rate.

In order to achieve this, the first element of the exit route from the spectator accommodation should be no wider than any subsequent element.

For new construction: exit routes in new construction should comply fully with the above principles.

For existing construction: narrowing in the exit routes may occur at existing constructions. However, this should be acceptable only when the narrowing is preceded by an open space or 'reservoir area', where the holding capacity is sufficient to contain those people held up because of the difference in the rate of passage into and out of the reservoir area.

Guidance on the calculation of capacities for reservoir areas follows in Section 10.4.

Management should conduct a risk assessment of any reservoir area to ensure that there are no potential hazards to people passing through.

Reservoir areas are not acceptable within, or in close proximity to, any combustible structure (for example, a timber stand).

If deviations from the recommendations in the *Guide* create potential dangers in any part of the exit route, that section of the route should be closed and the final capacity of that section of the ground reduced accordingly.

In areas of standing accommodation, the exit routes used for the purposes of calculating the exit capacity of a section should include only designated gangways. Notional gangways between staggered crush barriers cannot form part of the calculation.

10.3 Factors in design and management

When considering the design and safe management of exit systems and emergency evacuation systems, four factors have to be considered:

a. the widths of each part of the exit, or emergency exit route (see Section 10.4)

b. the rate of passage of people through the exit, or emergency exit system; this is a pre-determined figure (see Section 10.6)

c. the egress time; this is normally a maximum of eight minutes for calculation purposes (see Section 10.7)

d. the emergency evacuation time; this is a variable, maximum time, between two and a half minutes and eight minutes, based on a number of factors (see Section 10.9).

The above factors are used to help calculate the final capacity of a ground, or section of a ground (see Chapter 2).

10.4 Exit route widths and reservoir areas

The capacity of an exit system is limited by its most restrictive element. It makes no difference to the efficiency of the system where the most restrictive element is located; the capacity is always determined by it.

Exit route widths should meet the following requirements:

a. **For new construction:**
   The recommended minimum width of an exit route is 1.2m.

b. **For existing construction:**
    The minimum width of an exit route should be 1.1m.

Where reservoir areas are used as part of an exit system, their capacity should be calculated on the basis of the appropriate rate of passage (see Section 10.6) and the appropriate emergency evacuation time (see Section 10.9).

A density of 40 persons per 10 square metres of the area available for standing within the reservoir area is the maximum permitted for safety. It is the responsibility of management to ensure that this density is not exceeded.

Exit doors providing passage from executive boxes and some hospitality areas may form part of exit systems at sports grounds. The preferred effective exit door width in these areas should meet the following requirements:

c. **For new construction:**
    Not less than 800mm.

d. **For existing construction:**
    Not less than 750mm.

10.5   Rates of passage – method of calculation

The rate of passage is the number of people who can pass through a particular point in an exit system, or emergency evacuation system, in a given time.

The rate of passage therefore forms a fundamental part of the calculation of the capacity of both exit and emergency evacuation systems.

For calculating capacities for both normal egress and emergency evacuation, the Fourth (1997) Edition of the *Guide* recommended maximum rates of passage of 73 spectators per metre width per minute on all staircases and routes within seated accommodation and 109 spectators per metre width per minute in all other parts of the ground.

It was not always understood, however, that these rates should be regarded as maxima and are unlikely to be sustained for more than a limited period under ideal conditions. Management should therefore always observe and record the actual rates of passage. Where it is apparent that spectators cannot exit within the prescribed normal egress time (see Section 10.7) or emergency evacuation time (see Section 10.9), the capacity should be reduced accordingly (see Section 2.3).

Examples of how to apply rates of passage can be found in Annex A.

Factors affecting the rates of passage may include the following:

a. audience profile, children, elderly people and disabled spectators, availability of alcohol

b. the location and level of use of commercial, catering or other spectator facilities situated along the exit route

c. the design and physical condition of the exit system; for example, the number of stairways, the existence of flank walls, the design and projection of handrails, the quality of directional signs, lighting levels and underfoot conditions.

10.6 Recommended rates of passage

The informative annex of BS EN 13200-1:2003 (see Bibliography) for flow capacity advises that, for a width of 1.2m:

a. on a stepped surface 79 people can reasonably exit in 1 minute (equal to 66 spectators per metre width per minute)

b. on a level surface 100 people can reasonably exit in 1 minute (equal to 82 spectators per metre width per minute)

For new construction: it is recommended that new sports grounds or sections of grounds should be designed in accordance with the rates of passage in the British Standard.

10.7 Egress time

It is emphasised that there is a difference between egress times and emergency evacuation times.

The egress time is the total time in which all spectators can, in normal conditions, leave an area of viewing accommodation and enter into a free flowing exit system. It does not include the time taken to negotiate the entire exit route.

(For a definition of emergency evacuation times, see Section 10.9.)

The normal maximum egress time for sports grounds is eight minutes.

If for any reason – for example, there are not enough exits – spectators cannot exit within eight minutes, a reduction of the final capacity may be required (see Chapter 2).

The limit of eight minutes has been set as a result of research and experience, which suggests that within this period spectators are less likely to become agitated, or experience frustration or stress, provided they enter an exit system at an acceptable rate, or are familiar with the sports ground and/or can identify their point of exit.

In certain circumstances it may be appropriate to apply a shorter egress time than eight minutes; for example, if the design or management of the viewing accommodation is such that regular observation shows that spectators become agitated or experience frustration or stress in periods of under eight minutes.

It should also be recognised that in many circumstances spectators will willingly take longer than eight minutes to leave; for example, in order to watch scoreboards, hear additional announcements or simply wait for the crowds to disperse. This practice must not be considered a factor in the determination of the egress time.

10.8 Design and management of exit systems

The design and management of exit systems should take into account the following:

a. **Movement**
   Once spectators have passed into the exit system they should be able to keep moving throughout its length.

b. **Alternative exits**
   In the event of an incident which renders the usual exit route unusable, spectators should be able to use an alternative exit route or routes.

c.   **Direct exit routes**

Where there is a simple exit route, that is, a direct passage from the viewing area to the exit gate from the ground, every part of that route should be able to accommodate the flow from the terrace or stand exit.

d.   **Complex exit routes or networks**

For a more complex exit system which combines a number of exit routes and/or offers a choice of alternative routes, the system should be analysed in the form of a network. This is in order to check that the capacity of the exit route from the viewing area is sufficient to ensure a free flow of spectators to the various exits from the ground. Where branching of routes gives spectators a choice of paths, the proportion of the crowd likely to use each path should be assessed; for example, the exit closest to a railway or bus station may be likely to attract a higher proportion of spectators.

Grounds which have complex exit systems should have clear, illustrative plans of the network system which serves each section, identifying the capacity of the routes within the system. These plans should be kept with the drawings of the section of the ground to which they relate. Any changes to the ground which affect the entry/exit routes should be identified on the network plan. (A network plan is illustrated in Worked Example 1 in Annex A.)

e.   **Number and disposition of exits**

As stated in Section 10.1, in order to ensure a smooth, unimpeded passage for spectators through an exit system, there must be a sufficient number of exits in suitable locations (although no simple calculation of the number can be given which would apply to all situations). To avoid inconvenience and confusion, it is also important that the exits are easily accessible and not spaced too widely apart.

f.   **Keeping exit routes clear**

Exit routes should be kept clear of obstructions. Catering, sales or toilet facilities should be located in such a way that neither they, nor any queue or waiting they attract, obstruct an exit route. Where exit routes pass through car parks or other areas affected by vehicular movements, consideration should be given to suitable methods of traffic control.

g.   **Signposting**

All elements of the exit system should be clearly signposted in accordance with the requirements of the Health and Safety (Safety Signs and Signals) Regulations 1996 (see Sections 16.28 and 16.29). Directional signs should be provided to encourage crowds in any particular section to flow in one direction when leaving the ground and should, wherever practicable, provide information on the destination of the exit route (for example, 'Station', 'Town Centre' or 'Visitors' Coach Park') so as to provide confidence to people using them.

10.9   Emergency evacuation time

As stated in Section 10.7, there is a difference between egress times and emergency evacuation times.

The emergency evacuation time is a calculation which, together with the rate of passage, is used to determine the capacity of the emergency exit system from the viewing accommodation to a place of safety or reasonable safety, in the event of an emergency (see Section 15.16).

The maximum emergency evacuation time for sports grounds varies between two and half minutes and eight minutes.

The time set depends largely on the level of fire risk present. Spectator accommodation which has a high fire risk should have an emergency exit capacity based on an emergency evacuation time of not more than two and a half minutes. A longer emergency evacuation time, of between two and a half minutes and eight minutes, is acceptable for grounds or parts of grounds where the fire risk is reduced. For guidance on varying levels of fire risk, see Sections 15.5–15.7.

However, as stated in Section 15.2, rather than relying solely on a short emergency evacuation time, the aim should always be to introduce measures which will minimise the outbreak and spread of fire.

For new construction: while in practice spectators may evacuate onto the pitch or area of activity in an emergency, this should not form part of the calculation of the emergency evacuation time for newly constructed grounds or sections of grounds.

10.10 Design of emergency evacuation routes

Evacuation routes for use in emergencies may need to be provided in addition to normal exits. In all cases, the following points should be considered:

a. There should be more than one emergency evacuation route from a viewing area.

b. The system should be designed in such a way that the loss of one emergency evacuation route does not prevent access to an alternative.

c. Where a stairway or any other circulation route passes up, down or through any area used by spectators, unless it is in the open air, it should be in a fire-resistant enclosure separated from the remainder of the building by a structure having a fire resistance of not less then 30 minutes (see also Sections 9.3 and 15.11).

d. Emergency evacuation routes should discharge into a place of safety, preferably in the open air.

e. Where emergency evacuation is possible only by passing through an enclosed concourse (for example, from the upper tier of a stand), consideration should be given to the provision of fire separation to individual routes of escape (see also Section 9.3).

If the capacity of the exit route is considered insufficient for emergency evacuation purposes the final capacity of the section served may have to be reduced.

Where appropriate, the design of emergency evacuation routes should also take into account the needs of spectators with disabilities.

10.11 Management of emergency evacuation routes

Management is responsible for ensuring that emergency evacuation routes are capable of being safely and effectively used at all times when the ground is occupied. This requires such routes to be maintained as sterile areas, free from any blockages, temporary fittings or stored equipment.

In addition, as stated in Sections 3.17 and 3.18, management should prepare contingency plans. These plans should provide for the evacuation of all people in the event of an emergency from all areas of the ground to a place of safety. Such plans will require the designation of exits and emergency evacuation routes.

CCTV is a useful means of monitoring the exit and emergency evacuation routes (see Section 16.16).

All such routes should also be clearly signposted (see Section 16.28).

10.12 Management of evacuation of spectators with disabilities

It is essential to consider practical measures for the emergency evacuation of disabled spectators.

Detailed guidance on this matter is provided in the Building Regulations, British Standard 5588 Part 8 – *Code of Practice for Means of Escape for Disabled People* and Sports Grounds, Stadia Guide No.1 – *Accessible Stadia* and *Fire Safety Risk Assessment Supplementary guide – Means of Escape for Disabled People* (see Bibliography) (see also Section 15.17).

Disabled spectators must be accommodated without prejudicing their safety or the safety of others. Safety measures should not be construed in such a way as to place undue restrictions on disabled spectators.

Management should pay particular regard to the following matters.

a. **Information systems**
    Measures and information systems are required to help all spectators, in particular those with impaired vision, colour perception or hearing, find their way in an unfamiliar environment. Those with impaired mobility should have a choice of more than one means of ingress and egress.

b. **Refuges**
    Designers and management should provide refuges of a suitable size to accommodate known numbers of wheelchair users and to plan for their subsequent evacuation by means of suitable lifts or management procedures.

c. **Stairways**
    The preferred method of escape by most wheelchair users is horizontally to another fire compartment or to outside the building, or vertically by the use of an evacuation or fire-fighting lift. If those options are not available or not in operation, it may be necessary to carry a person up or down an escape stair. A width of 1.1m for existing (1.2m in new stands) is sufficient to accommodate a standard tubular steel wheelchair. (For further guidance on the design of stairways see Chapter 8).

    Detailed guidance on carry down process, including training, is available from the Department for Communities and Local Government (DCLG) (see Bibliography).

d. **Evacuation lifts**
    A lift provided for passenger use in the normal operation of the sports ground may only be used for emergency evacuation purposes if it meets the requirements of an evacuation lift, as specified in the relevant British Standards.

    While there is no requirement to provide evacuation lifts in sports grounds, such lifts reduce the need to evacuate disabled spectators down staircases. Evacuation lifts should be able to continue to operate with a reasonable degree of safety when there is a fire in the building.

    However a lift can still fail. It is crucial, therefore that, having reached a refuge at an evacuation lift, a disabled person can gain access to an adjacent suitable stairway should the conditions in the refuge become unacceptable. Contingency plans should therefore also allow for the careful carrying of disabled spectators down stairs without their wheelchairs, should the wheelchair be too large or heavy.

The location of evacuation lifts should be clearly indicated with signs on every floor level.

e. Fire-fighting lifts

A fire-fighting lift is essentially an evacuation lift that is provided principally for the use of the fire service and which meets the requirements of the current, relevant British Standard. Such a lift may, however, be used for the evacuation of disabled people.

Liaison with the relevant fire authority to co-ordinate procedures for the use of a fire-fighting lift for evacuation purposes is essential.

f. Wheelchair stairlifts

Wheelchair stairlifts should not be used for emergency evacuation. Nor should any part of a stairlift or its mechanism reduce the width of any stairway or escape route below the required minimum.

g. Ramps

Where ramps are necessary for the emergency evacuation of spectators in wheelchairs they should be as gentle as possible, preferably no steeper than 1 in 20 (see Section 8.11) and have signs identifying the change of level.

10.13 Use of the pitch or area of activity for emergency evacuation

In certain cases, forward evacuation onto the pitch or area of activity may form part of the emergency evacuation route, provided that it leads directly to an exit which itself leads to a place of safety.

The following requirements should also be taken into account:

a. Whether or not the emergency evacuation of spectators onto the pitch or area of activity forms part of the agreed emergency evacuation plan, wherever there is a pitch perimeter barrier or free-standing advertising material in front of spectator accommodation, other than in exceptional circumstances it must be fitted with a sufficient number of suitably designed gates or openings (see Section 10.14).

b. Where the playing surface is made of synthetic materials, advice should be sought from the authority responsible for enforcing fire safety legislation to establish whether it can be properly considered as an emergency exit route in the event of a fire. This is because some forms of artificial turf might constitute a hazard in the event of fire.

c. If the pitch or area of activity is wholly surrounded by covered accommodation, with no breaks in the roofing (see Section 15.11), it may not be a suitable route for emergency evacuation in the event of fire. In such cases advice should be sought from the authority responsible for enforcing fire safety legislation.

As stated in Section 10.9, for new construction, the use of the pitch or area of activity for emergency evacuation should not form part of the capacity calculation.

10.14   Provision of gates or openings in a pitch perimeter barrier

As stated above, where a pitch perimeter barrier or free-standing advertising material is in place in front of spectator accommodation, other than in exceptional circumstances it must be fitted with gates or openings allowing access onto the pitch or area of activity (see also Section 5.10.m).

If a viewing area is divided by structural means, each division must have sufficient gates or openings to evacuate all the spectators in that division within the emergency evacuation time set for that part of the ground.

Such gates or openings should:

a.   be a minimum width of 1.1m (1.2m recommended for new construction)

b.   align with radial gangways (where provided) and measure not less than the width of those gangways

c.   be appropriately stewarded.

Where gates are fitted, they should:

d.   open away from spectators

e.   be kept unlocked

f.   only be fitted with bolts or latches that can be released from both sides

g.   be clearly marked and painted a different colour from the rest of the pitch perimeter barrier.

10.15   Discounting an exit route for calculation purposes

There are no hard and fast rules as to whether or not an exit route should be discounted when calculating the emergency exit capacity of a sports ground or section of a ground. Each case needs to be determined in the light of local circumstances, taking into account the importance of a particular exit from an area of spectator accommodation and an assessment of the level of fire risk present.

If the fire risk assessment determines that there is a need to discount an exit, the exit to be discounted should be the widest one serving the area. If the fire risk is minimal and all elements of the exit system are suitably protected from the effects of fire, it may be unreasonable to discount an exit. (For guidance on fire risk assessment, see Sections 15.3–15.7).

10.16   Exit doors and gates

Exit doors and gates should meet the following requirements:

a.   All final exit doors and gates, unless secured in an open position, should be staffed at all times while the ground is used by the public.

b.   No door or gate forming part of an exit route should be locked or fastened in such a way that it cannot easily and immediately be opened by those using that route in an emergency.

c.   All final exit doors on a normal exit route should be secured in the fully open position before the end of the event. When open, no exit door should obstruct any gangway, passage, stairway or landing.

d. All exit doors and gates on an exit route should always be capable of opening outwards so that crowds can escape in an emergency without obstruction. In situations where the opening of the exit doors or gates would cause an obstruction on a public highway, they should be resited (that is, put further back) within the exit route they serve.

e. Where practicable exit doors and gates should be sited adjacent to entrances. There should be no obstructions and no changes in level at exit doors.

f. Sliding or roller-shutter gates should not be used because they are incapable of being opened when pressure is exerted in the direction of crowd flow, and they have mechanisms or runways which are vulnerable to jamming.

g. Reversible turnstiles or, preferably, pass doors should be provided in order to allow anyone to leave the ground at any time (including those ejected for breaching ground regulations). Such openings should be limited to allow the passage of only one person at a time.

h. Reversible turnstiles are not acceptable as a means of escape and should not form any part of the normal or emergency exit system.

i. Each exit door and gate should be clearly marked on both the inside and the outside with its identifying number so that resources can be quickly directed to wherever they may be required.

j. The safety officer should check or be informed when all the final exit doors and gates have been secured in an open position.

k. All exit doors and gates should ideally be monitored by CCTV.

10.17 Electronic securing systems

Where they are in place, electronic securing systems on exit doors and gates should meet the following requirements:

a. As stated in Section 10.16, no exit door or gate forming part of an exit route should be locked or fastened in such a way that it cannot easily and immediately be opened by those using that route in an emergency. This applies equally to exit doors and gates that are electronically secured.

b. All electronically secured exit doors and gates should be staffed by stewards at all times when spectators are in the ground.

c. The exit doors or gates should be capable of being de-energised individually by the steward.

d. The stewards should be specifically authorised to open their gates without further instructions in the event of a sudden local emergency.

e. Emergency telephones should be provided for instant communication, directly between the stewards staffing the exit doors or gates and the operator of the control panel (see below). All such telephones should be instantly accessible to the stewards without the use of a key.

f. The operation of each exit door or gate should be tested both electronically and manually immediately before each event and the result of each test recorded. The record should include all tests, any faults found, and any opening of any exit door or gate while spectators are present in the ground.

g. The control panel for the system should be located in the ground's control point and should be staffed continuously by a suitably trained and authorised person, who should have no other duties.

h. The base emergency telephone in the control point should be positioned so that the panel operator can answer it without having to leave his or her post.

i. Each gate should be clearly marked on both the inside and the outside with its identifying number. This identification should correspond to the identification of the switch on the control which releases it.

j. The exit doors or gates should be designed so that, in the event of a power failure, they are automatically de-energised and capable of being opened manually.

Before approving an electronic securing system, ground management or, where a safety certificate in force, the local authority, should consider carefully and take full account of the hazards associated with such a system. In particular, it should consider carefully what would happen if there was a major emergency and spectators had to force the exit doors open themselves.

11: Barriers

11.1 Definition and categories of barriers

A barrier (also referred to as a 'guard' or 'guard rail' in the Building Regulations) is any element of a sports ground, permanent or temporary, intended to prevent people from falling, and to retain, stop or guide people. This chapter is concerned with barriers in the following situations:

a.   barriers used in areas of seated accommodation and on stairways and ramps (see Sections 11.2–11.5, *Table 11.1* and *Diagrams 11.1 and 11.2*)

b.   barriers used in areas of standing accommodation, known as crush barriers (see Sections 11.6–11.12, *Table 11.2* and *Diagrams 11.3 – 11.5*)

c.   barriers used in spectator galleries (see Section 11.13 and *Table 11.3*)

d.   barriers used to separate spectator accommodation from the pitch or area of activity, known as pitch perimeter barriers (see Sections 11.14–11.15)

e.   barriers such as boundary walls, fences or gates used to enclose the sports ground or individual sections (see Section 11.17).

Sections 11.18–11.25 provide guidance on the risk assessment and testing of barriers.

When applying the recommendations in this chapter, the distinction between a barrier and a handrail, as outlined in Section 8.6, should be noted.

Further detailed guidance may be found in the European Standard BS EN 13200-3:2005 Spectator Facilities Part 3: *Separating Elements* (see Bibliography).

11.2 Barrier design and loading

Barriers at sports grounds should be designed to resist safely the minimum horizontal imposed loads specified in *Tables 11.1, 11.2 or 11.3*. It should be noted, however, that in all situations professional judgement should ensure that the loadings are sufficient for the barrier's intended purpose.

Regardless of the height of the barrier (see Section 11.4), the horizontal imposed load should be considered to act at a height of 1.1m above the datum, when applied as a static load at right angles to the longitudinal axis of the barrier. A component of the same load parallel to the longitudinal axis should also be considered, for example a 10° off-perpendicular component creates significant in-plane loading.

Designers should ensure that any construction or structure acting as a support for barriers is of adequate strength and stability to resist safely all applied loads, without excessive stress, deflection or distortion.

When using limit state design, the partial factors for loads and materials should be those recommended by the relevant British Standard for the relevant material.

Table 11.1 Horizontal imposed loads for barriers

types of barrier	horizontal imposed load
1. Crush barriers for standing accommodation	See Table 11.2
2. Barriers for spectator galleries	See Table 11.3
3. Barriers for gangways of seating decks, aligned at right angles to the direction of spectator movement	3.0 kN/m length
4. Barriers for gangways of seating decks, parallel to the direction of spectator movement	2.0 kN/m length
5. Barriers for seating decks, adjacent to the end row of seats and protecting spectators from falling sideways	1.0 kN/m length
6. Barriers for seating decks, behind a rear row of seats and protecting spectators from falling backwards	1.0 kN/m length
7. Barriers positioned within 530mm in front of seats	1.5 kN/m length
8. Barriers for stairways, landings and ramps, aligned at right angles to the direction of movement of spectators	3.0 kN/m length
9. Barriers for stairways, landings, and ramps, aligned with the direction of movement of spectators	2.0 kN/m length
10. Barriers for gangways in standing areas, aligned at right angles to the direction of spectator movement	5.0 kN/m length
11. Other barriers, including walls, boundary walls, fences and gates, that may be subject to crowd loading	See Section 11.17

Table 11.2 Horizontal imposed loads for crush barriers

angle of terrace or viewing slope	horizontal distance between crush barriers				
5°	5.0m	4.0m	3.3m	3.0m	2.0m
10°	4.3m	3.4m	2.9m	2.6m	1.7m
15°	3.8m	3.0m	2.6m	2.3m	1.5m
20°	3.4m	2.7m	2.3m	2.0m	1.3m
25°	3.1m	2.5m	2.1m	1.8m	1.2m
horizontal imposed load	5.0 kN/m	4.0 kN/m	3.4 kN/m	3.0 kN/m	2.0 kN/m

Table 11.3 Horizontal imposed loads for barriers in spectator galleries

depth of gallery measured perpendicular to barrier	3.4m	2.3m	1.7m
horizontal imposed load	3.0 kN/m length	2.0 kN/m length	1.5 kN/m length

General notes to Tables 11.1, 11.2 and 11.3

■ All barriers should be capable of resisting proof loads equivalent to 1.2 times the horizontal imposed loads listed in the tables.

■ Barrier testing methods and the criteria to be met are given in Sections 11.20–26.

■ Barrier foundations should be designed to resist the overturning moments and sliding forces induced by the horizontal imposed loads with a factor of safety of 2.

■ Loads specified in these tables should be treated as unfactored or characteristic loads for design purposes.

■ Refer also to the European Standard BS EN 13200-3:2005 Spectator Facilities Part 3: Separating Elements (see Bibliography).

Notes to Table 11.1

■ This table should be read in conjunction with Diagrams 11.1 and 11.2.

■ It is recommended that escalators should satisfy the same loadings as stairways.

■ All references to seats are to fixed seats (that is, any seat, tip-up or otherwise), attached to the main structure.

Notes to Table 11.2

■ Interpolation may be made between these figures.

■ Angles of slope in excess of 25° are potentially hazardous and should be avoided. Where they exist they should be subject to a risk assessment.

■ The maximum horizontal imposed load on a crush barrier should not be greater than 5 kN/m. This is because a transient load greater than 5 kN/m on the spectator immediately behind a crush barrier risks physical injury.

■ The horizontal distances specified are the maximum recommended according to the barrier strength and angle of slope, and should not be exceeded in new construction. If the distances at existing constructions exceed the maximum, the available viewing area (which forms part of the capacity calculation) should be limited to the area behind the barrier which falls within the maximum distance. The remaining space behind should be discounted, even though in practice spectators may stand in those areas (see worked examples 2 and 3 in Annex A).

Notes to Table 11.3

■ Interpolation may be made between these figures.

■ The required horizontal imposed load should be calculated according to the distance between the barrier and the gallery's rear wall, or any other restraint.

■ If the spectator gallery also forms part of an escape route, the barrier's horizontal imposed load should be no less than 2 kN/m length.

Diagram 11.1 Barrier design loads, heights and positions

This diagram illustrates the types of barriers used in seating decks, stairways and gangways. The type numbers correspond with those listed in Table 11.1

Type 4 side and lateral barrier, aligned parallel to the direction of spectator movement
Height: 1.1m
Design Load: 2.0 kN/m

Type 8 barrier on a stairway, aligned at right angles to the direction of movement
Height: 1.1m
Design Load: 3.0 kN/m

Type 3 barrier at the foot of a gangway
Height: 1.1m
Design Load: 3.0 kN/m

Type 9 barrier at the side of a stairway, aligned with the direction of movement
Height: 1.1m
Design Load: 2.0 kN/m

Type 7 barrier within 530mm in front of a row of fixed seats
Height: 800mm
Design Load: 1.5 kN/m

Type 6 barrier behind a rear row of seats
Height: 1.1m above level of seats.
Design Load: 1.0 kN/m

Type 5 barrier adjacent to end row of seats
Height: 1.1m
Design Load: 1.0 kN/m

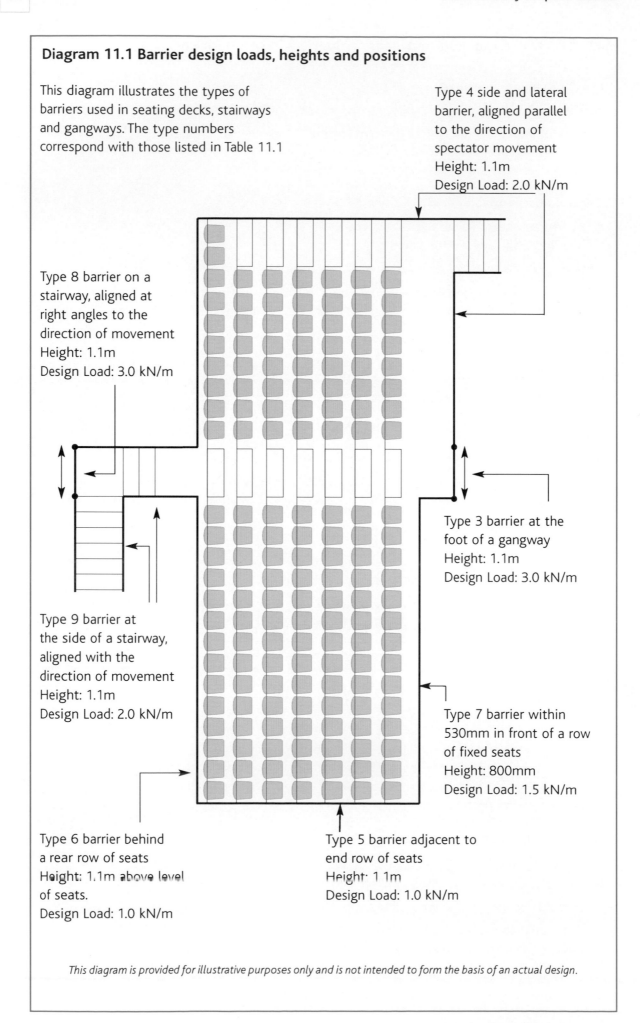

This diagram is provided for illustrative purposes only and is not intended to form the basis of an actual design.

Diagram 11.2 Barriers in front of and behind seating

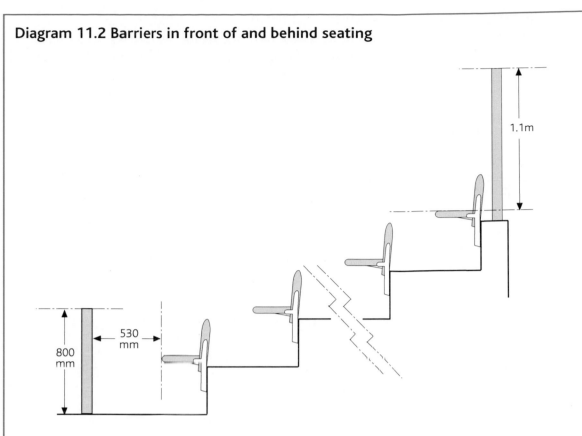

Type 7 barriers positioned within 530mm in front of a row of fixed seats should be a minimum height of 800mm above the datum and a recommended minimum of 200mm wide. If the barrier width is increased to 500mm the height above datum may be reduced to 700mm.

It also recommended that, where appropriate, the top surfaces of such barriers should be designed to prevent their use as shelves for items which might fall off and endanger spectators.

Where the rear of the stand is open type 6 barriers behind a row of seats should be a minimum height of 1.1m, measured from the seat level.

11.3   Barrier fixings

The strength of all fixings and joints should be adequate for the loading to which the barrier will be subjected. The design should avoid reliance wholly on the pull-out strength of a single fixing. It is also essential that fixing design takes account of the material into which the fixing is placed, the spacing between fixings, the edge distance and, where appropriate, the position of reinforcement in the concrete. The fixings should not create a trip hazard for spectators.

11.4   Barrier heights

Barriers used in areas of seated accommodation and on stairways and ramps should be designed to a height of not less than 1.1m, measured from the datum, unless they fall into one of the following three categories:

a.   Barriers within 530mm in front of fixed seating should be a height of 800mm above the datum (see *Diagram 11.2*) Note that this reduced barrier height is for seated spectators. If for any reason spectators regularly stand in this location consideration should be given to taking this row (and possibly others behind) out of use (see Section 12.20.e).

b.   Barriers immediately behind a row of seats should be a minimum height of 1.1m above the datum, which in this case is the level of the seat (see *Diagram 11.2*).

c.   Barriers designed to separate stairways into channels may be a minimum height of 1.0m above the datum (see Section 8.7.b and *Diagram 8.1*).

In all cases, as stated in Section 11.2, regardless of the height, the horizontal imposed load should still be considered to act at a height of 1.1m above the datum.

Further guidance on the height of crush barriers is provided in Section 11.10. Guidance on the heights of handrails for stairways and ramps is given in Section 8.8.

11.5   Barriers and sightline considerations

As stated in Section 12.2, all spectators in seated areas should have a clear, unobstructed view of the whole pitch or area of activity. However, it is recognised that even barriers meeting the height requirements listed in Section 11.4 may obstruct sightlines.

Careful consideration should therefore be given to the design and construction of any barrier forming part of a seating deck. This applies particularly to barriers placed within 530mm of fixed seating.

11.6   Crush barriers – main design criteria

This section and Sections 11.7–11.12 on crush barriers should be read in conjunction with Chapter 13, concerning the overall design and management of standing areas. Detailed reference should also be made to *Table 11.2*.

At sports grounds where standing accommodation is provided, many of the hazards arising from crowd pressure on terraces and viewing slopes can be eliminated by the provision of crush barriers that are appropriately designed and constructed.

The main considerations concerning the design and construction of crush barriers are detailed in the following sections, and can be summarised as follows:

a.   the angle of slope of the terrace or viewing slope, which in turn will determine the appropriate spacing of the crush barriers and the required horizontal imposed load for each crush barrier (see Section 11.7)

b. the configuration of the crush barriers in relation to gangways (see Sections 11.8 and 11.9)

c. the height and positioning of the crush barriers in relation to the treads or surfaces of the standing area (see Section 11.10)

d. the construction and condition of the crush barriers (see Section 11.11).

Section 11.12 summarises the consequences of any deficiencies or deviations from the requirements outlined in Sections 11.7–11.11.

11.7   Crush barriers – factors determining the horizontal imposed load

As stated in Section 11.6 above, the required horizontal imposed load for crush barriers is determined by the angle of the terrace or viewing slope, in relation to the horizontal distance between the crush barriers, as shown in *Table 11.2*.

Table 11.2 indicates that the steeper the angle of slope and the greater the horizontal distance between crush barriers, the greater the horizontal imposed load required for those crush barriers.

a. Angle of slope

The angle of slope (or gradient) is the first factor to be considered when determining the required horizontal imposed load for crush barriers.

For new construction: the angle of slope for newly constructed areas of standing should be designed according to the calculations for sightlines (see Section 13.11). Although for seated areas the angle can be as steep as 34°, for standing areas it should not exceed 25°.

For existing construction: the angle of slope will be pre-determined. However, it is strongly recommended that the angle of any standing area should not exceed 25° (see Section 11.12).

b. Horizontal distance between crush barriers

Having established the angle of slope, the spacing between crush barriers should then be considered.

For new construction: designers should use the figures in *Table 11.2* to determine the appropriate crush barrier loadings and spacings according to the desired angle of slope.

For existing construction: the horizontal spacing between crush barriers will be pre-determined, in which case the horizontal imposed load of the crush barriers must be in accordance with the requirements specified in *Table 11.2*. If the spacing proves to be excessive, the available viewing area should be reduced to those areas immediately behind each crush barrier, measured to a depth appropriate to the crush barrier's strength (see *Table 11.2* and Section 11.12).

Any crush barrier which fails to meet the horizontal imposed load requirements specified in *Table 11.2* should be removed and replaced, or strengthened and then re-tested (see Section 11.11).

11.8 Crush barriers – continuous crush barrier configuration

The configuration of crush barriers – that is, their layout in relation to each other and to the gangways – has a crucial influence on the safe management of spectators in standing areas.

Experience at sports grounds indicates that the safest configuration is to provide crush barriers along the full width of a terrace or viewing slope, with gaps only at the radial gangways. Because this configuration is considered to be the safest arrangement for guiding and controlling the movements of standing spectators, it is also the principal method by which ground management can aim to achieve the highest permissible capacity levels for a standing area.

For new construction: at all new stadia (see Glossary) where standing areas are to form part of the viewing accommodation, or at stadia where new standing areas are to be constructed, a continuous crush barrier configuration should be provided between radial gangways. It is acknowledged that at sports grounds where the spectators are ambulatory, for example horse racing, front loading terraces may load and empty quicker if there are staggered barriers but such a layout will result in a lower capacity. The use of such barrier configurations must be supported by risk assessment and effective monitoring to ensure that the safe capacities are not exceeded.

For existing construction: at all sports grounds where standing accommodation is already provided, consideration should be given to the conversion of existing standing areas so that they incorporate a continuous crush barrier configuration between radial gangways.

An example of a continuous crush barrier configuration is illustrated in *Diagram 11.3*.

As stated in Section 2.8, provided that the strengths of the continuous crush barriers are appropriate for the angle of slope and the spacings between the crush barriers, and the standing area is both in good condition and well stewarded, there should be no reduction in the calculation of its available viewing area, nor of its (P) and (S) factors, nor of its appropriate density, which should be the maximum of 47 persons per 10 square metres (as explained in Section 2.9).

Worked Example 1 in Annex A illustrates how a continuous crush barrier configuration results in a higher capacity than a standing area of an identical size but with a non-continuous configuration (as shown in Worked Example 2).

11.9 Crush barriers – non-continuous crush barrier configuration

Where non-continuous crush barriers are in place, the alignment of gaps in successive rows of barriers should form an angle of less than 60° to the barriers (see Worked Example 2).

There should be no more than two consecutive gaps in any line. These gaps should be at least 1.1m, and not more than 1.4m, in width.

11.10 Crush barriers – height and positioning

Research has shown that in order to locate the top rail of a crush barrier against that part of the body most able to tolerate pressure, and to accommodate a typical range of spectators, a reasonable height for the top rail is 1.1m.

Note, however, the need to evolve a management strategy for the safe accommodation of children, for whom the recommended barrier height might actually constitute a hazard (see Section 13.24.i).

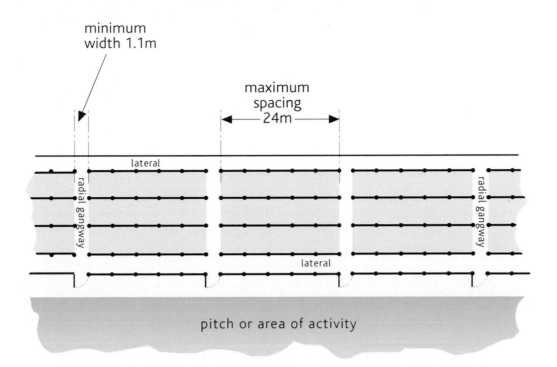

Diagram 11.3 Continuous crush barrier configuration

minimum
width 1.1m

maximum
spacing
24m

lateral

radial gangway

radial gangway

lateral

pitch or area of activity

Note that all spectators should be within 12m of a gangway or exit, hence the spacing of gangways 24m apart. Note also that for new construction the recommended minimum width for gangways is 1.2m.

At sports grounds where pitch perimeter barriers are positioned in front of standing areas, gates or openings should be provided to allow spectators to escape onto the pitch or area of activity in the event of an incident.

Where gates are fitted, as illustrated these should open away from the viewing accommodation.

Wherever practicable in standing areas, as stated in Section 11.15 and shown above, there should be a lateral gangway dividing the front row of crush barriers from the pitch perimeter barrier. However, where a continuous crush barrier configuration is provided, a front lateral gangway may not always be necessary, depending on local conditions.

For new construction: as illustrated in *Diagram 11.4*, to allow spectators sufficient room to stand safely and comfortably behind a crush barrier, new crush barriers should ideally be positioned immediately in front of a terrace step's riser, or if not, at the front of a step. In both cases, the 1.1m is measured from the step on which the spectator stands to the top of the crush barrier's rail

For barriers installed prior to 1997 a range of heights between 1.02m and 1.12m measured from the step to the centre line of the top rail, should still be regarded as acceptable.

However, any crush barrier not meeting the height requirement should be removed and replaced, or modified.

If the positioning of existing crush barriers leaves insufficient room for standing on the same step, as illustrated in *Diagram 11.4*, the height should be measured from the step immediately behind and the area of the step should not be included when calculating the available viewing area.

11.11 Crush barriers – construction and strengthening

Crush barriers should be constructed or strengthened taking into account the following requirements:

a.   For safety and comfort, there should be no sharp projections or edges.

b.   For safety and comfort, the crush barrier's top rail should be flat facing, measure 100mm in vertical depth and be designed to prevent it from being used as a shelf.

c.   As stated in Section 11.7, any crush barrier which fails to meet the horizontal imposed load specified in *Table 11.2* should be removed and replaced. If this is not possible and therefore strengthening measures are to be considered, care must be taken to avoid simply transferring the problem to another part of the crush barrier or its foundations.

If strengthening the crush barrier post, portal type bracing is recommended, as illustrated in *Diagram 11.5*.

All newly strengthened barriers must be tested before use.

11.12 Crush barriers – factors affecting the holding capacity

In addition to the reduction of the available viewing area resulting from the provision of a non-continuous crush barrier configuration (see Section 11.9), further deficiencies or deviations from the recommendations in the *Guide* may require a reduction of the holding capacity of the standing area (see Chapter 2).

A summary of the main concerns follows. Note that this list is not intended to be comprehensive, nor applicable in all circumstances.

A reduction in the holding capacity of a standing area may be necessary if:

a.   the angle of slope is above 25° (thereby requiring a reduction of the (P) or (S) factors)

b.   the crush barrier spacing is too great in relation to the angle of slope (thereby requiring a reduction of the available viewing area, and a possible reduction in the (S) factor)

Diagram 11.4
Positioning and height of crush barriers

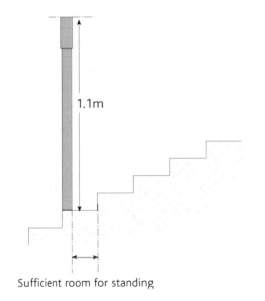

In the top two examples, the barriers are positioned, as recommended, at the front of the step. The recommended height of 1.1m is measured from the surface of the step to the top of the rail. For existing situations, the measurement can be taken from the step to the centre of the rail, and be between 1.02m and 1.12m.

Sufficient room for standing

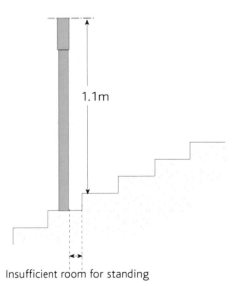

In this example the barrier is positioned in such a way as to make it difficult for a spectator to stand on the same step. For this reason the height measurement should be taken from the step behind. This positioning of barriers is not recommended for new construction. If there is insufficient space to stand on a step to which the barrier is fitted, this area should not be included when calculating the available viewing area.

Insufficient room for standing

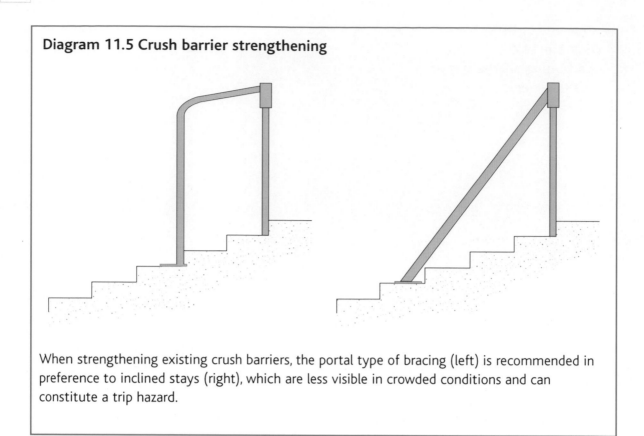

Diagram 11.5 Crush barrier strengthening

When strengthening existing crush barriers, the portal type of bracing (left) is recommended in preference to inclined stays (right), which are less visible in crowded conditions and can constitute a trip hazard.

c.   after testing, the barrier fails completely (see Section 11.25) and is removed but not replaced (thereby requiring a reduction in the available viewing area, and a possible reduction in the (S) factor).

It should be noted that there may be other aspects of the standing area which also require a reduction in the holding capacity. These might include the physical condition of the standing area, its safety management, the provision of partial cover only, or the inadequacy of sightlines. Further guidance on these concerns is provided in Chapters 2 and 13.

11.13   Barriers in spectator galleries

Viewing galleries for standing spectators are generally attached to hospitality areas at sports grounds staging sports such as horse or motor racing. Although the number of spectators who have access to such galleries is normally limited by the capacity of the hospitality area, the front barrier must still be designed to withstand crowd loading.

Table 11.3 specifies the required horizontal imposed loads, which vary according to the horizontal distance between the barrier and either the rear wall of the spectator gallery or any other restraint.

11.14   Pitch and activity area perimeter barriers

A perimeter barrier is a barrier installed to separate spectators from the pitch or area of activity. Such barriers can take the form of crush barriers, walls or rails.

The type, height and horizontal imposed load of a pitch perimeter barrier will vary according to its location and required function.

If spectators can lean on, or gather immediately behind, the perimeter barrier, it should be deemed a crush barrier and therefore meet the horizontal imposed load and height requirements as specified in Sections 11.6–11.12.

Even if a pitch perimeter barrier does not need to meet the horizontal imposed load requirements of a crush barrier, its height should ideally not exceed 1.1m (1.12m to the centre line in existing constructions). This is in order to facilitate spectator access to the pitch or area of activity in the event of an emergency. (This height requirement does not, however, preclude the need for gates or openings in pitch perimeter barriers, as stated in Section 10.14.)

Advertising hoardings placed along the side of pitch or activity area are not considered as pitch and activity area perimeter barriers and should not impair the function of any such barrier nor obscure spectators' views (see Section 19.3.h).

11.15 Pitch and activity area perimeter barriers and standing areas

Wherever practicable, pitch and activity area perimeter barriers should be separated from an area of standing accommodation by a lateral gangway, to assist circulation (see also *Diagram 11.3*).

An exception to this recommendation might be a standing area which has a continuous crush barrier configuration. In such cases an assessment of the need for a lateral gangway should be made, based on local conditions.

Wherever the standing area does descend directly to a pitch or activity area perimeter barrier, however, that barrier should meet the height and horizontal imposed load requirements of a crush barrier.

At certain sports grounds – for example those staging horse or greyhound racing – it is customary to allow spectators to view the event from level or near level standing areas commonly known as the lawns (see Section 13.19). Where such areas do not have a front barrier which meets the loading requirement of a crush barrier, it must be demonstrated through risk assessment, effective monitoring and appropriate safety management procedures that there is no forward movement or exerted pressure concentrated on the front rails (see Section 2.8.h). Even if all these measures are implemented, a careful assessment should be made of the (P) and (S) factors for each individual division or separate area of viewing accommodation.

11.16 Temporary barriers

Any temporary barrier or separating element should be of the same height and strength as any permanent barrier in a similar position.

11.17 Other load-bearing barriers

In addition to the barrier types already covered in this chapter, other load-bearing barriers subject to crowd loading at sports ground may include walls (including boundary walls), fences and gates.

If required to withstand crowd pressures, all such barriers should be designed, constructed and maintained to withstand those pressures safely.

Allowance should also be made for forces simultaneously and independently induced by other factors; for example, wind forces or attached installations.

11.18 Barriers and risk assessment

All barriers (including crush barriers) should be subject to an annual risk assessment to determine the time period or periods at which all barriers should be tested. Every barrier identified by the risk assessment as a potential risk should be tested immediately.

The risk assessment (which, in practice, will be carried out in a similar fashion to an annual inspection) should be conducted and recorded by a chartered engineer, architect or surveyor of the appropriate skill and experience. It should take into account all relevant recommendations in this *Guide*, combined with a detailed appraisal of each of the following specific considerations:

a.   any available recorded information concerning the barrier's design compliance

b.   the adequacy of the barrier's construction

c.   the age of the barrier

d.   any visual evidence of weakening or general deterioration of the barrier, including signs of corrosion, cracks, holes, misalignment, undue distortion, missing bolts or fittings

e.   the barrier's exposure to moisture

f.   the possibility of water or moisture ingress into hollow steel sections (see Bibliography)

g.   the barrier's location within the sports ground.

Those barriers which need to be tested immediately might include those whose theoretical strength is indeterminable, those which have suffered visible decay, and those where there is potential for undetected deterioration.

Responsibility for appointing a competent person to undertake and record the results of a risk assessment of barriers lies with the management of the sports ground.

11.19 Barrier tests – personnel and equipment

Having conducted the risk assessment and determined which barriers, if any, require testing, it is then the responsibility of management to ensure that the tests are carried out immediately.

The management is further responsible for ensuring that the testing is carried out by, or under the supervision of, a competent person of the appropriate skill and experience.

The competent person will then be responsible for ensuring that the tests are properly carried out and that all results are accurately recorded (see Section 11.20).

The competent person must be satisfied that the equipment used for the testing is suitable for the purpose and is used in the correct manner.

The equipment used should be capable of a level of accuracy of 5 per cent of the test load.

The deflection measuring equipment should be calibrated and be capable of a level of accuracy that reflects the magnitude of the deflections being measured.

11.20 Barrier tests – records

Detailed written records should be made and kept of all observations, loadings and deflection/recovery readings in respect of each barrier tested. The documentation should include a standard record sheet including the following information:

a. the identity of each barrier tested

b. its location, including a cross-reference to the ground plan

c. the date of inspection

d. all relevant results and comments arising from the test

e. a clear statement as to whether the barrier has passed or failed.

11.21 Barrier tests – methodology

The test method for barriers should be in two parts:

a. the 'bedding-in' cycle

b. the proof cycle.

Barriers that do not fulfil the requirements of both parts shall be deemed to have failed the test.

The deflection measuring equipment should be unaffected by any movement of the barriers, their supports, or the movements of personnel performing the test.

The deflections in the horizontal plane should be measured at relevant locations; for example, at the centre of a barrier rail or the top of an upright.

The loading procedure adopted shall result in each component part of any barrier being subject to levels of stress at least equal to the stresses that would occur were the structure subjected to the relevant uniformly distributed load at a design level of 1.1m.

11.22 Barrier tests – bedding-in cycle

In order to allow for bedding-in, the barrier should be loaded up to its horizontal imposed load as defined in either *Tables 11.1 or 11.2*. The bedding-in load should be applied in at least five equal increments and then removed. Deflections should be monitored at each increment of the load cycle and upon removal of the load. The barrier may be considered to have satisfactorily completed this part of the test if, on removal of the load, the recovery is at least 75 per cent of the maximum deflection, as measured from the original position prior to loading, or if the permanent deflection is less than 2mm.

If the barrier fails to achieve this level of recovery it shall be considered to have failed the test unless there is a satisfactory explanation for the results.

11.23 Barrier tests – proof cycle

The proof cycle is to consist of two consecutive applications of the proof load. The interval between each application shall be such as to enable complete unloading.

For crush barriers the proof load is equal to 1.2 x the horizontal imposed load specified in *Table 11.2*.

For other barriers the proof force is equal to 1.2 x the horizontal imposed load specified in either *Table 11.1* or *Table 11.3*.

The application of the proof load should consist of five equal increments.

The full proof load shall be maintained for five minutes and then removed.

A record shall be kept of:

a.   the deflection at each load increment

b.   the deflection after the five-minute application of the full proof load

c.   the residual deflection after removal of the load.

The procedure is then repeated.

If, on removal of the load after the second application, the recovery is at least 95 per cent in any measured deflection (as measured from the barrier position at the start of the proof cycle – that is, after the bedding-in cycle), the barrier should be considered to have satisfied the proof cycle loading requirement.

11.24   Barrier tests – further considerations

Comparisons should be made with the records available from previous testings of the barrier.

Comparison should also be made with the performance of other barriers of a similar type subjected to the same or similar tests. This is to establish whether there are indications of a reduction in overall performance, perhaps indicative of a developing weakness that necessitates either remedial action or more regular testing or inspection.

If the barrier satisfies the requirements of the testing procedure, but during that procedure doubt arises as to its safety, for any reason (including such matters as corrosion, distortion of connections and fittings, or cracking in the vicinity of supports), a further detailed investigation should be carried out. Unless the results of this detailed investigation remove the doubt, the barrier should be deemed to have failed.

11.25   Barrier tests resulting in failure

A barrier failing the test procedure should be removed and replaced, or strengthened and then retested.

As stated in Section 11.12, if a crush barrier fails, until it is replaced or strengthened the available viewing area of the standing area should be reduced, together with a possible reduction of the (P) factor, which in turn may lead to a reduction of the area's final capacity.

The removal of a crush barrier – particularly one placed where a high density of spectators may congregate – is likely to lead to uncontrolled movements and increased crowd pressure. In such situations, the reduction of the area's holding capacity should be much greater than if it were related to the non-replacement of an individual crush barrier elsewhere.

The non-replacement of a crush barrier will also require a management strategy to prevent overcrowding in the affected area.

Replacement, or repair, of the failed barrier should therefore always be the preferred option.

12: Spectator accommodation – seating

12.1 The provision of seated accommodation

At sports grounds where spectators are essentially non-ambulatory during the event – such as grounds staging football, rugby, cricket, athletics, tennis, hockey and motor racing – the provision of seated accommodation for all spectators is, wherever possible, recommended.

When considering new construction at such grounds, management should take this into consideration as part of its strategy for overall safety management.

It is recognised, however, that where spectators may be ambulatory during the event – such as at grounds staging golf, horse or greyhound racing – a combination of seated and standing accommodation is a fundamental design requirement.

The provision of seats is not, in itself, a guarantee of safe conditions for spectators. It is also necessary that seated areas are designed and managed to be safe.

Moreover, as stated in Section 2.6, the safe capacity of seated areas does not automatically correspond to the number of actual seats provided. It should instead be set at a number which the management can manage safely, and must always be assessed using the (P) and (S) factors. Guidance on the assessment of (P) and (S) factors for seated accommodation is provided in Chapter 2 and Sections 12.19 and 12.20.

Newly constructed seated accommodation should conform to any applicable Building Regulations, and to the appropriate requirements of the *Guide*, such as the design of circulation routes, barrier and handrail provision and fire safety. In addition, when designing and managing seated accommodation, the comfort and amenities of spectators, and their access to amenities, should be considered at all times.

It is therefore recommended that, in all matters relating to the design of seated accommodation, management seeks professional advice from competent persons of the appropriate skill and experience.

For further guidance reference may be made the European Standard BS EN 13200:2003 Spectator Facilities Part 1: *Layout Criteria for Spectator Viewing Area* (see Bibliography).

New and existing seated areas will need to provide accessible viewing areas to spectators with all kinds of disabilities, including the ambulant disabled. These areas must be located around the sports ground in adequate numbers and must be of appropriate viewing quality, to give all spectators a suitable range of viewing options. Provision and standards should be reviewed by management, in consultation with disabled supporters and local disability groups on a regular basis.

For further guidance, reference may be made to the Sports Grounds and Stadia Guide No.1 – *Accessible Stadia* (see Bibliography).

Prefabricated, temporary or demountable stands need to satisfy the same criteria for numbers, dispersal and viewing quality for disabled spectators as those required in a conventional construction (see also Chapter 14).

12.2   Viewing standards

The provision of adequate viewing standards is a key factor in ensuring that seated accommodation is both safe and serves its intended purpose.

Spectators in seated accommodation should have a clear, unrestricted view of the whole of the playing area or area of activity.

Designs should ensure that spectators are encouraged to remain seated and do not have to stretch or strain to view the event. (The only exceptions to this requirement are grounds staging such events as horse or motor racing, where clearly a view of the whole area of activity is difficult to achieve from any static viewing position.)

Viewing standards depend largely on three inter-related factors:

a.   the quality of sightlines (see Section 12.3 and *Diagram 12.1*)

b.   the existence of any restrictions (see Section 12.6)

c.   the viewing distance (see Section 12.20).

12.3   Sightlines

The term sightline refers to the ability of a spectator to see a predetermined focal point (on the pitch or area of activity) over the top of the heads of the spectators immediately in front. The better the quality of the sightline, the more likely it is that spectators will remain seated during the event. Ensuring adequate sightlines is therefore an important part of providing safe seated accommodation.

The quality of a sightline is often expressed as a 'C' value. *Diagram 12.1* shows how 'C' values are calculated. The recommended 'C' value for spectators varies according to the sport, as does the choice of focal point.

For example, it is important for spectators at football or rugby matches to be able to see the nearest touchline, so this should form the focal point. However, a focal point further infield may be acceptable for viewing cricket.

Because of the complex nature of sightline calculations in individual circumstances it is therefore recommended that management seeks professional advice from competent persons of the appropriate skill, and with experience of designing spectator accommodation for the sport (or sports) to be staged.

If spectators stand, they will, with the exception of the front row, experience a significant deterioration in the sightlines. The focal point will move further away, usually into the activity area. This is likely to prevent spectators who are standing in accommodation that was designed for seating from seeing the whole of the area, in particular that part closest to them. This is illustrated in *Diagram 12.2*.

This can lead to spectators stretching, straining, pushing, jostling and standing on tiptoes (and sometimes on the seats) in order to get a better view. The situation is compounded for those who are smaller and whose view is completely blocked.

Advice on the calculation of sightlines for different sports is included in the European Standard BS EN 13200:2003 Spectator Facilities Part 1: *Layout Criteria for Spectator Viewing Area* (see Bibliography).

Diagram 12.1 Sightlines for seated spectators

Key to diagram:

C = the 'C' value

D = the horizontal distance from the eye to the point of focus

N = the riser height

R = the vertical height to the point of focus

T = the seating row depth

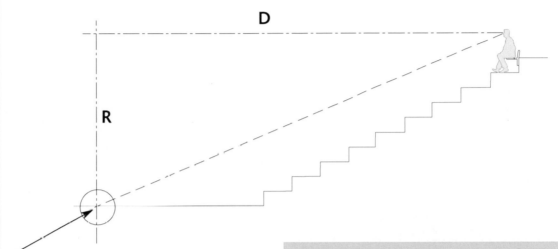

point of focus

typically the nearest touchline,
or outside lane of running track,
or boundary of area of activity

To calculate the appropriate 'C' value for the sport to be viewed, the following formula applies:

$$C = \frac{D\,(N + R)}{D + T} - R$$

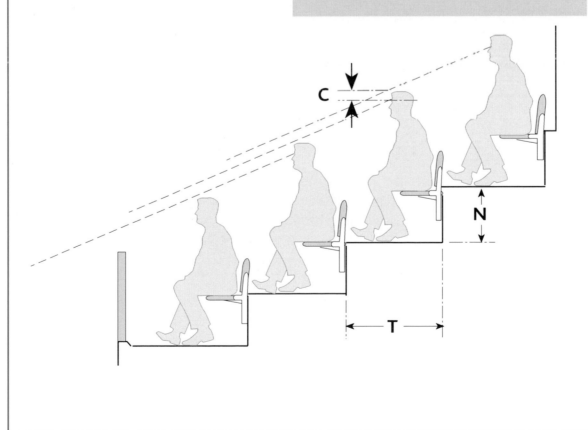

Diagram 12.2 Effect on sightlines on spectators standing in seated areas

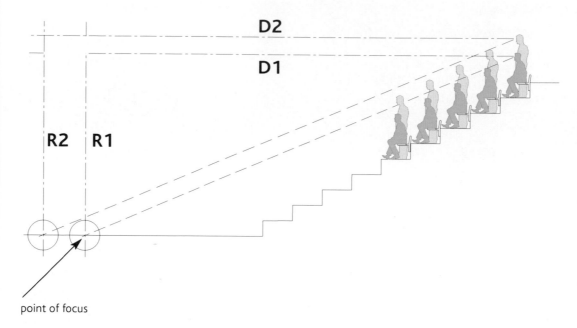

point of focus

typically the nearest touchline,
or outside lane of running track,
or boundary of area of activity

Key to diagram:

D1 = the horizontal distance from the eye to the point of focus for seated spectators

R1 = the vertical height to the point of focus for seated spectators

D2 = the horizontal distance from the eye to the point of focus for standing spectators

R2 = the vertical height to the point of focus for standing spectators

If spectators stand, they will, with the exception of the front row, experience a significant deterioration in the sightlines and "C" value. The focal point will move further away, usually into the activity area. This is likely to prevent spectators who are standing in accommodation that was designed for seating from seeing the whole of the area, in particular that part closest to them. The reduction in the visible part of the activity area can in practice be significant.

This can lead to spectators stretching, straining, pushing, jostling and standing on tiptoes (and sometimes unacceptably on the seats) in order to get a better view. The situation is compounded for those who are smaller, whose view is completely blocked.

12. 4 Sightlines for wheelchair users

The provision of areas located around the stadium designated for spectators in wheelchairs has implications for the sightlines of both disabled spectators and other spectators seated or standing nearby.

Wheelchair users may not be able to stand up to avoid having their view blocked. Any wheelchair seating area should be designed so that spectators in wheelchairs can still see the event when located behind standing accommodation or where people in front may stand up (see Bibliography).

Moreover, some wheelchair users cannot lean forwards or sideways in their seats or turn their heads like other spectators.

It is also acknowledged that at exciting moments during an event some seated spectators will stand. This can affect the quality of view of those in wheelchair spaces behind.

In order to create an acceptable viewing standard for those in wheelchairs, an increased height riser, or 'super riser', will be necessary which may be several times the height of a normal stepping riser.

It is recommended that there should be a minimum elevated position, as illustrated in *Diagram 12.3* which allows a person in a wheelchair to see the playing surface over any people standing in the row directly or diagonally in front. Spectators in wheelchairs must have a clear view of the whole pitch at all times, especially when seated spectators directly or diagonally in front stand up.

The helper seated adjacent to the wheelchair user should enjoy at least the minimum 'C' value even when the spectators in front are standing. The provision of seats behind the wheelchair spaces is only acceptable if adequate sightlines are maintained for those seated there.

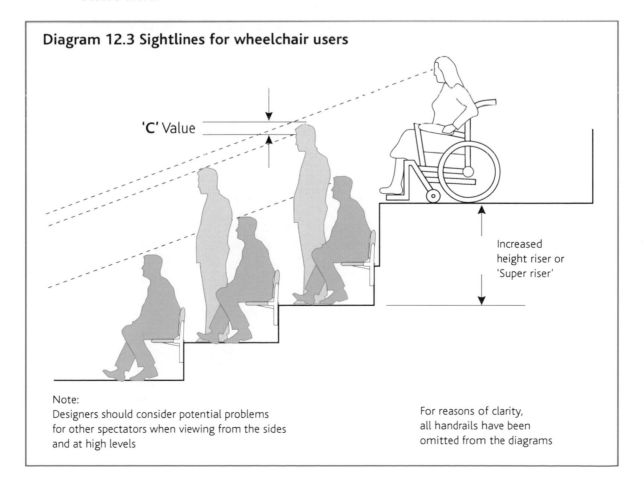

Diagram 12.3 Sightlines for wheelchair users

'C' Value

Increased height riser or 'Super riser'

Note:
Designers should consider potential problems for other spectators when viewing from the sides and at high levels

For reasons of clarity, all handrails have been omitted from the diagrams

It is equally important that the sightlines of other spectators behind and to the side of the wheelchair areas are considered, to ensure that their sightlines are not unduly affected.

Where the wheelchair spaces are positioned at activity level, or behind a lateral gangway, management should carefully assess the effect of spectator movement and any viewing restrictions – such as advertising hoardings – and ensure that all movements of staff and personnel are kept to a minimum.

12.5 Elevation of wheelchair viewing areas

One of the principal requirements of the relevant British Standard is that disabled people should have access to any storey of a new non-domestic building. In the context of sports grounds, this means that spectators with disabilities should gain a far greater choice of viewing location.

12.6 Restricted viewing

As stated previously, all spectators should have a clear, unrestricted view of the whole of the playing area or area of activity. Although there are exceptions to this requirement (see Section 12.2), the causes of potential restrictions should be considered at all sports grounds. These may include:

a.   inadequate sightlines

b.   roof supports or roof structures

c.   the flanking walls, screens or overhanging upper tiers of stands

d.   barriers serving gangways

e.   segregation barriers or fences

f.   structures such as floodlights, scoreboards or temporary camera platforms

g.   advertising hoardings

h.   the passage of other spectators or ground personnel in front of seats or in lateral gangways

i.   the positioning of media personnel (such as photographers and camera operators), stewards and any other personnel (such as promotional staff, bookmakers and their umbrellas)

j.   sports equipment, goal netting, protective netting and support devices.

Note that the provision of pitch perimeter fences in front of seated areas is not recommended unless specifically required for the protection of spectators from the activity taking place (as, for example, in hockey).

Management is responsible for assessing the effects of restricted viewing from every seat to which spectators have access, and for taking the appropriate action where necessary (see Section 12.6).

In carrying out this assessment, it is recommended that the following criteria are applied:

Partial restriction

This applies to seats from which the view may be restricted, for example by a roof support, but not to the extent that spectators have to strain or are encouraged to stand in order to gain an improved view.

Serious restriction

This applies to seats from which the view is sufficiently restricted, for example by inadequate sightlines or advertising hoardings, to encourage spectators to stand.

12.7   Management strategies towards restricted viewing

For new construction:

No newly constructed stands should have any seats offering views with serious restrictions. Every effort should also be made to ensure that partially restricted views are eliminated.

Furthermore, it is the responsibility of both the management and designers to ensure that the viewing standards provided are adequate and appropriate for the sports or events to be staged. For this reason, management may wish to request that designers provide written assurance to that effect.

For existing construction:

Where views are partially restricted and the restrictions cannot be removed, consideration should be given to marking tickets for the affected seats with the words 'Restricted View'. Management should ensure that people are advised of this before they purchase such tickets. Where a safety certificate is in force, this course of action may be required by the local authority on safety grounds.

Where views are seriously restricted and the restrictions cannot be removed, the affected seats should not be made available to spectators and should be excluded from the holding capacity (see Chapter 2).

If, despite carrying out the measures recommended above, it is observed that spectators in certain seats continue to stand for extended periods during an event, there should be a reduction in the (S) factor, thus leading to a possible reduction of the final capacity of the stand (see Section 12.20).

12.8   Provision of cover

Although at grounds staging certain sports it is recommended that all seated accommodation be covered, it is recognised that full protection from the elements is hard to achieve in all situations and in all weather conditions; for example, owing to the height of the roof or the direction of prevailing winds. It should be noted that any form of contamination, for example rainwater, will adversely affect the slip resistance of the seating deck. Detailed guidance on slip resistance can be found in the CIRIA publication – *Safer surfaces to walk on* (see Bibliography).

Where the protection provided is only partial, or there is no cover at all, the following strategies should be considered:

a.   **Partial cover**

Experience shows that where partial cover only is provided and spectators are able to migrate from an uncovered section to a covered section, congestion can occur. In such situations management might consider the following options:

i.   to extend the roof; if such an extension adds to the number of roof supports, however, these could adversely effect the viewing standards of a larger number of spectators

ii. to provide a new roof covering the whole area

iii. to install appropriate barriers, to prevent or control migration, and/or

iv. to adopt appropriate stewarding strategies to control the migration.

If none of the above options are implemented, or if either options iii. or iv. are implemented but the problems of migration and overcrowding continue, consideration should be given to limiting the final capacity of the affected section to those seats under cover.

b.   No cover
At sports ground where uncovered seats are provided, management should ensure that spectators seeking shelter do not overcrowd other areas of the ground (such as covered stands and concourses).

c.   Ticketing
As a general principle, tickets for seats which are not covered should be marked with the words 'Uncovered Seat'. Management should ensure that people are advised of this before they purchase such tickets. Where a safety certificate is in force, this course of action may be required by the local authority, on safety grounds.

Wherever possible, wheelchair spaces should be sited in viewing areas that provide adequate shelter. If separate shelter is provided (for example, for an area of wheelchair spaces), the roof level should not restrict views of other spectators, but should still be sufficiently high to allow people, such as carers and stewards, to enter the shelter and move around as normal.

12.9   Gangways in seated areas – general requirements
As stated in Section 12.1, the provision of seats alone is not, in itself, a guarantee of safe conditions for spectators. It is also necessary that seated areas are designed and managed to be safe.

Although it is recognised that, compared to standing spectators, people in seated areas are generally less hurried and more orderly in terms of their circulation – largely owing to the layout of seating rows – careful consideration must still be given to the design and provision of ingress and egress routes, including both radial and lateral gangways.

In general, the design of gangways in seated areas should meet the following requirements:

a.   They should be provided so that no spectator in any part of a seated area should have to travel more than 30m from their seat in order to enter an exit system, measured along the line of the seating row and gangway. (For example, in stands with vomitories this distance would be measured from the seat to the entrance of the vomitory.) It should also be noted that the normal maximum egress time for all areas of viewing accommodation, standing or seated, is eight minutes (see Section 10.7).

b.   As for all areas of spectator accommodation, gangways in seated areas should be a minimum of 1.1m wide (1.2m recommended for new construction); should be even and free from trip hazards; and their surfaces should be slip-resistant.

c. Any stepped side gangway (that is, with viewing accommodation on one side only) should be provided either with a barrier which meets the requirements of *Table 11.1*, or if a barrier is not necessary (see Section 8.7), a handrail which meets the requirements detailed in Section 8.8.

Further guidance on circulation can be found in Chapters 6–10, and in the following sections.

12.10 Lateral gangways in seated areas

The design and management of lateral gangways in seated areas requires particular attention.

a. Front lateral gangways

Spectators seated in the front rows of stands which have front lateral gangways at the same level as the first row of seats, may have their views restricted by the passage of people along the gangway.

Where such a situation exists, the management should make every effort to ensure that spectators are not encouraged to stand. If the restriction of views cannot be managed effectively, a reduction in the (S) factor may have to be considered, or access to the affected seats prohibited (see Section 12.20).

b. Mid-level lateral gangways

Where spectators in seats immediately behind mid-level lateral gangways have their views restricted by the passage of people along the gangway, the same considerations as above should be applied.

In addition, designers should recognise that when incorporating mid-level lateral gangways, the geometry of the design should ensure that sightlines for spectators in the rows behind such gangways are not adversely affected.

12.11 Radial gangways in seated areas

As stated in Section 8.2, for the purpose of design and assessment, the criteria applying to radial gangways are, in part, different to those pertaining to stairways. The main difference is that the dimensions of the goings and risers of radial gangways will be determined by the gradient of the seating rows (although they should not exceed that achieved by the step dimensions for stairways; that is, 34°).

Taking this into account, the following requirements should apply:

a. The goings of steps in radial gangways should not be less than 280mm, and should be uniform.

b. The risers of steps in radial gangways should not be more than 190mm, and should also be uniform, although for ambulant disabled spectators this should preferably be between 150mm and 170mm.

However, in order to provide adequate sightlines in larger tiers of stands, it is often necessary for seating rows, or series of seating rows (sometimes called facets), to be constructed with riser heights which increase incrementally from the front to the rear of the tier. Accordingly in such situations, the riser heights of steps in radial gangways will also increase incrementally.

This is acceptable practice, with one proviso. If the resultant radial gangway steps do not comply with the specified minimum or maximum dimensions, compensatory measures should be considered in order to ensure safe passage. Examples of compensatory measures may include hand holds or intermittent central handrails.

These hand holds or handrails should be robust, securely fixed, and their fixings designed to be fit for the purpose. Such compensatory features will also be of benefit to ambulant disabled and more elderly spectators.

c.   In order to minimise the discomfort of spectators, it may be preferable to shorten the length of excessively long radial gangways on steeply angled upper tiers by diverting the flow along lateral gangways.

d.   The nosings of steps in radial gangways should be clearly identified for the benefit of spectators.

e.   Radial gangways in seated areas should not contain winders (that is, tapered treads).

f.   Any barrier (including walls, fences or gates) at the foot of radial gangways in seated areas should be 1.1m high and have the design load shown in *Table 11.1* (that is, 3.0 kN/m length).

12.12   The importance of seat dimensions

As stated in Section 12.3, the provision of adequate and appropriate sightlines requires a complex calculation which, as illustrated in *Diagrams 12.1 and 12.2*, involves a number of different factors relating to seat dimensions.

In addition, the safety, comfort and amenity of spectators will be determined by the amount of space provided for each individual seat.

For new construction: it is the responsibility of management to ensure that sightlines and seat dimensions are provided to the highest standard that can be reasonably achieved, and that these factors are incorporated into the design by competent persons of the appropriate skill and experience.

For existing construction: although it may be difficult to improve upon the sightlines or seat dimensions in existing constructions, wherever practicable management should consider upgrading areas where the provision is clearly inadequate. If reconstruction of the particular areas is impracticable, consideration might be given to the installation of more appropriate seat types, or to the adjustment or adaptation of the existing seats. In all cases, management should seek guidance from competent persons.

For an explanation of the terms used in the following sections, see *Diagram 12.4*.

12.13   Seat widths and seating row depths

For new construction:
The minimum space allotted to each seated person should be as follows:

Seat width: 460 mm (40mm greater if fitted with armrests)

Seating row depth: 700 mm

With the population generally becoming larger, it is strongly recommended that, for comfort and accessibility the seat width should be increased to at least 500 mm. In line with the European Standard BS EN 13200:2003 Spectator Facilities Part 1: *Layout criteria for Spectator Viewing Areas* it is recommended that the seating-row depth should be at least 800mm. These recommendations apply particularly in the following circumstances:

a. where spectators require, and/or the management hopes to facilitate, easy movement to and from seats during an event (for example, to purchase refreshments)

b. where the sport being staged is of a lengthy and continuous nature

c. where it is the custom of spectators to place refreshments, bags or hampers on the seating row tread

d. at sports grounds where it is intended to stage events such as concerts, for which a greater level of accessibility and comfort may be desirable

It should also be recognised that designing new construction to the minimum recommended dimensions may preclude the upgrading of facilities in the future; for example, the provision of more advanced seat types.

For existing construction:
The minimum space allotted to each seated person should be as follows:

Seat width: 460 mm (40mm greater if fitted with armrests)

Seating row depth: 610 mm – for bench seating only

This figure of 610mm, derived from early editions of the *Guide* is unlikely to be acceptable for seating with backs. It is questionable whether seating with a row depth of less than 660mm can now be regarded as acceptable. Where such seating exists, the ground management should demonstrate that it does not encourage people to stand.

12.14 Clearways

As illustrated in *Diagram 12.4*, the clearway (B) is the distance between the foremost projection of one seat and the back of the seat in front of it. This measurement is also known as the seatway, and is included in the seating row depth. The size of the clearway determines how safely and freely spectators and other personnel (such as stewards or first aiders) can move along rows of seats.

For new construction:
The minimum clearway should be 400mm. This may be reduced to 305mm where there are not more than seven seats in a row served by a gangway on one side, or not more than 14 seats in a row served by gangways on both sides.

For existing construction:
The minimum clearway should be 305mm.

The following points should also be considered:

a. Where tip-up seats are fitted, the clearway is measured with the seat in its tipped up position.

b. A tip-up seat will provide a greater clearway than a fixed seat and may affect the design and selection of seating row depth.

c. Where fitted, armrests must not project into the clearway to such an extent that they reduce the clearway to below the specified minimum.

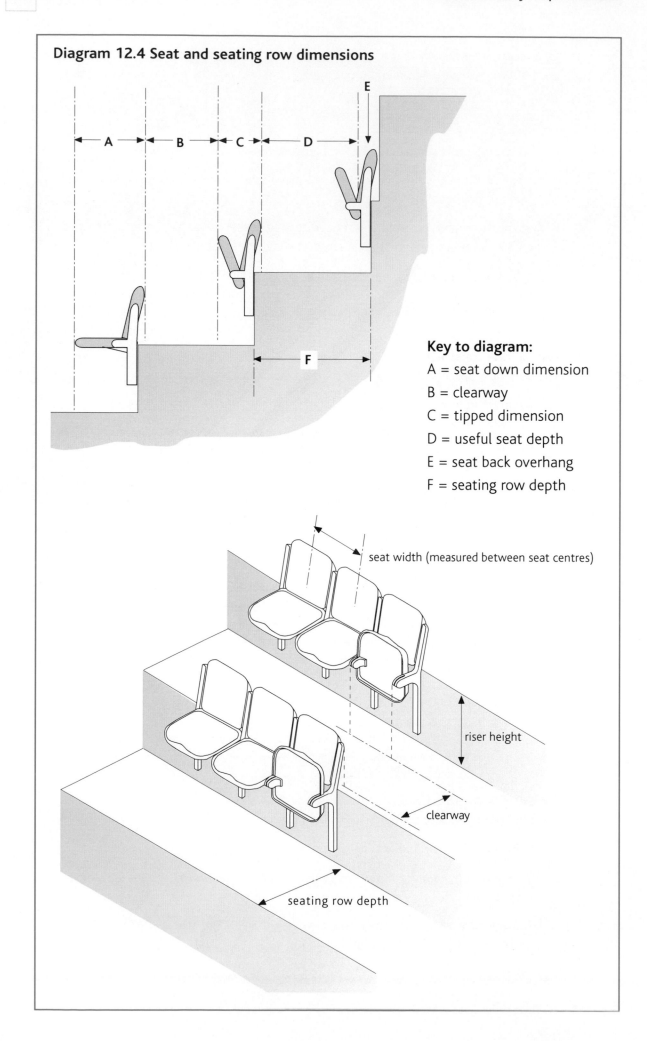

Diagram 12.4 Seat and seating row dimensions

Key to diagram:

A = seat down dimension

B = clearway

C = tipped dimension

D = useful seat depth

E = seat back overhang

F = seating row depth

seat width (measured between seat centres)

riser height

clearway

seating row depth

12.15 Useful seat depths

Another dimension which needs careful consideration is the useful seat depth (D in *Diagram 12.4*). This is an important factor in the comfort and accessibility of seats. The useful seat depth is the horizontal distance between the back of the seat, measured at seat height, and the rear of the seat in front.

The selection of a seat with a narrow tipped dimension (C in *Diagram 12.4*) will result in an improved useful seat depth.

12.16 Number of seats in rows

It is recommended that the number of seats in a row should not exceed:

a.   14 where there is a gangway at one end only

b.   28 where there is a gangway at both ends.

Deviations from this guidance should be permitted only if a risk assessment demonstrates the acceptability of the proposals, taking into account the requirements of both the normal egress time and the maximum recommended travel distance (see Sections 10.7 and 12.9).

12.17 Seat design

When selecting and installing seats, the following requirements should be met:

a.   **Fixing**
All seats should be securely fixed in position. The fixings should not present any trip hazards on the treads. They should be vandal proof and contain no sharp projections or edges.

b.   **Flame retardancy**
All seats, irrespective of the material used, and whether upholstered or not, should satisfy the ignition source requirements specified in the relevant British Standards.

c.   **Physical injury**
All seats should be designed not to cause injury to the user.

Reference may also be made to the European Standard BS EN 13200:2003 Spectator Facilities Part 4: *Seats – Product Characteristics* (see Bibliography).

12.18 Design of wheelchair spaces

A wheelchair space should meet the following requirements:

a.   Wheelchair users should be able to manoeuvre easily to a space that allows them a clear view of the event (see Sections 12.1 and 12.4).

b.   Wheelchair users should be provided with a choice of sitting next to a disabled or non-disabled companion.

c.   Some seats should be located so that an assistance/guide dog can accompany its owner and rest in front of, or under, the seat.

Although an individual wheelchair place can be provided by a clear space with a width of at least 900mm and a depth of at least 1400mm, it is recommended that each designated place should ideally measure 1400mm x 1400mm to allow space for one helper per wheelchair space to sit alongside in a fixed or removable seat.

12.19   Assessment of (P) factors for seated areas

As stated throughout the *Guide* (and in particular in Sections 2.4 and 12.1) the safe capacity of all areas of seated accommodation will be partly based on an assessment of their physical condition, namely the (P) factor. It should be noted, however, that the (P) factor can only be applied after the number of useable seats has been established – that is, the actual number of seats, less those affected by seriously restricted views and those found to be inadequate or damaged (see Section 2.6).

The (P) factor is then used to calculate the holding capacity of the area, which in turn forms part of the calculation of the final capacity of the area.

The following are some of the main requirements that will need to be met if the (P) factor is not to be reduced. It is stressed that this list is neither comprehensive nor applicable in all situations. Nor is it presented in order of importance.

a.   Physical condition

This concerns not the condition of the seats (since those which are damaged or inadequate should already have been excluded from the calculation), but the condition of all gangways, seating row treads, barriers and handrails.

(Damaged seats should be repaired, replaced or removed; whichever is appropriate to maintain safe conditions in the seated area. Where tip-up seats are not working properly nor being maintained and the clearway is being affected then the egress of spectators along the row could be impeded).

b.   Structures

Management should ensure that any structures or parts of structures with which seated spectators could come in contact are made safe and secure. Where necessary, protective measures should be taken to avoid potential injury; for example, from low roof beams at the back of seated areas or from sharp edges of seat fixings.

c.   Sightlines

If the sightlines are inadequate, thus encouraging spectators to stand, an assessment should be made of the risks to safety and, if necessary, the (P) factor reduced accordingly (see Section 12.20.e).

Wherever doubts arise as to the physical condition of a seated area, consideration should be given to a reduction in the (P) factor.

12.20   Assessment of (S) factors for seated areas

In addition to (P) factors, the calculation of a safe capacity for all areas of seated accommodation will be partly based on an assessment of their safety management, or the (S) factor.

The (S) factor is used to calculate the holding capacity of the area, which in turn forms part of the calculation of the final capacity of the area.

The following are some of the main requirements that will need to be met if the (S) factor is not to be reduced. It is stressed, however, that this list is neither comprehensive nor applicable in all situations. Nor is it presented in order of importance. (Further general guidance on (S) factors is also provided in Section 2.5.)

a.   Ticketing

Management should ensure that tickets are issued only for useable seats, and that the information on the tickets corresponds exactly with the correct number and row. As stated in Section 12.8, management should also ensure that tickets for seats with partially restricted views and either partial or no cover, are marked accordingly and the purchaser warned in advance. Reference should also be made to the recommendations in Section 7.10 concerning the sale of unreserved tickets.

b. **Seat and row identification**

Each individual seat and seat row should be clearly, neatly and accurately identified for the benefit of spectators and stewards. The seat identification marks should be fixed so as to make their removal difficult. Where there is no seat and/or seat row identification there should be reduction of the seating capacity in accordance with Section 7.10.d.

To avoid congestion and confusion, where tip-up seats are installed, for ease of reading, seat identification marks should ideally be located on the front of the back rest, rather than on the underside of the seat.

c. **Good housekeeping**

Clean and tidy seated areas are not only safer, but they also assist in promoting good behaviour and a more favourable attitude among spectators towards the facilities provided.

Each seat should therefore be cleaned before spectators are admitted. This is particularly important in exposed situations where seats may collect moisture or dust. Where seats are exposed to rain, ground staff should be provided with suitable means for wiping each seat immediately before it is occupied, so that spectators are not encouraged to stand in order to avoid coming into contact with a wet surface.

A useful practice for rain affected seats is for management to provide facilities for spectators to obtain disposable capes.

d. **Stewarding**

Stewards should be familiar with the layout of all areas of seated accommodation, the location of specific rows and seats, and the location of exits, emergency exits and amenities.

If reserved seats are sold, stewards should be trained and briefed to ensure that spectators sit in their designated seats. If unreserved seats are sold, they should be able to encourage spectators to sit in concentrated groups, so as to make it easier to direct latecomers to unoccupied seats.

While allowing for the natural tendency of spectators to stand up at key moments during an event, stewards should also be trained and briefed to deal effectively with spectators who persistently stand up (see also Section 12.20.e).

e. **Standing in seated areas**

Persistent standing by spectators in seated areas raises significant safety, crowd management and customer care issues which are usually interrelated. Where these are likely to arise, the ground management should prepare a comprehensive risk assessment and plans for resolving them.

Local authorities should take these into account when agreeing the appropriate (S) factor for the accommodation and/or event concerned. Local authorities should also consider whether the capacity should be reduced to counter particular safety problems, for example obstructed gangways or spectators standing in the front rows of upper tiers.

Guidance is available on the Football Licensing Authority website.

f. **Keeping gangways clear**
It is essential that gangways, both lateral and radial, are kept clear, especially in areas where the passage of spectators and other personnel obstructs the views of seated spectators, including spectators using wheelchairs. In addition to the efforts of stewards, spectators should be informed of this requirement by signs and other means; for example, by announcements in event programme and via the public address system.

g. **Migration – viewing distances**
As stated in Section 12.2, one of the factors determining viewing standards is the viewing distance. This is the distance between the spectator and the playing area or area of activity.

Viewing distances are not, in themselves, a safety matter. However, the distance may influence spectators' behaviour at key moments during an event. For example, management may need to ensure that spectators in areas closest to the pitch or area of activity are not encouraged to leave their seats and surge forward, particularly in response to the actions of players or participants in the event.

This should be achieved by the use of high-profile stewarding, clear signs and public address announcements. As recommended in Section 12.6 pitch perimeter fences should not be erected in front of areas of seated accommodation.

If observation indicates that forward migration is a persistent problem, a reduction in the (S) factor may be necessary. Alternatively, the use of front row seats can be prohibited.

For certain sports there may also be a need to protect spectators near the front from the activity taking place.

Where the viewing distances are long, management should ensure that spectators in the rearmost rows are also not encouraged to migrate forwards at key moments of an event in order to obtain a closer view.

Guidance on optimum viewing distances for various sports can be found in Stadia: A Design and Development Guide and the European Standard BS EN 13200:2003 Spectator Facilities Part 1: *Layout Criteria for Spectator Viewing Area* (see Bibliography).

h. **Migration – partial cover**
Management should ensure that the migration of spectators as a result of partial cover does not lead to congestion or to a breakdown of safety management procedures.

i. **Removal or control of potential restrictions**
Before and during an event, management should ensure that any restrictions to viewing are removed or controlled. Such restrictions are listed in Section 12.6.

In addition, provision should be made for the accommodation of any stewards or members of staff who may not be on duty during an event. Such personnel should not be allowed to stand in vomitories or in areas where they might restrict views or obstruct gangways or exits.

j. **Segregation methods**
If it is necessary to segregate tiers of seats into sections for different groups of spectators, care should be taken to ensure that the dividing methods used do not restrict views.

In all cases it is recommended that the methods used should be flexible, so that differing numbers of spectators can be segregated according to the needs of the event. Such methods may include the use of stewards and/or a line of tape or suitable, fire-resistant material draped over a width of several seats from the front to the back of the tier of seating.

Care should be taken to ensure that the positioning of any temporary means of segregation does not result in more than 14 seats in a row with a gangway at one end only (see Section 12.16).

For further guidance on the segregation of seated spectators, see Sections 3.26 and 9.6.

13: Spectator accommodation – standing

13.1 The provision of standing accommodation

Standing accommodation is recognised as presenting a special safety problem at sports grounds. For this reason, although the problems have mainly been associated with football grounds, as stated in Section 12.1, wherever possible the provision of safe seated accommodation for all spectators is recommended.

When planning a new standing area, management should therefore consider the possibility of converting it to seats at a later date (see Section 13.25).

Wherever standing accommodation is provided – be it in the form of terraces, viewing slopes, level areas or spectator galleries – it should be designed and managed to be safe. The comfort and amenities of spectators – and their access to amenities should also be considered, in as much detail as they would be for seated areas.

Account should also be taken of the nature of the event and the varying patterns of crowd movement at different types of event; for example, at horse racing compared to football.

It is therefore recommended that in all matters relating to the design of standing accommodation, management seeks professional advice from competent persons of the appropriate skill and experience.

Newly constructed standing accommodation should conform to any applicable Building Regulations, and should be designed in accordance with recommendations contained elsewhere in the *Guide*, particularly those in Chapter 11, concerning the provision of barriers (including crush barriers and pitch perimeter barriers).

13.2 The importance of good design

Owing to the complex patterns of crowd circulation and movement to which standing areas are subject – at many grounds, continuously throughout the occupancy of the area – their design cannot be considered simply in terms of their individual elements. Instead, they should be regarded as a finely balanced network of inter-related elements, including entry systems, gangways, terrace steps, crush barriers, exit systems and emergency evacuation routes. Design faults or deterioration in any one of those elements shifts additional pressures onto the others, which, as experience shows, has often led to accidents, occasionally with fatal consequences.

To provide reasonable safety, standing areas and the circulation routes which serve them should therefore be designed taking the following conditions into consideration:

a. Spectators should be able to gain access to their desired standing position from the point of entry to the ground via a properly designed and constructed route.

b. Spectators should be able to leave their viewing position by a clearly defined and properly designed and constructed route at any time during the event, to gain access to toilet and other facilities. They should also, within reason, be able to return to their viewing position at any time during the event.

c.   Spectators should be able to leave the viewing area and exit from the sports ground at any time during, or at the end of, the event, via a properly constructed and defined exit route.

13.3   Viewing conditions for standing spectators

The provision of adequate viewing standards for standing spectators will be similar to those described in Section 12.2.

Once spectators are in position, the design and management of the standing area should ensure that they are able to view all elements of the event in such a way that they are not subjected to:

a.   excessive pressures from crowd surges

b.   excessive pressure from a high density of spectators

c.   forces that cause spectators to lose control of their own movement, so that they step forward in an uncontrolled manner

d.   physical stresses caused by poorly constructed terracing, such as sloping treads, uneven surfaces or broken or damaged terracing

e.   restricted viewing, necessitating frequent changes of position or excessive movement, which might affect other spectators.

The assessment of (P) and (S) factors for all existing standing areas should start by considering whether, by design and management, the conditions listed above and in Section 13.2 are being met.

Further guidance on the assessment of (P) and (S) factors for standings areas is provided in Chapter 2 and Sections 13.23 and 13.24.

13.4   Gangways in standing areas – general requirements

As in seated areas, radial and lateral gangways should provide the means for spectators to proceed in a uniform, orderly manner into, around and out of standing areas. However, because spectators often have more freedom of movement in standing areas, the provision of suitably designed and clearly marked, designated gangways is a vital part of achieving safe standing conditions.

In general, the design of gangways in standing areas should meet the following requirements:

a.   They should be provided so that all spectators are within 12m of a gangway or exit as measured along a line of unobstructed travel from the viewing position, so that they can move quickly into the exit system. It should be noted that the normal maximum egress time for all areas of viewing accommodation, standing or seated, is eight minutes (see Section 10.7).

b.   All gangways in standing areas, lateral and radial, should be clearly delineated by the application of a non-slip paint in a conspicuous colour. This not only makes them easier for spectators to identify in congested situations, but also aids those who are responsible for keeping the gangways clear.

c.   As for all areas of spectator accommodation, gangways in standing areas should be a minimum of 1.1m wide (1.2m recommended for new construction), should be even and free from trip hazards, and their surfaces should be slip resistant.

d.   Any stepped side gangway (that is, with viewing accommodation on one side only) should be provided either with a barrier which meets the requirements of *Table 11.1*, or, if a barrier is not required, a handrail which meets the requirements detailed in Section 8.8.

Further guidance on circulation can be found in Chapters 6–10, and in the following sections.

13.5   Lateral gangways in standing areas

Spectators should not be allowed to stand in lateral gangways because this disrupts the passage of spectators along them and may restrict the views of those standing on the steps behind, causing them to stretch or strain in order to see the event.

In order to assist management in achieving this, the following design requirements should be considered:

a.   To discourage standing in lateral gangways, the surfaces should be sunk approximately 150mm.

b.   Wherever possible, the front steps of standing areas behind mid-level lateral gangways should start at a level higher than the section in front, to ensure that views from the rear areas are not restricted.

c.   Crush barriers should be provided behind the lateral gangway, but not immediately in front.

d.   As stated in Section 11.15, in order to assist circulation, wherever practicable a lateral gangway should be provided between the front row of crush barriers and the pitch perimeter barrier.

13.6   Radial gangways in standing areas

The design and management of radial gangways is of particular importance in standing areas, owing to the tendency of spectators to stand in them for viewing, and because of the potential for crowd surges down the gangway. For this reason it is stressed that management should ensure that radial gangways are always kept clear.

This responsibility should be much easier to discharge where continuous crush barriers are provided between radial gangways (see Sections 11.8 and 13.7).

Wherever reasonably practicable, the following requirements should apply to all radial gangways in standing areas:

a.   Whatever the crush barrier configuration, all areas of standing accommodation should have clearly marked, designated radial gangways.

b.   As stated in Section 13.4, all spectators should be within 12m of a gangway or exit. The spacing of radial gangways should also take into account the future possibility of the standing area being converted to seating (see Section 13.25).

c.   Where the gangway is stepped, the goings should be uniform and the step dimensions compatible with those for the terrace which they serve (see Section 13.9).

d.   To minimise the risk of crowd surges, it may be preferable to shorten excessively long radial gangways by diverting the flow along lateral gangways.

e.   The nosings of steps in radial gangways should be clearly identified for the benefit of spectators.

f.   Radial gangways should not contain winders (that is, tapered treads).

g.   Any wall, barrier, fence or gate at the foot of radial gangways in standing areas should be the same height as crush barriers (1.1m) and have the maximum horizontal imposed load for crush barriers (that is, 5.0 kN/m length, as shown in *Table 11.1*).

13.7   Crush barriers

Crush barriers are vital elements in the design and management of standing areas.

As stated in Section 11.8, crush barriers should be provided along the full width of a standing area, with gaps only at the radial gangways. These barriers should be designed and spaced according to the recommendations given in Chapter 11. An example of continuous crush barrier configuration is illustrated in *Diagram 11.3*.

If the provision of crush barriers conform to this recommendation, many of the other elements required for the design and management of standing areas should be simpler to provide as part of an integrated and smoothly functioning network.

In addition, there is a much greater likelihood that the capacity calculation can be based upon the maximum appropriate density of 47 persons per 10 square metres (see Chapter 2).

a.   **For new construction:** at all sports grounds where standing accommodation is provided, to achieve the highest permissible capacity levels for a standing area, a continuous crush barrier configuration must be provided.

b.   **For existing construction:** if all other elements of the standing accommodation are in good condition and the safety management is effective, non-continuous crush barrier configurations may still be regarded as acceptable. However, as stated in Section 2.8, the capacity will still have to be significantly reduced. This reduction is explained further in Worked Examples 2 and 3 in Annex A. Wherever possible, and wherever the highest permissible capacity levels for a standing area are desired, the existing standing areas should be redesigned to incorporate continuous crush barriers between radial gangways.

c.   **Standing areas without crush barriers**
Standing areas without crush barriers cannot be considered as safe unless the capacity is set at such a level that the risks are minimised. For guidance on how to calculate the capacity in such situations, see Section 2.8 and Worked Example 5.

Section 13.20 and Worked Example 6 also show how to calculate capacities in situations such as are common at racecourses, where adjoining standing areas both with and without crush barriers may form part of a larger enclosure.

13.8   Design of terrace steps

When designing new terraces, or assessing the (P) factor of existing standing areas, it should be noted that:

a.   The dimensions of terrace steps, and therefore the angle of slope, have a direct correlation with the spacing of crush barriers, as detailed in *Table 11.2*.

b.   Angles of slope, or gradients, in excess of 25° are potentially hazardous and should be avoided. Where they exist, consideration should be given to a reduction in the (P) factor or the provision of additional crush barriers.

c.   Excessive variations in the gradient of a terrace are potentially hazardous and should be avoided.

d.   The surface of terrace steps should be slip-resistant (see Bibliography).

e.   The surface of each tread should be uniform, and designed so that rain or water does not accumulate, thereby leading to deterioration. This can be achieved by creating a slight fall on each tread.

f.   An excessive fall on terrace treads will reduce the comfort of spectators and possibly lead them to step forward in an uncontrolled manner.

Further guidance on the assessment of (P) factors for standing areas is provided in Chapter 2 and Section 13.23.

13.9   Dimensions of terrace steps

For new construction:

The dimensions of terrace steps for a newly constructed standing area should be as follows:

a.   Tread depth: 350 mm minimum   400 mm maximum

Designing to these dimensions will also enable the terrace, if required, to be converted to seating more easily at a later date (see Section 13.25).

b.   Riser height: 75 mm minimum   170mm maximum

It should be noted that when designing new standing areas, the exact dimensions of riser heights are not pre-determined. Rather, they depend on the calculation for sightlines.

For existing construction:

The dimensions of terrace steps for existing terraces should be as follows:

a.   Tread depth: 280 mm minimum   400 mm maximum

b.   Riser height: 75 mm minimum   180 mm maximum

If any riser height is greater than 180 mm, a crush barrier should be provided at the top of the riser.

13.10 Viewing standards

As stated in Section 13.3, the provision of adequate viewing standards is a key factor in achieving safe standing conditions. Viewing standards are explained more fully in Sections 12.2 and 12.3, and in relation to standing accommodation, are illustrated in *Diagram 13.1*. As for seated spectators, viewing standards for standing spectators depend largely on three inter-related factors:

a. the quality of sightlines (see Section 13.11 and *Diagrams 12.1 and 13.1*)

b. the existence of any restrictions (see Section 13.12)

c. the viewing distance (see Section 13.24).

13.11 Sightlines

The provision of adequate and appropriate sightlines for standing spectators is an important part of achieving safe standing conditions.

The better the sightline, the more likely it is that standing spectators will not have to stretch or strain in order to view the event. If the sightlines are poor, resulting in excessive crowd movement and pressure, the (P) factor for the standing area should be reduced. This in turn will lead to a reduction of the appropriate density and may result in a reduction of the final capacity (see Chapter 2 and Section 13.23).

As stated in Section 12.3, the quality of a sightline is often expressed as a 'C' value. 'C' values for seated spectators are calculated for every row. However, for standing spectators they may be calculated for every second tread. This is because standing spectators have more freedom to re-adjust their position, and the variation of eye level is greater across the range for standing spectators than for seated spectators.

Advice on the calculation of sightlines for different sports is included in the European Standard BS EN 13200:2003 Spectator Facilities Part 1: *Layout Criteria for Spectator Viewing Area* (see Bibliography).

When calculating sightlines it should be noted that the maximum recommended angle of slope for standing accommodation is 25°, compared with 34° for seating.

13.12 Restricted viewing

All standing spectators should have a clear, unrestricted view of the whole of the pitch or area of activity. Although there are exceptions to this requirement (for example at events such as horse or motor racing), the causes of potential restrictions are likely to be the same as those listed in Section 12.6.

Management is responsible for assessing the effects of restricted viewing from every part of the standing area to which spectators have access, and for taking appropriate action (see Section 13.13). This assessment should take into account any restrictions, such as fences or advertising material, between the spectators and the pitch or area of activity.

In carrying out the assessment, the following criteria should be applied:

a. **Partial restriction**
   This applies to areas from which partial restrictions force standing spectators to stretch or strain in order to gain an improved view, but without significantly changing their position or affecting other spectators.

b. **Serious restriction**
    This applies to areas from which standing spectators have seriously restricted, or even completely obstructed views of part of the playing area or area of activity, necessitating significant changes of position or excessive movement, thereby risking the possibility of crowd surging.

13.13   Management strategies towards restricted viewing

For new construction:
Newly constructed standing accommodation should be designed so that it has no areas with viewing restrictions.

As is the case for seated areas, it is, furthermore, the responsibility of both the management and designers to ensure that the viewing standards provided are adequate and appropriate for the sports or events to be staged. Management may therefore wish to request that designers provide written assurance to that effect.

For existing construction:
Where views are partially restricted and the restrictions cannot be removed, an assessment of the potential risk of crowd movement should be made, and if considered necessary, the affected area should be discounted from the available viewing area (see Chapter 2).

Where views are seriously restricted and the restrictions cannot be removed, the affected areas should be discounted from the available viewing area and consideration given to them being prohibited for the purposes of viewing. These areas may either be sealed off, or their boundaries marked clearly on the actual terrace surface and stewarded accordingly.

If, despite carrying out the measures recommended above, it is observed that areas with seriously restricted views continue to be occupied by standing spectators, and this results in excessive crowd movement, there should be a reduction in the (S) factor, thus leading to the possibility of a further reduction of the final capacity of the standing area (see Chapter 2 and Section 13.24).

13.14   Provision of cover
Although it is recommended that at certain sports grounds all standing accommodation should be covered, as stated in Section 12.8, it is recognised that full protection from the elements is hard to achieve in all situations and weather conditions.

Where the protection provided is only partial, or there is no cover at all, the following strategies should be considered:

a. **Partial cover**
    Experience shows that where partial cover is provided, in poor weather conditions standing spectators will, whenever possible, migrate to covered areas. In certain circumstances this can result in unacceptable local concentrations of spectators, particularly where the covered area is smaller than the uncovered area. Additional safety concerns arise when conditions under the roof are inferior to those on the rest of the standing area. In such situations management might consider the following options:

    i.   to extend the existing roof or provide a new roof covering the whole area

    ii.   to install appropriate barriers, to prevent or control migration

iii. to adopt appropriate stewarding strategies to manage or control the migration, preferably with the assistance of CCTV monitoring.

If none of the above options are acted upon, or if either options ii. or iii. are implemented but the problems of migration and overcrowding continue, further consideration should be given to the following options:

iv. to limit the final capacity of the whole section by restricting the available viewing area to the area under cover

v. to limit the final capacity of the whole section by a reduction of the (S) factor.

Management and, where a safety certificate is in force, the local authority, will need to judge carefully all the circumstances before deciding which of the above options to pursue.

b. No cover

At sports grounds where uncovered standing areas are provided, management should ensure that spectators seeking shelter do not overcrowd other areas of the ground (such as covered stands and concourses).

c. Admission

As a general principle, people should be advised before seeking admission to standing areas which are not covered. Where a safety certificate is in force, this course of action may also be required by the local authority.

13.15 Division of standing accommodation

Large areas of standing accommodation, or physically adjoining areas of standing accommodation, are subject to migration, which in turn can lead to dangerous overcrowding. In such cases it will be necessary to introduce structures and/or management controls to separate the areas into divisions.

If such areas are not divided, or if the divisions are not adequately arranged or managed as recommended below, a reduction of the capacity or capacities should be enforced by reductions of the (P) and/or (S) factors (see also Sections 13.23 and 13.24). This reduction should also apply when assessing the effect of migration in standing areas with only partial cover (see Section 13.14).

For situations where a free movement of spectators between divisions is desirable, see Section 13.16.

It is strongly recommended that any division of standing accommodation complies with the following requirements:

a. Each division must have its capacity assessed separately.

b. Entry to each division must either be controlled by its own designated turnstiles, or by other entry arrangements which allow management to keep an accurate count of the number of spectators admitted.

c. As with any other separate area of spectator accommodation, in order to alert staff and stewards at the entry points when a division is nearing capacity, and then when it is full – and for the purposes of overall safety management – it should be possible to monitor the numbers of spectators in each division from the control point, by counting systems, and by stewarding and/or CCTV.

d. Once the capacity of the division has been reached, further entry should be denied and spectators re-directed to other available areas.

e.   When dividing areas of standing accommodation, the siting of dividing barriers, walls or fences should be such that each division functions safely as a separate unit, in terms of its crush barrier configuration, gangways, and its means of ingress, egress and emergency evacuation (including pitch perimeter gates or openings).

f.   Each division should also be self-contained in terms of its toilet and refreshment facilities.

g.   Consideration should be given to providing additional access from one division to another for use in an emergency evacuation. However, such access will not normally be taken into account in any exit capacity calculation.

h.   If required to withstand crowd pressures, all barriers (including walls or fences) used to divide one section from another, should be designed, constructed and maintained to withstand those pressures safely.

In situations where dividing structures might be vulnerable to crowd pressures, the use of brick, blockwork or other solid structures is not recommended. Where they are used, they should be subject to regular appraisal by competent persons of the appropriate skills and experience.

i.   Where the separation is achieved by means of radial divisions, gangways should be provided on either side to discourage lateral movement and prevent spectators pressing up against the dividing structures. These gangways should be suitably stewarded and kept clear at all times.

j.   Dividing structures should be designed or sited in such a way that they do not restrict the views of spectators. If they do, the affected areas should be discounted from the available viewing area (see Chapter 2).

13.16 Allowing free movement of spectators between divisions

At certain sports grounds – for example those staging horse or greyhound racing – it is customary to allow spectators to move freely between various areas of spectator accommodation.

However, if free movement of spectators is to be allowed between standing areas, or between standing areas and any other areas of spectator accommodation (including circulation areas), management should ensure that appropriate measures are taken to control and monitor the situation at all times and in all weather conditions, to ensure that the capacity of each area is not exceeded. As stated in Section 13.15.c this should be achieved by control of entry points between each section, by effective stewarding, and by monitoring from the control point (by CCTV if appropriate).

Even if all these measures are implemented, where free movement of spectators is allowed, a careful assessment should be made of the (P) and (S) factors for each individual division or separate area of viewing accommodation.

13.17 Segregation of standing accommodation

Where areas of standing accommodation are divided in order to segregate different groups of spectators, the requirements for the design and management of divided areas listed in Section 13.15 should be met in full.

It is emphasised that whichever form of dividing (or segregation) structure is used, the structure should not restrict the views of spectators.

Flexible means of segregation, such as are recommended for seated areas (see Section 12.20), can also be used in standing areas, provided that the stewarding arrangements, barrier configurations and gangway layouts are suitable.

However, all segregation methods should be the subject of consultation between the ground management, the local authority and the police.

13.18 Viewing slopes

A viewing slope is defined as a non-stepped sloping area providing standing accommodation for spectators. Wherever possible their use should be avoided at grounds staging sports where spectators maintain an essentially fixed position for the duration of the event (such as football or rugby).

However, where they are provided, in order to be considered suitable for standing spectators, viewing slopes should comply with the following requirements:

a.   The surface should be properly drained and such that spectators do not lose their footing or balance.

b.   The angle of slope should ideally be no greater than approximately 10° (compared with the maximum angle recommended for terraced areas of 25°).

c.   If the angle of slope is greater than 10° continuous crush barriers should be provided between radial gangways.

d.   The spacing of crush barriers should be the same as for those on terraced areas (see *Table 11.2*).

13.19 Level standing accommodation

As stated in Section 2.8.g, it is recommended that whatever the loading of any front barrier, the available viewing area allowed when calculating the capacity of a level standing area should be no greater than 1.5m. This is the equivalent of approximately four persons deep. Beyond this depth viewing is too seriously restricted to be considered as part of the viewing accommodation.

An example of the capacity calculation for a level standing area is provided in Worked Example 5.

It is further recommended that level areas for standing do not normally form part of the spectator accommodation for new construction.

However at certain sports grounds – for example those staging horse racing – it is customary to allow spectators to view the event from level or near level standing areas commonly known as lawns.

It is acknowledged that at horse racing sightline requirements can differ from those at other sports. The nearest point of focus is likely to be raised off the ground which reduces the amount of stretching and straining necessary to view the event. In addition raised video screens are often provided to compensate for any restriction to the view.

Similar considerations apply where the pitch or activity area is temporarily converted for a concert to level standing viewing accommodation.

13.20 Combined standing and circulation areas

Lawns at racecourses may be used for both viewing and circulation, have no crush barriers, and are occupied by persons such as bookmakers and vendors. They often also allow a free movement of spectators between other areas of spectator accommodation, such as seated stands or terraces for standing spectators. Worked Example 6 illustrates such an area.

In such situations, it is stressed that although spectators may freely move from the enclosure into a stand or terrace, the holding capacity of the stand or terrace should still be calculated separately from the adjoining enclosure or lawn. As stated in Section 13.16, management should also ensure that the capacity of each area is not exceeded.

As is the case for any section of a sports ground where free movement of spectators is common, a reduction in the (P) factor will be necessary in order to facilitate safe movement.

This reduction may be severe where there is not only free movement but where viewing areas are used also for circulation. In this respect it should be noted that research indicates that spectators can only circulate freely when crowds are no denser than approximately 15 persons per 10 square metres. It is acknowledged that some groups of spectators will congregate at densities of or about 20 persons per 10 square metres but free circulation will become more restricted at these densities.

In order to assess the capacity of the enclosures, or lawns, it will therefore be necessary to assess both the (P) and (S) factors, taking into account all the usual factors, but with particular attention to local circumstances.

This will require assessment of the following:

a. When calculating the available viewing area a reasonable assessment should be made of those parts of the area in which viewing, rather than circulation, actually takes place.

b. Those areas clearly used only for circulation should not form part of the available viewing area.

c. Discounts from the available viewing area should be made to allow for areas occupied by bookmakers, vendors and other personnel.

d. Those areas from which viewing does take place should be assessed as to the underfoot conditions, the quality of sightlines, the existence of any restrictions and any other relevant physical characteristics which may affect the safety of standing spectators.

e. The ability of stewards to prevent congestion or overcrowding.

The above list is not comprehensive nor intended to apply in all circumstances or in all weather conditions.

Regular monitoring may also be required to ensure that a safe capacity limit is set, appropriate to the viewing area's particular characteristics.

13.21 Spectator galleries

Galleries in which spectators stand are usually accessed from hospitality areas, whose capacities are already limited by their size and design. These capacity limits should be strictly applied.

However, spectator galleries should still be subject to an assessment of (P) and (S) factors, and all barriers should comply with *Table 11.3*.

13.22   Standing accommodation and disabled spectators

Disabled spectators are entitled to gain access to standing areas in existing or new sports grounds. The issues in respect of numbers, location and sightlines within standing areas are the same as those within seated areas (see Section 12.4).

Refer also to the Sports Grounds and Stadia Guide No. 1 – *Accessible Stadia* (see Bibliography).

13.23   Assessment of (P) factors for standing areas

As stated throughout the *Guide* (in particular Sections 2.4 and 2.9), the calculation of capacities for all areas of standing accommodation will be partly based on an assessment of their physical condition, or the (P) factor.

The following are some of the main requirements that will need to be met if the (P) factor is not to be reduced. It is stressed that this list is neither comprehensive nor applicable in all situations. Nor is it presented in order of importance.

a.   Physical condition of standing areas

Management should ensure that all surfaces, treads, risers and nosings, and all gangway markings are maintained in good condition. Any alterations or repairs to surfaces should avoid creating additional trip hazards (due to unevenness) and all gangway markings should be reinstated.

All barriers and crush barriers, and their fixings, should be maintained, inspected and tested as recommended in Chapter 11.

Particular attention should be made to:

i.   crumbling of the surface due to age or poor maintenance

ii.   unevenness of the terrace due to poor construction, settlement or repair work

iii.   irregular terrace tread depths or riser heights

iv.   poor drainage, leading to standing water and/or icing.

b.   Structures

Management should ensure that any structures or parts of structures with which standing spectators could come in contact, are made safe, secure and, where appropriate, non-climbable. Where necessary, protective measures should be taken to avoid potential injury, for example, from low roof beams at the back of covered terraces.

Any structure located in a standing area, be it permanent or temporary – for example floodlight pylons or television camera platforms – should be protected from potential crowd pressures, by the provision of suitably designed barriers.

c.   Sightlines

If the sightlines are poor, thus encouraging spectators to stretch or strain, an assessment should be made of the effects upon spectator movement. If this movement is considered to be excessive, or leads to any of the pressures detailed in Section 13.3, a reduced (P) factor will in turn reduce the numbers allowed to occupy the area.

d.   Lighting

Where standing areas are to be used during non-daylight hours, they must be sufficiently lit to enable spectators to identify hazards.

Wherever doubts arise as to the physical condition of a standing area, consideration should be given to a reduction in the (P) factor.

13.24 Assessment of (S) factors for standing areas

In addition to (P) factors, the calculation of capacities for standing areas will be partly based on an assessment of their safety management, or the (S) factor (see Section 2.5). The following are some of the main requirements that need to be met if the (S) factor is not to be reduced. It is stressed that this list is not comprehensive or applicable in all situations. Nor is it presented in order of importance.

a. **Admission**
    Management should ensure that the number of people admitted to standing areas, or divisions of standing areas, is counted and strictly controlled, according to the capacities set for those areas.

b. **Stewarding**
    Stewards should be familiar with the layout of all areas of standing accommodation and the location of exits, emergency exits and amenities. They should be trained and briefed to ensure that spectators do not stand in gangways, do not climb on barriers, fences or other structures, and do not behave in such a way as to endanger other spectators.

c. **Keeping gangways clear**
    As stated above, it is essential that gangways, both lateral and radial, are kept clear. In addition to the efforts of stewards, spectators should be informed of this requirement by signs and other means; for example, by means of announcements in event programme and via the public address system.

d. **Distribution of spectators**
    Using suitably trained, qualified and briefed stewards and, where appropriate, CCTV, management should ensure that spectators are evenly distributed. This is particularly important in popular standing areas – for example, behind the goals at football grounds or close to the finishing post at racecourses – where concentrations of spectators are prone to gather.

    Monitoring and controlling the distribution of spectators is also particularly important if non-continuous crush barriers are provided, owing to the greater risk of crowd surges in the gaps between crush barriers, or if there are no crush barriers at all.

e. **Migration – viewing distances**
    As stated in Section 13.10, one of the factors determining viewing standards is the viewing distance. This is the distance between the spectator and the pitch or area of activity. Viewing distances are not, in themselves, a safety matter. However, the distance may influence spectators' behaviour at key moments during an event. Management should therefore ensure that spectators in areas closest to the pitch or area of activity are not encouraged to surge forward, particularly in response to the actions of players or participants in the event.

    Similarly, where standing spectators are a long distance from the playing area or area of activity, management should ensure that they are not encouraged to migrate forwards at key moments of an event in order to obtain a closer view.

f. **Migration – partial cover**
    For guidance on safety management of standing areas offering only partial cover, see Section 13.14.

g. **Large standing areas**
    Although the determination of the available viewing area (see Chapter 2) will have already taken the crush barrier strengths and configuration into account, on large

standing areas with inadequate crush barriers this can still result in a considerable capacity. In such situations, special attention should be paid to the ability of management to cope with migration and congestion in popular areas.

h. **Removal or control of potential restrictions**
Before and during an event, management should ensure that any restrictions to viewing are removed or controlled. Such restrictions are listed in Section 12.6. In addition, provision should be made for the accommodation of any stewards or members of staff who may not be on duty during an event. Such personnel should not be allowed to stand in vomitories or in areas where they might restrict views or obstruct gangways or exits.

i. **Provision for children**
The presence of young children on standing areas raises particular concerns, because, in common with smaller adults and elderly people, they may have neither the strength nor stature to deal with crowd movement. They may also be vulnerable when pressed up against standard 1.1m height crush barriers.

It has traditionally been common for children to migrate to the front of terraces, with or without adults, in order to obtain a better viewing position. Where non-continuous barriers are provided, this can create additional safety concerns, because at the front, children are clearly more vulnerable to maximum pressure.

Ground management should recognise these potential dangers and develop a strategy to ensure the safety of children and indeed any vulnerable adults in such situations.

The ideal strategy is to create a well-managed and appropriately designed children's or family enclosure where children can remain free from crowd pressures and movement, and obtain a clear view of the pitch or area of activity. Wherever possible, these areas should have their own entry and exit points, to avoid children having to pass through other areas of terracing.

j. **Signs**
The provision of clear, informative and suitably elevated signs, illuminated where necessary, is particularly important in standing areas (see Chapter 16).

k. **Crowd behaviour**
This is a factor where crowd behaviour is such that it creates safety risks on a regular basis, and management proves unable to deal with the problem.

Wherever doubts arise as to the safety management of a standing area, consideration should be given to a reduction in the (S) factor.

13.25 Conversion of terraces to seating

Although primarily a matter of design, as stated throughout this chapter, when planning the construction of new standing areas or the refurbishment of existing ones, management and designers should take into account the possibility of future conversion to seating.

If all the recommendations listed in this chapter for new constructions are followed, the conversion should be relatively simple.

However, as is the case for all matters relating to the design of standing or seated accommodation, it is recommended that management seeks professional advice from competent persons of the appropriate skill and experience.

The following is a summary the main considerations.

a. If the future conversion of the terrace to seating is achieved by the usual method of creating one seating row from every two terrace treads (see *Diagram 13.1*) designers should work out the sightlines for:

   i.   standing spectators, and

   ii   seated spectators in advance of the terrace being constructed.

   By doing this the sightlines will be adequate and appropriate both for the standing spectators and, after conversion, for seated spectators.

b. By designing new terracing to the appropriate dimensions recommended in Section 13.9, future conversion to seating will be much simpler and meet the requirements for seating listed in Section 11.1.

c. If radial gangways provided for standing areas are to be appropriately sited for future use in a seated area, to avoid additional costs, they should be spaced 13 – 14m apart, rather than 24m as would be the case for standing areas.

d. If a roof is already in place, advanced calculations of sightlines will be necessary to ensure that, once converted to seating, the roof will not require replacement or remodelling in order to avoid restricted views.

Diagram 13.1 Conversion of terracing to seated accommodation

By designing new standing areas to the appropriate dimensions (see Section 13.9), the future conversion to seating will be much simpler.

As illustrated, this can be achieved by creating one seating row for every two terrace treads.

If this approach is taken, as stated in Section 13.25, designers should work out the sightlines for standing spectators, and seated spectators in advance of the terrace being constructed By doing this the sightlines will be adequate and appropriate both for the standing spectators and, after conversion, for seated spectators.

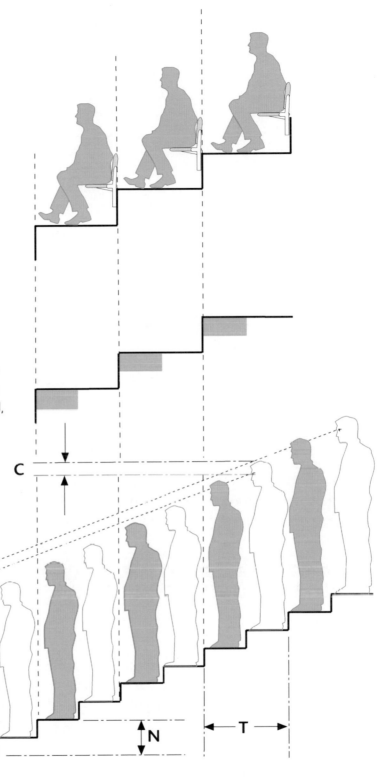

Note that, as illustrated, regardless of whether the terrace is going to be converted to seating at a later date, or when assessing existing standing areas, 'C' values for standing spectators need only be calculated for every second tread (see Section 13.11 and Diagram 12.1).

14: Spectator accommodation – temporary demountable structures

14.1   Responsibility for safety

As stated in Chapter 1 responsibility for the safety of spectators lies at all times with the ground management. The management will normally be either the owner or lessee of the ground, who may not necessarily be the promoter of the event.

This responsibility extends to any temporary demountable structure erected at the sports ground. Management cannot delegate the responsibility to the event promoter, to the designers of the structure, or to the contractors responsible for assembling the structure.

Ground management should therefore put in place procedures for ensuring the safe design, assembly and usage of any such structures. If management does not itself possess sufficient expertise in specific matters relating to temporary demountable structures, it should require the event promoter or contractor to produce certificates from competent persons of the appropriate qualification and experience.

14.2   Need to meet standards

The construction and configuration of temporary demountable structures – such as grandstands, standing decks, hospitality suites and marquees – vary considerably, as do the materials used in their construction. Some structures may be erected for a single event only and may be commissioned at short notice. Structural components are lightweight, rapidly assembled, readily dismantled, and reusable.

Nevertheless, the fact that a structure is designed for temporary use does not justify acceptance of lower margins of safety than those required for permanent structures.

The design and construction of temporary demountable structures should, wherever possible, meet the standards for new construction, as specified in the *Guide*.

It is recognised, however, that there is a considerable amount of proprietary stock currently in use. When used at sports grounds this should at least meet the standards of the *Guide*, and should satisfy all relevant British Standards.

All the principles of the *Guide* including those in respect of entry and exit systems, seated and standing accommodation, barriers and fire safety, are also applicable to temporary demountable structures. The need for lightning protection should also be noted (see Section 17.9).

Reference should be made to *Temporary Demountable Structures – Guidance on Procurement, Design and Use*, published by the Institution of Structural Engineers and to the European Standard BS EN 13200-6:2006 *Spectator Facilities: Demountable (temporary) stands* (see Bibliography).

14.3 Independent design check

Prior to assembly, the design of a temporary demountable structure should be subject to an independent check by a chartered structural engineer of the appropriate skills and experience. The supplier of a temporary demountable structure may appoint the structural engineer responsible for the independent design check.

In the case of proprietary systems, the results of an independent design check should remain valid provided no subsequent modifications are made to the system. If significant changes are made, further independent design checking will be required; for example if the proprietary structure is supported by tubular scaffolding.

All temporary demountable structures should be erected and used in strict accordance with their approved design criteria. Any changes in layout, dimensions or loading will necessitate a new, independent design check.

Furthermore, ground management is responsible for ensuring the integrity of such structures after their assembly, and before spectators are permitted to occupy them.

14.4 Design performance and suitability

Temporary demountable structures should be designed in three dimensional form, to be robust and stable, and to support design loadings for the required period with an adequate margin of safety. Guidance is available from the Institution of Structural Engineers (see Sections 5.5 and 14.2). The following main points should also be considered:

a. By virtue of their lightweight construction and use, temporary demountable structures are often exposed to a greater risk of accidental damage, such as by vehicles, unauthorised removals and alterations. This fact should be carefully considered when assessing stability and when considering the management of such structures (see Section 14.6).

b. The robustness of temporary demountable structures should be such that the effects of accidental damage are not disproportionate, thereby leading to progressive collapse.

c. Having assessed the structure's overall stability, where necessary, ballast and/or anchorage to the ground should be provided to ensure adequate resistance to overturning.

14.5 Consultation

Even when not formally required to do so under the terms of a safety certificate, management should consult the relevant authorities regarding enforcement responsibility, and any special local regulations, certificates, licences or permissions. Consultation should also take place with the fire authority concerning access for fire fighting purposes.

14.6 Management of temporary demountable structures

The special characteristics of temporary demountable structures require that management adopt specific strategies to ensure the safety of spectators. Such measures include the following:

a. Management should ensure that the structure is used strictly for the purpose for which it was designed. If used for any other purpose, or modified in any way, it should be the subject of an independent design check before it may be occupied by spectators.

b. Stewards should be briefed to pay close attention to the circulation and behaviour of spectators around the structure, so as to ensure that no-one is allowed to climb up or underneath any part of the structure, or behave in such a way that any elements or components may be damaged or removed.

c. At events where there is a possibility of synchronised spectator movement, stewards, assisted by public address announcements, should ensure that spectators are suitably warned. If potentially dangerous synchronised movements do occur, the event organiser should ensure that the movement is halted and, if appropriate, any part of the event which stimulates the movement, is curtailed.

d. The occurrence of high winds immediately prior to or during an event may require management to consider prohibiting spectators from occupying the temporary demountable structure, or, if necessary, cancelling the event.

e. Management should ensure that maintenance is carried out in strict accordance with written instructions, which should be provided by the designer or manufacturer.

14.7 Telescopic stands

The design, construction and maintenance of telescopic stands should, wherever possible, meet the standards for new construction, as specified in the *Guide* and should satisfy all relevant British Standards. Reference should be made to the European Standard BS EN 13200-5:2006 *Spectator Facilities: Telescopic stands* (see Bibliography).

14.8 Other temporary demountable structures

For guidance on other uses for temporary demountable structures at sports grounds, see Chapter 19 on media provision and Chapter 20 on alternative uses for sports grounds.

15: Fire safety

15.1 Fire safety legislation

The Regulatory Reform (Fire Safety) Order 2005 requires management to plan, organise, control, monitor and review the necessary preventive and protective measures and record these arrangements in writing. The Fire (Scotland) Act 2005, as amended and the Fire Safety (Scotland) Regulations 2006, introduced broadly equivalent requirements in Scotland but with some differences in respect of application, terminology and the detailed provisions.

Detailed guidance on the above legislation, including enforcement responsibilities, has been published by DCLG and the Scottish Executive (see Bibliography).

The legislation also requires a responsible person (in Scotland the duty holder) to undertake a risk assessment. It is incumbent on ground management to identify such a person who should lead or be part of the management team.

The DCLG publication *Fire Safety Risk Assessment – Large Places of Assembly* (see Bibliography) provides guidance on how to undertake such a risk assessment. It refers the reader back to this *Guide* for specific advice on sports grounds. For guidance in respect of sports grounds in Scotland, reference should be made to the Scottish Executive publication *Practical Fire Safety Guidance for Places of Entertainment and Assembly* (see Bibliography).

15.2 Achieving safety from fire

Having undertaken the risk assessment, the fire strategy for the premises should be developed to:

a.   adopt measures designed to minimise the fire risk (see Section 15.10)

b.   ensure that measures are taken to restrict the rate of early fire growth and fire spread (see Section 15.11)

c.   provide and protect sufficient emergency evacuation routes (see Sections 10.11, 15.11 and 15.16)

d.   provide appropriate fire detection and warning systems (see Section 15.13)

e.   provide appropriate fire-fighting equipment (see Sections 15.14 and 15.15)

f.   ensure that all staff receive appropriate training in fire safety and the use of fire fighting equipment (see Section 15.18).

Once the above measures have been taken and the level of fire risk has been reduced, it is then possible to determine the appropriate times for both normal egress and emergency evacuation for each area of spectator accommodation. These times will then form part of the capacity calculation, as explained in Chapter 2.

When considering fire safety, it should be noted that:

g. The maximum travel distance for seated spectators is 30m from the seat to the nearest exit from the viewing area (see Section 12.9), and for standing spectators is 12m from the standing position to a gangway or point of entry to the exit system (see Section 13.4).

h. The maximum normal egress time for a sports ground is eight minutes (see Section 10.7).

i. The maximum emergency evacuation time varies between two and half minutes and eight minutes, according to the level of fire risk (see Sections 10.9 and 15.5–15.7).

However, it is stressed that, rather than relying solely on a short emergency evacuation time, management should always aim to introduce measures which will minimise the outbreak and spread of fire.

In addition to these factors, achieving safety from fire also requires the preparation of contingency plans (see Sections 3.17 and 3.18), and the provision of a suitable system of internal and external communications (see Chapter 16).

15.3   Fire risk assessment

In order to determine the fire risk, ground management must ensure that the responsible person (in Scotland the duty holder) conducts a fire risk assessment of all accommodation and involving all parties who are working within the sports ground, at least once a year (see *diagram 15.1* and also Section 3.6).

The method of undertaking the risk assessment is as follows:

a. Identify the location of combustible materials and any sources of ignition to identify those parts of the ground where fire is likely (see Sections 15.10).

b. Identify people especially at risk and ensure that their needs in an emergency are provided for in the management's contingency plans. People especially at risk might include:

   i.   children and disabled spectators who might need help to escape, and may have difficulties in using escape routes, particularly stairs

   ii. staff or stewards who may have to assist others.

c. Identify reasonable steps that can be taken to minimise the fire risk (see Section 15.10).

d. Having identified the categorisations of risk and hence emergency evacuation times, record significant findings and action taken (see Section 15.9).

e. Keep the assessment under review and revise it where necessary (see Section 15.9).

15.4   Levels of risk

The fire risk assessment should assess all structures and installations at the ground, including all areas of spectator accommodation, taking into account their form of construction, usage, facilities, location and management. This assessment will determine for each structure or area of accommodation the appropriate level of fire risk; that is, low risk, normal risk or higher risk.

Diagram 15.1 The steps of fire risk assesment.

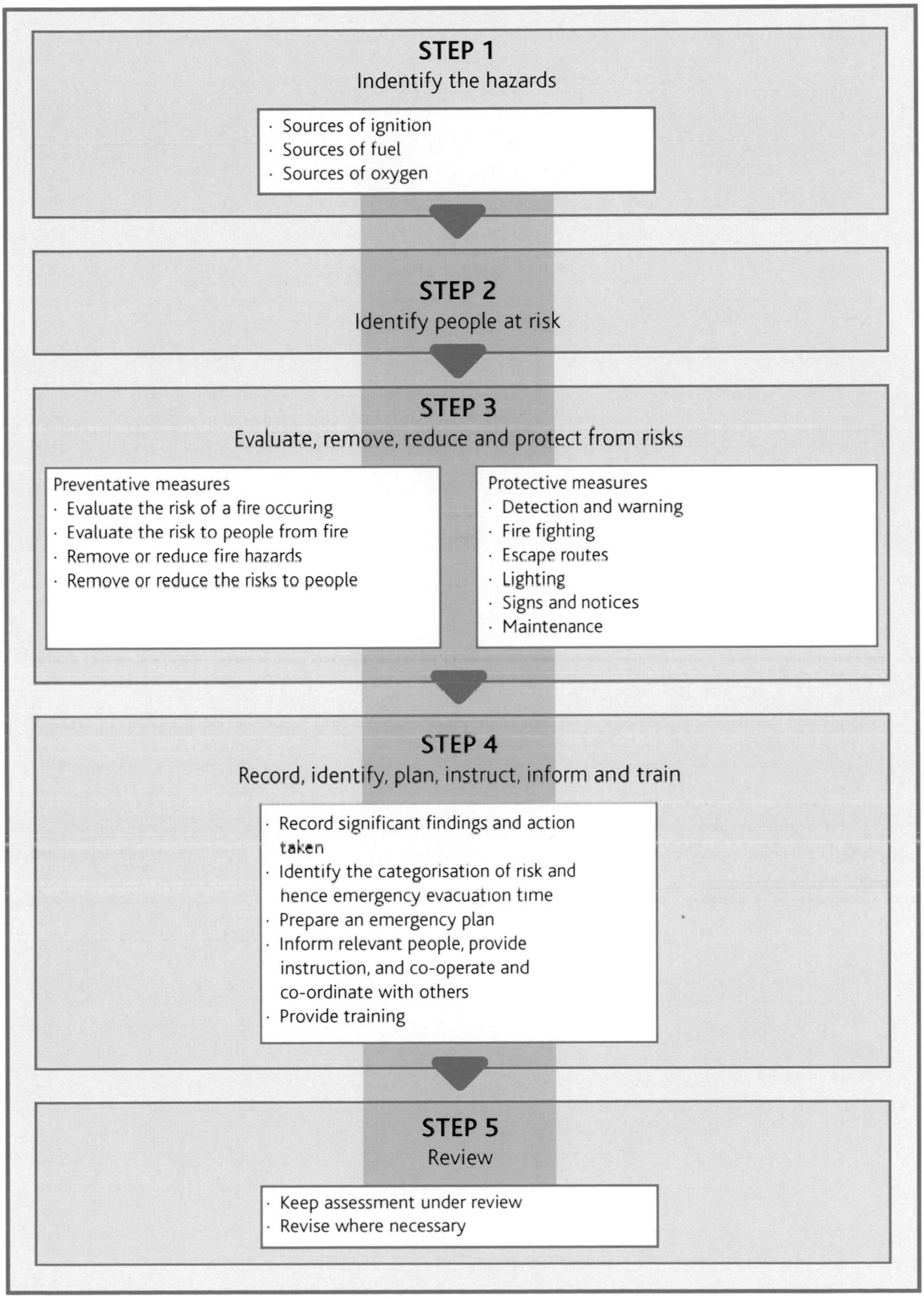

STEP 1
Indentify the hazards

- Sources of ignition
- Sources of fuel
- Sources of oxygen

STEP 2
Identify people at risk

STEP 3
Evaluate, remove, reduce and protect from risks

Preventative measures
- Evaluate the risk of a fire occuring
- Evaluate the risk to people from fire
- Remove or reduce fire hazards
- Remove or reduce the risks to people

Protective measures
- Detection and warning
- Fire fighting
- Escape routes
- Lighting
- Signs and notices
- Maintenance

STEP 4
Record, identify, plan, instruct, inform and train

- Record significant findings and action taken
- Identify the categorisation of risk and hence emergency evacuation time
- Prepare an emergency plan
- Inform relevant people, provide instruction, and co-operate and co-ordinate with others
- Provide training

STEP 5
Review

- Keep assessment under review
- Revise where necessary

The assessment should also take into account the availability and location of a place or places of safety or reasonable safety from fire (see Glossary) and the proximity of other buildings or installations which might themselves carry a risk of fire.

Examples of each level of fire risk follow in Sections 15.5–15.7.

The level of fire risk will determine the emergency evacuation time, which in turn will form part of the calculation of the final capacity of the ground or sections of the ground (see Chapter 2).

If the fire risk assessment indicates that the area's holding capacity is too large to enable all spectators to evacuate the area and reach a place of safety or reasonable safety within the emergency evacuation time appropriate to the level of risk, or if undue congestion or psychological stress are likely to result, the capacity should be reduced accordingly.

Note also that the conditions within a particular ground may call for interpolation between the emergency evacuation times referred to in the following sections.

In all cases, the advice should be sought from the authority responsible for enforcing fire safety legislation.

15.5   Categorisation of low fire risk

A low fire risk seated or standing area at a sports ground is likely to be one where:

a.   the risk of a fire occurring is low, and

b.   in the unlikely event of a fire, the potential for the fire, heat or smoke generated by it, to spread, is negligible, and

c.   there is a minimal risk to life.

Such structures might include open terraces and stands constructed of non-combustible materials with fully protected catering outlets.

For low risk seated and standing areas, the emergency evacuation time for all spectators to reach a place of safety or reasonable safety should be no more than eight minutes.

15.6   Categorisation of normal fire risk

A normal fire risk seated or standing area is likely to be one where:

a.   the risk of a fire spreading is low

b.   should a fire occur it is likely to be confined to a room or its place of origin

c.   there is in place an effective fire suppression or containment system.

For normal risk seated and standing areas, the emergency evacuation time for all spectators to reach a place of safety or reasonable safety should be no more than six minutes.

15.7   Categorisation of higher fire risk

The type of spectator accommodation most at risk from fire is the covered stand. A higher fire risk seated or standing area is likely to be one where one or more of the following characteristics apply:

a.   the construction consists of combustible materials

b.   structural features could promote the spread of fire, heat and smoke

c. there are voids under seating decks, floors or terraces where waste or litter may accumulate

d. there are several storeys, with exiting systems from the upper levels routed through hospitality areas

e. the concourse areas have inadequate fire separation between retail and/or catering facilities and the emergency evacuation routes

f. highly flammable or explosive materials are present

g. people in the area are at risk from an incident occurring in an adjacent premise.

For higher risk seated and standing areas, the emergency evacuation time for all spectators to reach a place of safety or reasonable safety should be no more than two and a half minutes.

It is stressed that the list of characteristics summarised in Sections 15.5–15.7 above are for general guidance only. Any fire risk assessment must take into account all relevant local circumstances.

15.8 New or refurbished stands or structural alterations

Any new or refurbished stands or alterations to the use of a structure will need to take account of the overall fire safety arrangements in the sports ground. As part of the design process the designer should carry out a fire risk assessment to identify areas where a fire might occur. Management should also ensure that the responsible person (in Scotland the duty holder) carries out a fire risk assessment of the new or refurbished construction, before the premises are occupied. This risk assessment will of necessity make assumptions about the conditions after occupation and so it should be reviewed shortly after occupation to ensure it is accurate.

15.9 Recording, monitoring and reviewing the fire risk assessment

The findings of the risk assessment must be recorded and taken into account when planning and managing fire safety arrangements at the ground. The location of all people especially at risk (see Section 15.3), together with any special arrangements put into place to ensure their safety if a fire occurs, should also be recorded.

The risk assessment must be continually monitored to ensure that the fire safety arrangements remain adequate, and should be reviewed in the following circumstances:

a. there is a significant change of staff

b. there is a change to the safety management arrangements

c. building, refurbishment or alterations are planned or in progress

d. there is a significant increase of combustible materials, or sources of heat in the ground

e. there is any other reason to believe that the fire risk assessment is no longer valid.

Where the review indicates that the risk to people has changed, a new fire risk assessment should be carried out.

As stated in Section 15.1, having completed a fire risk assessment, the next stage is to reduce those risks, wherever possible. The following sections detail how this may be achieved.

15.10 Minimising fire risk

The following measures and practices should be considered when seeking to minimise fire risk:

a. **Sources of ignition**

As stated in Section 15.2, the fire risk assessment should identify all potential sources of ignition at the ground. Where possible, those sources should be removed or replaced with safer forms. Where this cannot be done, the ignition source should be kept well away from combustible materials, be adequately guarded or made the subject of management controls. Ignition sources may include:

    i. cooking appliances

    ii. central heating boilers

    iii. room heaters

    iv. light fittings

    v. certain electrical apparatus, especially if not maintained

    vi. smoking materials (see Section 15.10.b).

b. **Smoking**

Whilst legislation prohibits smoking in certain areas, management should ensure that if smoking is permitted in other areas it does not increase the risk of fire. Management should therefore adopt and enforce a clear policy on smoking for both staff and spectators. The policy should be supported by suitable signs and use of the public address system to inform spectators.

In areas which are constructed of, or contain, combustible or flammable items or materials, smoking should be discouraged or even prohibited.

Stewards and safety personnel should not smoke during an event.

c. **Flares and fireworks**

Management should adopt and enforce a clear policy prohibiting spectators from bringing flares or fireworks into the sports ground. Indeed this is illegal at many football matches.

Any activities which include pyrotechnic displays must be included in the fire risk assessment and a method statement prepared.

d. **Voids**

Voids under seating decks or terraces, or under the flooring itself, are often used for the unauthorised storage of combustible materials. They may also accumulate waste or litter. To counter this, all voids should either be sealed off or be kept entirely open to allow easy access for inspection and the removal of the combustible materials.

It may be necessary to consider ventilation of some large voids where the possibility of flammable or explosive atmospheres may arise.

Voids which are unusable, for example, where the viewing deck is built over a slope, should, if practicable, be filled with a non-combustible material.

e. **Waste and litter**
The accumulation of waste and litter (such as programmes and food and drink packaging) should be avoided. All parts of the ground should therefore be inspected before, during and after each event. Any accumulation of waste or litter should be removed without delay or kept in a fire-resistant container or room, pending removal.

Sufficient waste and litter bins should be provided and arrangements made for their frequent emptying during a match or event.

f. **Furnishings, upholstered seating and cushions**
The use of furnishings, upholstered seating and cushions which are easily ignited or have rapid spread of flame characteristics should be avoided. If present, they should be taken into account when determining the acceptability of escape routes. All furnishings, upholstered seating and cushions should conform to relevant British Standards.

When stored in bulk, certain types of cushioning (which is distributed or hired for event use), and foam mats (used at athletics events), pose a risk of a rapid fire growth and should therefore be stored in a fire-resistant container or room.

g. **Storage**
Rooms or buildings used for the storage of waste, litter, upholstered seating or hazardous materials should:

i.   be accessible directly from the open air

ii.   ideally, be well away from public areas

iii. if forming part of a stand or structure, be separated from any other part of the building by construction having a fire resistance of at least 30 minutes

iv.   if measuring 6m or more in depth, be provided with an alternative means of escape

v.   be kept locked shut when not in use.

h. **High risk fire areas**
High fire risk areas should be separated from any other parts of spectator accommodation by a construction having a fire resistance of at least 30 minutes. Such areas may include:

i.   kitchens

ii.   catering outlets

iii. hospitality areas

iv.   boiler rooms, oil fuel stores and general stores

v.   enclosed or underground car parks.

i. **Catering facilities**
Wherever possible, all catering facilities should be located in permanent structures. If located within other structures they must be separated by fire resistant construction and provided with adequate ventilation. Any temporary or mobile catering facility must be included in the fire risk assessment.

Flues should be separated as they pass through the structure, should have an adequate degree of fire separation, and terminate at a point where the emissions can disperse in the open air.

For further guidance on catering facilities at sports grounds, refer to the *Guide to Control over Concessionaire Facilities and Other Services at Sports Grounds*, published by the District Surveyors Association (see Bibliography).

j. Fuel or power supply

Special care should be taken to ensure that any fuel or power supply used for cooking or heating, in particular liquefied petroleum gas (LPG) cylinders, is safely stored and used, in accordance with the advice of the authority responsible for enforcement. Any assessment of a potential LPG installation should include reference to the relevant British Standard. Further guidance on the keeping and use of LPG in mobile catering units is available from the Health and Safety Executive and Nationwide Caterers Association (NCASS) (see Bibliography).

k. Hazardous materials

If it is necessary to utilise hazardous materials, such as fuels (whether in containers or within fuel tanks and machinery), fertilizers, weed killers, paints or gas cylinders used for medical purposes, they should, if held within or near to spectator facilities, be stored in a fire resistant room.

l. Temporary structures and ancillary activities

Any temporary accommodation or facility must be included within the fire safety risk assessment. Any ancillary activity not included in the overall fire safety risk assessment must be the subject of a site-specific risk assessment.

15.11 Restriction of fire growth and spread

It is vital to ensure that, in the event of a fire, the rate of fire growth is restricted in its early stages. It should also be noted that most measures which restrict the rate of fire growth in its early stages will also serve to restrict the fire spread in its later stages. These measures include:

A. Viewing accommodation should be separated from adjacent areas or voids by a construction which has a fire resistance of at least 30 minutes. This is so that any fire underneath or in an adjacent area cannot easily break through into the spectator accommodation.

   Where stands incorporate hospitality facilities, any additional separation must be determined by the level of fire risk.

B. Where a stairway, vomitory, passage or any other part of an emergency evacuation route passes up, down or through a stand or other structure used by spectators, unless it is in the open air, it should be in a fire resistant enclosure separated by a construction having a fire resistance of not less than 30 minutes. For further guidance on vomitories and concourses, see Chapter 9.

C. Walls and ceiling linings within spectator accommodation, together with ceiling linings beneath the floor of that accommodation, should have a flame spread classification of not less than Class 1 when tested in accordance with the relevant British Standard. Walls and ceiling linings in emergency evacuation routes and circulation areas should have a flame spread classification of Class O.

D. Any door forming part of the enclosure to an escape route should be self closing and have a fire resistance of not less than 30 minutes.

E. Where the roofs of buildings are close together or connected to each other, smoke or flame can easily spread. This risk should be eliminated by fire prevention measures, or by adequate fire separation.

F.   For some roof configurations, venting systems may offer a means of reducing the spread of fire (including the movement of flames under the roof) and the spread of smoke and toxic gases. The science of fire and smoke venting is, however, complex and advice from the fire authority should be sought on whether venting systems would be advantageous in a particular case.

G.   Where the roof contains flammable materials it should be replaced by non-combustible materials. Where this is not practicable, the roof should be underdrawn with non-combustible board.

H.   Shops, or catering outlets containing deep fat fryers or hot food cooking facilities, should be separated from other internal areas or spectator accommodation areas by a construction which has a fire resistance of at least 30 minutes. Where roller shutters are used these should be capable of operating both manually and by fusible link. Where a fire detection or fire alarm system has been installed, the roller shutter should also be designed to close on the activation of the system.

New or substantially altered structures should comply with the appropriate Building Regulations or relevant British Standards which may require higher levels of fire protection than those outlined above.

15.12   Fire resistance in existing constructions

Existing stands and others areas of spectator accommodation will vary considerably according to age, condition and the materials used in their construction. It may therefore be difficult in some cases to improve the fire resistance of an existing structure to any significant extent. But it should be done wherever possible, even though, in some cases, substantial alterations may be needed to provide reasonable protection from fire.

Where not possible, alternative compensatory measures will need to be considered. These might include:

a.   provision of an extensive early fire warning system

b.   improvements to the exit and emergency evacuation systems

c.   installation of a suitable fire suppression system

d.   a reduction of the travel distances

e.   a reduction of the final capacity.

15.13   Fire warning and fire detection systems

All buildings to which the public or staff have access and which might pose a fire risk should be provided with a manually operated electrical fire warning system to alert staff. Consideration should also be given to the installation of an automatic fire detection (AFD) system in all high risk fire areas (see Section 15.10.h) and also in any unoccupied areas that contain a normal fire risk.

These systems should:

a.   be designed to accommodate the emergency evacuation procedure.

b.   give an automatic indication of the fire warning and its location. If this warning is directed to a part of the ground other than the control point (for example, to the secretary's office), there should ideally be a repeater panel sited in the control point.

c.   be designed, installed, commissioned, maintained and tested by competent persons in accordance with the advice given in the relevant British Standard.

Where the public address system is part of the fire warning system it should be connected to an auxiliary power source to ensure the continued use of the system in the event of fire or other emergency.

Whichever warning or detection systems are in place, however, if a fire occurs the fire service should always be called immediately.

The procedures adopted to notify the fire service should also form part of the management's contingency plans and of staff training.

15.14 Automatic fire extinguishing systems

Consideration should be given to the provision of automatic fire extinguishing systems, particularly in high risk fire areas, such as large storerooms and enclosed or underground car parks situated under or adjacent to spectator accommodation. Such systems should:

a. be designed, installed, commissioned, maintained and tested by competent persons in accordance with the advice given in the relevant British Standards

b. provide for the activation of the system to be automatically communicated to the control point.

In all cases, the advice should be sought from the authority responsible for enforcing fire safety legislation.

15.15 Fire fighting facilities and equipment

All sports grounds should be provided with appropriate fire fighting equipment. For the majority of grounds, portable fire fighting equipment, that is, fire extinguishers, fire blankets and hose reels, will be sufficient. However, at some larger grounds it may be necessary to provide a suitable water supply for fire fighting, in the form of hydrants, rising mains and/or sprinkler systems.

Advice on the type, the level of provision and the siting of fire fighting equipment should be sought from the authority responsible for enforcing fire legislation.

Responsibility for the provision of appropriate fire fighting equipment lies with the management. It is also the responsibility of management to check that all fire fighting equipment is in the correct position and in satisfactory order before each event.

When providing such equipment, the following should be considered:

a. Hose reels, where appropriate, should be sufficient to provide adequate protection to the whole floor area, and should be installed in a suitable position by entrances, exits and stairways.

b. Where hose reels are not provided, sufficient portable fire extinguishers should be installed to give adequate cover. The number and type will depend upon the size, layout, fire separation and risk in each structure.

c. Fire blankets and appropriate fire extinguishers should be provided in all catering facilities and outlets.

d. Portable fire fighting equipment should be located so that it cannot be vandalised but is readily accessible to staff in the event of fire (see Section 9.7e).

e. All portable fire fighting equipment should be designed, installed, maintained and tested in accordance with the advice given in the relevant British Standards.

15.16 Emergency evacuation and places of safety

As stated in Section 10.7, a clear distinction should be made between the emergency evacuation time and the normal egress time at the end of an event.

The emergency evacuation time is a calculation which, together with the appropriate rate of passage, is used to determine the capacity of the emergency exit system from the viewing accommodation to a place of safety or reasonable safety, in the event of an emergency (see also Section 10.9).

As stated in Section 15.4, the fire risk assessment should take into account the availability and location of one or more places of safety or reasonable safety.

A place of safety (see Glossary) may be a road, walkway or open space adjacent to, or even within, the boundaries of the sports ground.

Within a large sports ground there may also be a need to designate a place or places of reasonable safety where people can be safe from the effects of fire for 30 minutes or more, thus allowing extra time for them to move directly to a place of safety.

A place of reasonable safety (see Glossary) may include:

a. an exit route that is protected throughout its length by a construction having a fire resistance of 30 minutes

b. a stairway that is in the open air and protected from fire breaking out onto or below it

c. the pitch or area of activity. As stated in Section 10.13, however, this should be considered only in certain circumstances and only after consultation with the authority responsible for enforcing fire safety legislation.

It should also be noted that if the fire risk assessment indicates that an emergency evacuation exit could be affected by fire, that exit may have to be discounted when calculating the capacity of the emergency exit system (see Section 10.15).

15.17 Emergency evacuation of spectators with disabilities

Contingency plans for emergency evacuation should take into account the special needs of spectators with disabilities. Separate emergency evacuation routes for disabled spectators will allow for all spectators to be evacuated at the same time.

If separate escape routes for disabled spectators cannot, for practical reasons, be provided, the contingency plans need to consider how disabled and non-disabled spectators are to be evacuated. For further detailed guidance see the Bibliography.

Warning systems may consist of an evacuation signal, announcements over the public address system, and, where appropriate, visual instructions on electronic scoreboards or video screens.

The fact that some people have a hearing impairment does not mean that they are necessarily insensitive to sound. Many people with severe impairments have enough perception of conventional audible alarm signals to require no special provision. In most situations it is reasonable to plan on the basis that most spectators with impaired hearing will rely on others for warning.

For further guidance on managing the evacuation of spectators with disabilities see Section 10.12.

15.18   Staff awareness and training

Management should ensure that all staff working at a sports ground or event are aware of the need to guard at all times against fire, including the possibility of arson. The staff should be trained in how to respond to any incident. In particular, they should understand what action to take on discovering a fire:

a.   to raise the alarm

b.   to await further instructions

c.   to tackle any fire before the arrival of the fire service without placing themselves in any danger

d.   to evacuate the ground (for which they should recognise any coded warning messages).

15.19   Other fire safety considerations

When considering fire safety in the overall context of the design and management of sports grounds, reference should also to be made to the following sections:

a.   Section 6.8 (access for emergency vehicles)

b.   Chapter 10 (egress and emergency evacuation)

c.   Chapter 17 (particularly Section 17.13 concerning emergency lighting and 17.14 on the use of lifts for evacuation and fire fighting).

16: Communications

16.1 Management responsibility

Clear, efficient and reliable communications are an integral part of any safety management operation. This applies regardless of the type of sports ground or the nature of the event.

It is stressed that good communications are not solely dependent on the provision of advanced equipment or modern systems. The skills, awareness and efficiency of management, stewards and other personnel form a vital part of all links.

The management responsibility for communications can be summarised as follows:

a. to provide, operate and maintain the necessary means of communication

b. to provide, equip, maintain and manage the operation of a control point

c. to keep open and maintain all necessary lines of communication, in both normal and emergency conditions

d. to ensure that all safety personnel and stewards are competent and suitably trained in the practice of good communications, with or without equipment, as conditions allow.

16.2 Lines of communication

Whatever the means of communication utilised (see Section 16.3), there are essentially seven lines of communication needed at all grounds These are communications between members of the safety management team (in particular the safety officer) and

a. the stewards and other safety personnel

b. all points of entry (including the monitoring of counting systems) and all points of exit

c. the police, other emergency services and medical agencies

d. spectators, inside and outside the ground

e. other members of staff

f. officials in charge of the actual event

g. officials from the British Transport Police, the Highways Agency and public transport companies where necessary.

16.3 Means of communication

This chapter provides guidance on the principal means of communication, in terms of their technical and operational requirements.

Precise requirements will depend on the type of ground, the nature of the sport, and the number of people in attendance. Professional advice and expertise should therefore be sought from competent persons of the appropriate skills and experience. In general, the provision of all communication systems should also be determined after consultation with the emergency services, and, where a safety certificate is in force, the local authority. Communication systems should also conform to the relevant British Standards or Codes of Practice.

The principal means of communication outlined in this chapter are as follows:

a. radio communications

b. telephone communications (internal and external)

c. public address systems

d. closed circuit television systems (CCTV)

e. scoreboards, information boards and video boards

f. signs

g. written communications (via tickets, signs and printed material)

h. inter-personal communications.

16.4 Provision of a control point

Regardless of the type or size of a ground, a control point should be provided, and equipped to meet the reasonable requirements of the ground. Such a facility should form the hub of the safety management's communications network.

At larger grounds, particularly football grounds, the control point is currently referred to using terms such as 'stadium control room' or 'ground operations centre.' But whatever the term employed, it is emphasised that the provision and equipment of the control point is the responsibility of management.

If the police and other emergency services are required to be present at the ground, all decisions relating to the location, design and equipment of the control point must be made in consultation with representatives of those services. This is in order to ensure that the control point will also meet the needs of the police and others in both normal and emergency conditions. Where a safety certificate is in force, consultation concerning the control point should also take place with the local authority.

16.5 Functions of a control point

As stated in Section 16.4, the control point should form the hub of the safety management's communications network.

It is needed for the following five main functions:

a. to monitor the safety of people inside the ground and its immediate vicinity

b. to co-ordinate responses to specific incidents and emergencies

c to provide, if required, a monitoring facility for the emergency services

d. to monitor public order

e. to assist the management in the staging of events.

16.6   Location of control points

The location of the control point should, as far as possible, meet the following requirements:

a.   It should command a good, unrestricted view of the whole ground; that is, the whole playing area or area of activity, and as much of the viewing accommodation as possible. (It is recognised, however, that this may not be possible at certain grounds, for example multi-tiered large grounds or those staging horse or motor racing or where there are multiple areas of activity).

b.   It should be conveniently accessible for all authorised personnel in normal and emergency conditions, without depending on circulation routes or emergency evacuation routes used by large numbers of spectators.

c.   It should be capable of being readily evacuated in an emergency.

d.   Its presence should not restrict the views of any spectators. Nor should it have its own views restricted by the close proximity of spectators.

e.   Its location should take into account any long term plans for the ground, to ensure that, wherever possible, construction work and new structures will not disrupt its operation.

f.   It should not be located adjacent to an area of high fire risk that might compromise its function during an emergency.

16.7   Command of control points

In normal conditions, command of the control point and its communication systems should be the responsibility of a representative of the ground management, who will usually be the safety officer (see Sections 3.11 and 3.12).

If the police are on duty in the control point, there should be a clear, unequivocal understanding of the division of responsibilities between their personnel and the ground's own safety management team. This understanding should be recorded as part of the written statement of intent (see Section 3.24).

16.8   Design of control points

For both new construction and existing grounds, as stated in Section 16.4, it is important to match the size, facilities and equipment of the control point with the reasonable requirements of the sports ground.

It should be recognised, however, that a control point is often occupied for long periods and that under the relevant legislation it may be classified as a workplace. As such, both for the efficacy of the ground's safety management operation and for the health and safety of its occupants, the facility should be designed and fitted with due regard to these considerations.

Further detailed guidance on all aspects of the design and safety management of new and existing control points is available in the Sports Grounds and Stadia Guide No. 2 – *Control Rooms* (see Bibliography). Although written primarily for stadia, the publication contains much general advice applicable to all sports grounds.

16.9   Secondary control point

Management should plan how the safety management operation will continue to be effectively managed if the primary control point is rendered unusable owing to fire or other emergencies. It is suggested in Section 16.15.a that siting the public announcer's room away from the control point would allow for emergency public address messages to continue to be relayed to spectators in the event of the control point facility becoming inoperable. Other potential locations for a secondary control point could be a hospitality box or an office within the sports ground. However, whatever site is chosen, it is important that systems are put in place to ensure the control team will be able to continue to operate effectively. Management's contingency plans should therefore identify how the flow of information to and from the secondary control point will be maintained if the purpose-built facility is unavailable or has to be evacuated in an emergency.

16.10   Equipment of control points

As stated earlier, it is important to match the equipment of the control point with the reasonable requirements of the sports ground. Certain means of communication included in the following sections may not therefore apply to all sports grounds.

However, regardless of the means of communication utilised in individual circumstances, it is essential that the seven lines of communication summarised in Section 16.2 are available to personnel working in the control point.

The means employed may include communication by radios, telephones, coded announcements over the public address system, electronic systems, written and spoken messages, provided that the lines of communication remain open in all normal conditions, and are clear, efficient and reliable.

The following sections provide guidance on the communications network as operated to and from the control point (but see Section 16.14 concerning public address systems).

16.11   Radio communications

Dependent on the scale of the stewarding operation and the sports ground, radio usually forms the main means of communication between the control point and stewards (or stewards' supervisors). If telephone links are not provided, radio might also be used for communication with other personnel such as the crowd doctor, turnstile controllers, members of the emergency services and car park or traffic controllers.

It is recommended that a licensed frequency should be used for radio communication. Unlicensed frequencies can be interrupted by external radio traffic, and may compromise important safety messages. Advice on the use of licensed frequencies is available from the Office of Communications.

When considering radio communications, the following points should be taken into account:

a.   Radio links may operate from either a radio base station or simply by hand held radios. Where appropriate, if a base station is provided, it should be located adjacent to the communicator's workstation, to assist in the exchange of information.

b.   A separate command channel between the control point and key safety personnel, such as the chief steward and supervisors, may be desirable.

c.   If possible there should also be a back up radio channel within the system.

d.   Any police radio facilities available for the maintenance of law and order should augment and not be regarded as a substitute for the ground's own communications system.

e.   The police will advise on the extent of their own radio requirements, which may be more extensive than the system needed for the ground's own safety needs. The police system may also require extra space to be provided in the control point; for example, for more than one police communicator, and for the provision of a voice recording facility.

f.   Consideration should be given to the provision of space for any ambulance or voluntary aid society radio equipment, in the event of this equipment being operated from within the control point or from an adjacent room.

g.   Personnel who operate two-way radios require an environment in which they can hear comfortably and avoid having to raise their voices. Good quality equipment, including the provision of appropriate headsets and microphones, should therefore be considered.

h.   The location of aerials should take into account the possibility of radio interference.

16.12   Telephone communications – internal

Ideally, but particularly at larger grounds, two forms of designated telephone systems should be provided; internal (a key point telephone system – see Glossary) and external (see Section 16.13).

To complement (or in certain cases to take the place of) radio communications, the internal telephone system should provide the link between the control room and key points around the ground.

Where possible, the internal system should meet the following requirements:

a.   It should be independent of any other internal telephone system operating at the ground.

b.   It should be possible for the operator in the control point to select which line to talk to without being blocked by other calls.

c.   Telephone lines provided for emergency use should meet the relevant British Standard; that is, no person who has need of the system should have to travel more than 30 metres to reach an emergency telephone.

d.   Key points of the ground linked to the control point by telephone might include:

   i.   the turnstiles (or banks of turnstiles)

   ii.   all steward control points

   iii. the public address operating booth

   iv.   the office of the Secretary, Clerk of the Course or equivalent senior official

   v.   the referee or event official's room

   vi.   lighting control points

   vii. any security office

   viii. the first aid room

        ix.   any police room

        x.   any rendezvous points

        xii. the ticket office.

e.   For safety related communications, the use of mobile telephones should be discouraged. In emergencies their use may not be possible owing to the network becoming overloaded.

16.13   Telephone communications – external

In addition to, and independent of, the internal system, telephone lines should also be available for direct and immediate telephone communication between the control point and the fire service and/or other emergency services. External telephone lines designated for emergency purposes should not be used for any other purposes.

16.14   Public address system – guidance and specifications

Other than direct personal contact with staff and stewards (see Section 16.31), or through the circulation of written material (see Section 16.30), the public address system will usually provide the main form of communication between the management and spectators.

There are a number of relevant British Standards with which public address systems at sports grounds should comply.

Although clear, audible public address announcements are of benefit to all spectators, they are vital for the safety and enjoyment of people with impaired vision. Although people with impaired hearing may experience difficulty in hearing messages on the public address system, they may still be sensitive to sound and to conventional alarm signals. It is also reasonable to expect spectators around them to warn those with impaired hearing in the event of an emergency (see also Section 16.23). Where a hearing enhancement system is installed to provide match commentaries for visually or hearing impaired spectators it should also be used for relaying important safety information.

In general, the public address system should meet the following requirements:

a.   **Intelligibility**
The system should be intelligible, so that broadcast messages can be heard under reasonable conditions (including emergencies), by all persons of normal hearing in any part of the ground to which the public has access.

b.   **Zoning**
The system of the public address system should generally be designed to broadcast to individual areas outside and inside the ground, to groups of areas, and to the whole ground. The system should also be capable of broadcasting to the pitch, if that forms part of the management's emergency evacuation procedure.

The operation of any zoning system should be part of a pre-determined contingency plan to ensure that only the appropriate parts of the sports ground are targeted.

Whether zoning is possible or not, however, at smaller sports grounds it may be preferable to make important announcements to the whole ground. Experience has shown that in these situations spectators sometimes think that they might have missed an announcement because the sound intended for one zone has carried partially into another. In such circumstances an assessment should be made before establishing any firm policy and, for example, a message of reassurance might be sent to the unaffected zones.

Repeating the evacuation and the alert messages to the relevant zones will reduce any likelihood of confusion.

c. **Override facility**

As explained in Section 16.15, it is recommended that the public address system should not be operated from the control point. However, it should be designed so that an operator – either from the management or police, as agreed in the contingency plans – can override the system in order to broadcast emergency messages, either to the whole ground or to particular zones only.

Similarly, if there are areas of the ground which have the facility for turning down the output from the public address system – such as hospitality boxes or lounges – the system should be designed to override these volume controls automatically when emergency messages are broadcast.

d. **Fire warning**

Emergency use of the public address system as part of the fire warning system requires full compliance with the relevant British Standard.

e. **Back up power supply**

The back up power supply to the public address system should be such to enable it to continue to function at full load in an emergency, such as a fire or a failure of the mains supply, for up to three hours (see Sections 16.25 and 17.11).

f. **Back-up loud hailers**

In the event of a failure of the public address system, loud hailers should be available for the use of stewards and police in all parts of the ground, including the control point, for directing or instructing spectators. It is vital that that all personnel are trained in their use, and that the batteries are kept fully charged.

g. **Inspections and tests**

Once installed, the public address system should be confirmed as meeting current standards by the issue of a commissioning certificate. It should be inspected and tested annually, in addition to the regular pre-event checks, and an inspection certificate obtained. Where a safety certificate is in force, the inspection certificate should be available for inspection by the local authority.

16.15 Public address system – operation

As stated in Section 16.1, good communications are not solely dependent on the provision of advanced equipment. This is particularly true of public address systems. The operation of the system, and the skills of the operators, are equally important.

The following considerations should be taken into account:

a. **Provision of a separate booth**

It is recommended that the general public address announcer should not be stationed within the control point, although it should be possible for personnel in the control point to override the system in the event of an emergency (see Section 16.14.c).

A separate booth may have the advantages of being used as a secondary control point in the event of the primary control point becoming unusable (see Section 16.9).

If a separate operating booth or facility is provided, it should command a good view of the playing area or area of activity, and be linked to the control point by telephone, via a land line. Ideally, this link should also include the provision of a clearly visible red light, so that the general announcer can see instantly when someone in the control point is trying to make contact.

This latter form of communication will not be necessary if the public address booth is located immediately adjacent to the control point, in which case there should be a sliding glass window, so as to enable more immediate contact.

Whatever arrangement is provided, it is vital that public address announcements can be heard clearly in the control point.

As ambient noise may adversely affect the audibility of the public address system, it is important to ensure that the sound levels are suitably adjusted to take account of any changes during an event. This can be achieved automatically by the installation of an ambient noise sensing system. Where such a system is installed it is important that it fails safe to maximum power, with the option of reduced power if it fails when the ground is only partly filled.

b. **Agreement on emergency announcement procedures**

As stated in Section 16.14.c, in addition to the provision of an override facility, there should be an agreed operational policy stating whether a representative of the management's safety team or a representative of the police, broadcasts announcements in the event of an emergency. This agreement should be recorded in the management's contingency plans.

c. **Pre-announcement signal**

Important announcements relating to crowd safety should be preceded by a loud, distinct signal to catch the attention of the crowd, whatever the level of noise in the ground at the time.

The following recommendations should be considered:

i.   Experience has shown that a three-event two-tone chime (that is, 'bing bong bing') is most effective. This signal should be different to, and distinct from, any other signals which may be in general use on the public address system.

ii. While the pre-announcement signal is being relayed, it is essential that the public address system's control panel clearly indicates that the microphone is temporarily muted. Ideally there should be two coloured indicators; one for 'wait' and the other 'speak now'.

iii. All ground officials, stewards, police, fire, ambulance and any other emergency personnel should be made aware of the pre-announcement signal.

iv. The signal should be tested before the start of each event.

v.   The signal should be sounded shortly before the start of the event as part of a general announcement on safety procedures, to reach the maximum possible number of spectators.

vi. The existence of this signal should be explained in every event programme printed for circulation to spectators.

d. **Tone and content of announcements**

In the event of an emergency it is essential that clear, accurate information is given to spectators at the earliest possible time. Messages should be positive, leaving those to whom they are addressed in no doubt as to what is required of them. The messages should be scripted in advance with the agreement of the police, fire authority and, where a safety certificate is in force, the local authority. It may also be appropriate to pre-record certain standard messages, for use in emergencies.

In all cases it is recommended that the announcer practices using the public address system, while assessors comment on the audibility, tone and effectiveness of their delivery. It is also important that the announcer is familiar with the layout of the sports ground and the agreed evacuation procedures.

Management should ensure that for certain international events, announcers able to speak the appropriate language are in post at the ground, and are briefed on the use of the system and the content of any safety announcements.

16.16 Closed circuit television – provision

The installation of closed circuit television systems (CCTV) is strongly recommended as an effective method of monitoring crowd movement and behaviour, particularly at larger sports grounds.

The primary advantage of CCTV is that it allows personnel in the control point to identify incidents – either by viewing the monitor directly or after receiving reports – and then, by use of the system, to make a more detailed appraisal.

However, a CCTV system should never be considered as a substitute for good stewarding or other forms of safety management.

Although not the primary purpose of CCTV systems at sports grounds, recordings made may also be used for evidential purposes. Reference should therefore be made to *Guidance Notes for the Procurement of CCTV for Public Safety at Football Grounds* and *Digital Imaging Procedure* both produced by the Home Office Police Scientific Development Branch (see Bibliography).

16.17 CCTV – assessment of need

When considering the installation of a CCTV system, or the upgrading of an existing system, management should undertake a detailed assessment of the needs of the ground as a whole and in particular those specific areas that need to be closely monitored, in order to assess the likely benefits of having such a system.

The areas to be assessed will include those immediately outside the ground, plus all turnstile areas, entry routes, concourses, areas of seated and standing accommodation, and exit routes. Ideally the system will cover all these areas. The assessment should also take into account when specific areas need to be monitored; that is before, during and/or at the end of an event.

If it is decided to install a new CCTV system, or upgrade an existing one, a detailed specification should be drawn up to meet the operational requirements of the management, before contractual negotiations and procurement commence.

As outlined in the following sections, there are essentially three stages in the drawing up of a specification for CCTV systems:

a. risk assessment

b. statement of operational requirement

c. tender document.

16.18　CCTV – risk assessment

In order to establish which areas need to be covered by CCTV, a detailed risk assessment of every part of the ground is required.

This assessment should identify the level of risk in each area. For example, a turnstile area at the end of a confined space may be assessed as a high risk, and a hospitality lounge a low risk.

The assessment should also take into account the nature of the risk, the likelihood of an incident occurring and the potential consequences.

Such an assessment will help management to establish whether alternative methods can be adopted to monitor areas of risk, or, if CCTV coverage is considered necessary, the level of coverage required.

The risk assessment should be recorded in the form of a plan of the ground, identifying the following points for each area:

a.　the type of risk; for example, overcrowding, crushing or the existence of a steep slope or escalator

b.　the level of risk

c.　whether CCTV is required

d.　the image required for monitoring purposes in the control point; for example, a general view, long shot, or closer view showing head and shoulders

e.　the number of images that might need to be viewed in detail and simultaneously, in the event of an incident or incidents (this may determine the number of cameras in a specific area)

f.　whether the image should be monochrome or colour

g.　the levels and types of lighting in specific areas, in both normal and emergency conditions.

Where there are significant changes to the operation of a sports ground, for example the relocation of visiting supporters or the use of the pitch or activity area for a concert, a risk assessment should be carried out to determine whether any changes to the CCTV system are necessary.

Generally, the risk assessment requires no technical knowledge of CCTV. Only in respect of parts (f) and (g) is there a need for some technical expertise. It is, however, recommended that the risk assessment is undertaken with the assistance of the relevant authorities, or where a safety certificate is in force, the local authority.

16.19　CCTV – operational requirement and tendering

The findings of the risk assessment, together with the annotated ground plan and any associated paperwork, should be combined to provide a clear statement of the CCTV system's operational requirement.

Additional points which should be considered are as follows:

a.　The images provided should be sufficiently clear and distinct to enable personnel in the control point to monitor effectively the areas covered.

b.　The system should make provision for video recording all CCTV coverage.

c.   Where a CCTV system is to be used for other purposes; for example, for 24 hour site security, care should be taken to ensure that the equipment is suitable for extended use. Otherwise, prolonged use may result in the system's failure at a crucial period during an event.

The statement of operational requirement should form the basis of any tender documents prepared for contractors to bid for the installation of the CCTV system.

However, the statement must be supported by additional technical specifications detailing aspects of the expected use and performance of the installation; for example, the need for weather protection of cameras, the quality of monitors, and the facilities required for video recording.

Advice on the drawing up of tendering documents is available in the Home Office publication *Guidance Notes for the Procurement of CCTV for Public Safety at Football Grounds* (see Bibliography).

16.20   CCTV – operation

Where CCTV cameras are installed the images produced must be capable of being monitored and recorded by personnel in the control point.

Personnel operating the system should be suitably trained and, where appropriate, qualified in the operation of CCTV systems. They should also be skilled in the interpretation, use and storage of the data provided.

The positioning of monitors requires careful consideration to ensure that the images are not adversely affected by light or glare from windows or from overhead lighting.

Whilst it may be desirable to monitor the CCTV system from other locations; for example, a security office, it is essential that total control of the system is maintained by personnel in the control point.

An auxiliary power supply should be provided to ensure continued operation of the CCTV system in the event of a power failure.

16.21   Monitoring the number of spectators entering the ground

As stated in Section 7.1, all spectators entering all sections of the ground, including VIP and lounge areas, should be accurately counted at their time of entry, and their number controlled in order to ensure that overcrowding does not occur.

Whether manual, mechanical or computerised, the counting system used should be designed to ensure that personnel in the control point are informed immediately when a predetermined number of spectators has been admitted through each turnstile, bank of turnstiles or point of entry serving each section of the ground (see Section 7.5).

In addition, the following points should be considered.

a.   Where a computerised counting system is installed, the display monitor should be sited in the control point, where it can be viewed by the safety officer and, if present, the police commander.

b.   In the absence of computerised screen displays or read-outs, an efficient system of communication must be established between the turnstiles and/or points of entry and the control point, using runners, land-lines or radios, with clear, written records kept at regular intervals using wipe boards and/or pro-formas.

c.   All read outs or written records should indicate the section of the ground, the number of spectators occupying that section and the time of the count.

d.   All read outs or written records need to be immediately available to the safety officer and, if present, the police ground commander.

e.   Contingency plans should cover the failure of the computerised system.

f.   The installation of a back up monitor.

16.22   Fire warning systems

The fire alarm master panel should be in a location that is both accessible and visible to the fire service. If this is not in the control point, a fire alarm repeater panel should also be located in the control point.

The repeater panel should run silently, or have a mute facility, so that if it goes off it will illuminate a prominent red or flashing light rather than audibly. This is so that there will be no extra noise to disrupt communications within the control room.

If the repeater panel is located elsewhere, it will require a designated individual to monitor it constantly during events (see also Section 15.13).

16.23   Scoreboards and other display boards

Where electronic scoreboards or video display boards are in use, management should pre-arrange and script the contents of all safety related and emergency messages. These should be displayed in co-ordination with the broadcast of prepared public address announcements.

People with impaired hearing rely on the presentation of clear, informative visual information on scoreboards, electronic boards and video boards.

Operation of the scoreboard or video display board should be from a place other than the control point; for example, from the same booth or room used by the general public address announcer.

The contents and graphics of the messages should be agreed in consultation between the management, the police, the emergency services and, where a safety certificate is in force, the local authority.

16.24   Electronic securing systems

At grounds where electronic securing systems – also known as automated exit gate release systems – are installed, a designated exit gate supervisor should be stationed in the control point.

As stated in Section 10.17, the sole duty of this person should be to operate and monitor the main console or computer display installed as part of such systems.

Written records of the operation should be maintained, and made immediately available to the safety officer and, where appropriate, the police ground commander.

16.25   Auxiliary power

It is essential that power is maintained to provide the continuous operation of all control point functions and selected communications systems in the event of a power failure, fire or other emergency.

Auxiliary power should therefore be provided, sufficient at the very least to enable emergency lighting, the public address system, CCTV and all other safety-related installations to function for a minimum of three hours after the failure of the normal supply.

It is essential to test the necessary communication systems to ensure that they do continue to function normally when the auxiliary power takes over.

As stated in Sections 3.17 and 3.18, management should also prepare contingency plans to cover the possibility of a power failure. These should include, as stated in Section 16.14, the provision of loud hailers.

If, as recommended above, the auxiliary power is capable of supplying the entire load for the ground for a minimum of three hours, it may be possible to continue the event, provided it is scheduled to finish and the ground be cleared of spectators within this period, and no other emergency exists. In such cases, the auxiliary power supply must itself be provided with additional back-up power.

16.26 Displayed communications within the control point

Depending on the size and type of the ground, a certain amount of information will need to be displayed inside the control point. This is best achieved by the use of display and deployment boards. Such boards might display the following:

a. a plan of the ground and its immediate approaches

b. a plan showing the location of fire alarm points and fire fighting equipment

c. a list of key point telephone extensions

d. a wipe board for the deployment of stewards

e. a wipe board for the deployment of police officers

f. a wipe board showing the location of ambulance service, voluntary agency and crowd doctor

g. where no computerised or mechanical readouts are available, a wipe board to display the number of spectators passing through the turnstiles.

16.27 Documentation to be stored in the control point

As an aid to communications within the control point, storage space should be provided for documentation that might be required for instant reference. Such documentation is likely to include:

a. a copy of the ground's contingency plans (see Sections 3.17 and 3.18)

b. relevant details of the emergency plan (see Section 3.20)

c. where there is one in force, a copy of the safety certificate, and any other records required as a condition of the safety certificate

d. where possible, copies of detailed scaled drawings of each section of the ground (see Section 5.16).

16.28 Signs – forms and categories

A vital part of the communications system is the provision of sufficiently large, clear, legible and suitably positioned signs.

There are essentially three forms of signs, as follows:

a. Safety signs

Safety signs appear in five different categories, and should meet the shape and colour requirements specified:

i. prohibition signs; for example, 'No Smoking' (circular shape, with a black pictogram on a white background, red edging and a red diagonal line through the pictogram)

ii. warning signs; for example, 'Low Headroom' or 'Uneven Steps' (triangular shape, with a black pictogram on a yellow background, with black edging)

iii. mandatory signs; for example, 'Spectators must not cross this line' (circular shape, with white pictogram on a blue background)

iv. emergency Escape or First Aid signs (rectangular or square shape, with a white pictogram on a green background)

v. fire-fighting equipment signs (rectangular or square shape, with a white pictogram on a red background).

All signs in this category should be easily seen and understood. In conditions of poor natural light it may be necessary to provide either artificial illumination and/or to make the signs using reflective material.

It is emphasised that safety signs are not a substitute for other means of controlling risk. They are to warn of any risk that may remain after all engineering controls and safe systems of working have been put in place.

The provision of signs that communicate a hazard warning or safety related message may, in certain situations, be mandatory under the Health and Safety at Work etc. Act 1974, and in such cases should conform to the guidance provided within the Health and Safety (Safety Signs and Signals) Regulations 1996.

Further guidance on these regulations and on safety signs in general is available from the Health and Safety Executive (see Bibliography).

b. Information signs

These are signs communicating information relative to the ground, to the event, or to specific restrictions. Such signs include:

i. ground plans; it is recommended that simplified ground plans are displayed at suitable locations, such as by ticket offices and main entrances, and, where appropriate, in places where they might benefit supporters of visiting teams. The ground plans should display any colour coded information relating to ticketing and entry requirements.

ii. ground regulations, including information on prohibited items.

iii. directional signs, both outside and inside the ground.

iv. seat and row indicators.

Signs in this category should not use predominant colouring which could lead to their being confused with safety signs. Neither should they be placed in such a way that they obscure or dominate over safety signs.

c.   Commercial signs and hoardings
Care should be taken that signs and hoardings in this category are located in such a way that they do not obscure or detract from safety or information signs; for example, by being too close, by blocking the line of vision, or by the over-use of predominant colours utilised in the safety or information signs.

16.29   Signs – general provision and maintenance

All signs, and particularly signs relating to fire safety and emergency evacuation, should be presented and sited so that they can be easily seen and readily distinguished by those with impaired vision or colour perception. Only a minority of the general population has perfect vision, therefore clear, well designed signage will be of benefit to all spectators. Advice on this matter is available from the Royal National Institute for the Blind or the National Federation of the Blind of the UK. Further guidance can be found in Sports Grounds and Stadia Guide No. 1 – *Accessible Stadia* (see Bibliography).

Signs at sports grounds should also meet the following general requirements:

a.   All signs should be securely fixed, including temporary signs used on an event basis only.

b.   Signs should not be fixed in such a way that they restrict spectator viewing or impede the circulation of spectators.

c.   All signs should be kept clean.

d.   Handwritten signs should be avoided.

e.   It might be necessary to confirm with the appropriate authority that signs do not contravene the fire resistance or fire loading requirements of particular areas of a ground, such as emergency evacuation routes or concourses.

16.30   Tickets and programmes

Wherever possible, the written information provided for spectators should be used as a means of communicating safety related information.

As stated in Section 3.29, a clear plan of the ground should be provided on the rear of the ticket.

That part of the ticket retained by the spectator after passing through a ticket control point or turnstile should clearly identify the location of the accommodation for which it has been issued. Colour coding of tickets, corresponding to different sections of the grounds, should be considered.

As stated in Section 7.9, the design of the ticket should also ensure that the key information printed – such as turnstile, block, seat and row number or, in the case of racecourses, enclosure – is clear and easy to read for the spectator, turnstile operators and stewards.

Management should ensure that the same information is provided to those using an electronic card entry system.

Clear and concise information about the ground's layout and safety procedures should also be printed in the event programme.

Management may also wish to issue periodically written material that provides further information of interest and relevance to spectators; for example, concerning changes of procedure or future arrangements. Such material may be issued with tickets.

16.31 Inter-personal communications

As stated in Section 16.1, good communications are not solely dependent on the provision of equipment or systems.

In all exchanges between members of the safety management team, individuals should recognise the need for clear, concise and constructive communication. Training and briefing should ensure that there is no confusion as to the use of specific terms, or to the meaning of instructions or directions.

It should also be remembered that for many spectators the only direct contact they have with representatives of management may be with staff or stewards. It is therefore crucial that any information imparted to spectators is clearly given, accurate and in accord with the policies of the safety management team.

False or confusing information, rudeness or unhelpfulness are all examples of poor communication, and are thus a weak link in the safety chain.

17: Electrical and mechanical services

17.1 Introduction

This Chapter covers a number of permanent or temporary electrical and mechanical installations likely to be in place at a sports ground, many of which are either safety-related or have their own safety implications. However, reference to other electrical and mechanical installations and systems may also be found elsewhere in the *Guide*, as follows:

a.   public address, CCTV and emergency telephone systems (see Chapter 16)

b.   fire warning and other fire safety systems, and catering installations (see Chapter 15)

c.   turnstile monitoring systems (see Chapter 7)

d.   sound systems (see Section 20.6).

Further reference may be made to the *Guide to Electrical and Mechanical Services in Sports Grounds*, published by the London District Surveyors Association (see Bibliography).

17.2 The importance of maintenance

All electrical and mechanical installations at a sports ground are liable to gradual deterioration, particularly those situated in outdoor or exposed environments. It is therefore vital that management ensures that such installations are properly maintained by competent persons with the appropriate skills and experience.

It is imperative that maintenance procedures for both new and existing installations are properly understood. Management should prepare a detailed planned preventative maintenance schedule covering the testing, inspection, commissioning and servicing of all such installations in accordance with:

a.   the written instructions and schedules provided by the manufacturer

b.   where appropriate, the relevant British Standards

c.   where a safety certificate is in force, the requirements of the local authority.

A planned preventative maintenance schedule demonstrates that the management is taking its responsibilities for maintenance seriously. It may be relevant when assessing the overall (S) factor.

17.3 Inspections and tests

Unless specified to the contrary by the manufacturers' written instructions or other relevant documentation, all electrical and mechanical installations should be inspected and tested at least annually by competent qualified persons, and an inspection certificate supplied to ground management. This annual inspection and test will be in addition to the regular pre-event tests (see Sections 5.9 and 5.10). The results of all inspections and tests should be recorded in writing.

17.4   Event-day staffing

Management should ensure that there is a competent person or persons either on site or readily available on an event day to deal with any problems which might arise in relation to the electrical or mechanical installations at the ground. Contact details should be included in the contingency plan (see Section 3.18).

17.5   Anti-vandalism

A number of electrical and mechanical installations associated with safety systems, including auxiliary power units, may be vulnerable to vandalism. This should be taken into consideration when fixing and securing such installations.

17.6   Electrical installations

All electrical installations should comply with current regulations. New electrical installations should also comply with the relevant British Standards, and wherever practicable, existing installations should be upgraded to comply with those standards.

An Electrical Installation Completion Certificate prescribed by the Institution of Electrical Engineers (IEE) should be retained by the management. Each Completion Certificate should be accompanied by a current Periodic Inspection Report. Any new part to the electrical installation should, in the first instance, have a separate Completion Certificate. Further guidance is available from the IEE (see Bibliography).

17.7   Circuit diagrams

Main electrical circuit diagrams should be provided, clearly labelled to indicate:

a.   all main switches, circuit breakers and fuseways in distribution boards and the circuits which they control

b.   the location of all switch rooms and distribution boards.

The circuit diagrams should be kept in a location easily accessible to technical staff, be protected from defacement or damage, and be updated as necessary.

17.8   Protection of cables

All cables should be sited so that they are, as far as practicable, inaccessible to the public. Where necessary, cables should also be enclosed throughout their length in a protective covering of material which has sufficient strength to resist mechanical damage. The following wiring systems are acceptable:

a.   mineral insulated metal sheathed cables

b.   steel wire or tape armoured cables

c.   insulated cables in screwed metal conduit

d.   insulated cables in metal trunking.

Notwithstanding the above, alternative wiring systems may be acceptable; for example, insulated cables in rigid PVC conduit which complies with the relevant British Standard. However, PVC conduit or PVC served cables should not be used in confined areas (such as catering outlets or emergency evacuation routes), because of their fire smoke hazard. The use of PVC conduit should also be discouraged in exposed areas, because of its susceptibility to vandalism.

Where wiring systems do not meet the above requirements, consideration should be given to a programme of phased replacement.

17.9   Lightning protection

Lightning protection for structures, both permanent and temporary, should be provided in accordance with the relevant British Standard. The lightning protection should be tested annually by competent persons, and a certificate supplied to the ground management. Floodlighting towers should be bonded to earth in accordance with the relevant British Standard.

17.10   Lighting

The lighting in all parts of a sports ground accessible to spectators should allow them to enter, to leave and move about the ground in safety. This is particularly important in relation to entry and exit routes and stairways used by the public.

At all times when the daylight in any section of a ground accessible to the public is insufficient, or if the ground is to be used in non-daylight hours, adequate artificial lighting should be provided. This lighting should be sufficient to illuminate all signs, in accordance with relevant European Union Directives (see also Section 16.28).

Consideration should also be given to the lighting required for CCTV systems to operate satisfactorily (see Sections 16.16–16.20).

The minimum level of illumination should be as recommended by the Chartered Institute of Building Services Engineers. (For details of guides produced by CIBSE, see Bibliography. For guidance on emergency lighting, see Section 17.13.).

17.11   Provision of auxiliary power

As stated in Sections 3.17 and 3.18, management should prepare contingency plans to cover the possibility of a power failure.

Where appropriate, auxiliary power should be provided, sufficient at the very least to enable emergency lighting, the public address system, CCTV and all other safety-related electrical installations to function for at least three hours after the failure of the normal supply.

An auxiliary power system designed to supply emergency and safety systems should be independent of any other wiring systems.

17.12   Auxiliary power equipment

Auxiliary power equipment should be located in a secure room or building to which the public does not have access. The room or building should be of a construction having a fire resistance of not less than 30 minutes.

Auxiliary power equipment should be installed, maintained and tested in accordance with the manufacturers' written instructions and relevant British Standards. As stated in Section 5.9, it should be inspected and tested 24 hours before each event, and should also be capable of operating on the failure of a single phase.

For further guidance on auxiliary power, see Section 16.25.

17.13 Emergency lighting

At sports grounds used to stage events in non-daylight hours, emergency lighting for use in the event of a failure of the general lighting, should be provided in all parts of the ground to which the public have access, including along all exit and emergency evacuation routes, with exit signs clearly illuminated.

Emergency lighting at sports grounds should meet the following requirements:

a. Where emergency lighting systems are not separate from the normal lighting system, a risk assessment should be carried out to determine the adequacy of the chosen system in emergency conditions.

b. The emergency lighting system should operate automatically on the failure of the normal lighting system.

c. Where the emergency lighting is a non-maintained system, such lighting should be designed to operate on the failure of a circuit or sub-circuit.

d. Along all exit and emergency evacuation routes, the emergency lighting should afford a level of illumination sufficient to enable people to leave the premises. For guidance on the level of illumination required, reference should be made to the CIBSE *Emergency Lighting* guide (see Bibliography).

e. Unless, exceptionally, two entirely independent supplies can be obtained from outside sources, the emergency circuit should be connected to a source of auxiliary power located on the premises.

f. If a generator is used, it should be able to operate the full emergency lighting load within not more than five seconds of start-up.

g. The system should be capable of maintaining the necessary level of illumination for a period of three hours from the time of failure of the normal supply.

17.14 Passenger lifts and escalators

Passenger lifts and escalators should be maintained and tested in accordance with the manufacturers' written instructions and schedules and the relevant British Standards. Ground management should be familiar with the Lifting Operations and Lifting Equipment Regulations 1998.

The following general requirements should be considered:

a. Lift alarms should be audible under event conditions.

b. For new lift installations, consideration should be given to providing a duplicate alarm in the ground's control point.

c. As stated in Section 10.12.d, a lift provided for passenger use in the normal operation of the sports ground may only be used for evacuation purposes if it meets the requirements of an evacuation lift, as specified in the relevant British Standard. Among other requirements, this means that it should be able to operate in reasonable safety when there is a fire in the building.

d. Where provided, a fire fighting lift may also be used for emergency evacuation (see Section 10.12.e).

e. Among the recommendations for the safe guarding of evacuation lifts, as required by the relevant British Standard, the following points should be noted:

i. An evacuation lift should be situated within a protected enclosure consisting of the lift well itself and a protected lobby at each storey served by the lift. The protected enclosure should also contain an escape stair.

ii. Except for lifts serving two storeys only, evacuation lifts should be provided with a switch which brings the lift to the final exit storey (usually ground level), isolates the landing call buttons and enables an authorised person to take control.

iii. The primary electrical supply should be obtained from a sub-main circuit exclusive to the lift. It should also have a secondary supply from an independent main or emergency generator and an automatic switch to change over from one to the other.

iv. Any electrical sub-station, distribution board or generator supplying the lift should be protected from the action of fire for a period not less than that of the enclosing structure of the lift shaft itself.

17.15 Gas fired installations

All natural gas and LPG installations (see also Section 15.10), including heating and cooking appliances, pipework and meters, should comply with current gas safety legislation, as follows:

a. The Gas Safety (Installation and Use) Regulations 1994, as amended, covering matters related to meters, appliances, and the pipework connecting appliances to meters. These regulations allow only CORGI registered installers to carry out work on these parts of gas installations.

b. The Pipework Safety Regulations 1996, covering matters related to service pipework connecting meters to gas distribution mains.

17.16 Boilers and other heating devices

As stated in Section 15.10 rooms containing boilers may be considered as high risk fire areas. For this reason, boilers (and other heating devices) should meet the following requirements:

a. Boilers should be installed by a competent person in accordance with the relevant British Standard. They should be housed in a fire resistant enclosure, and, where appropriate, separated from areas of spectator accommodation by a construction having a fire resistance of at least 30 minutes.

b. To prevent over-heating, boilers, generators, air heaters and other similar appliances should be fitted with a fusible link or similar device that will automatically cut-off energy supplies.

c. Boiler or generator rooms should have adequate air supply for the safe operation of the appliances, and be generally ventilated.

d. The location of both combustion air intakes and ducts, and flue pipes and exhaust systems for boilers and generators, should not prejudice the means of escape for spectators, and should not cause a nuisance by emission into spectator accommodation.

e. Where it is necessary for ducts and pipes to pass through areas occupied by spectators, they should be of the same fire resistance as the room to which they are connected, until they reach a safe place of emission or supply.

17.17 Oil storage and supply

Oil storage and oil supply systems should comply with the relevant British Standard. To reduce the risks on event days, the amount of oil stored within the boiler or generator room should be limited to essential requirements.

17.18 Ventilation, air conditioning and smoke control systems

The installation of any mechanical ventilation, air conditioning or smoke control systems should be subject to detailed design and installation by competent persons with the appropriate qualifications and experience.

The provision of such systems will form an important part of any fire safety risk assessment (see Chapter 15).

Where provided to help facilitate safe evacuation (for example, smoke extraction in a concourse), they should be linked to an auxiliary power supply.

18: Medical and first aid provision for spectators

18.1 Management responsibility and consultation

The measures described elsewhere in the *Guide* should, if followed, help to prevent a serious incident. However, in order to discharge fully its safety responsibilities, ground management should ensure that appropriate medical, nursing, paramedic and first aid provision are available for all spectators.

Management must commission a medical risk assessment from a competent person or organisation (see Section 18.2) who should consult the local ambulance service NHS trust or other NHS authority (in Scotland the Scottish Ambulance Service), medical and first aider providers and crowd doctors as appropriate.

Where a safety certificate is in force the consultation should be arranged through the local authority.

From the results of the medical risk assessment, management must produce a written medical plan defining the levels of medical and first aid provision for spectators at the sports ground (see Section 18.3).

18.2 Medical and first aid risk assessment

The risk assessment should take account of (but not be limited to) the following factors:

a.   Physical factors
   i.   the physical layout of the sports ground and its surroundings (including roads, car parks and waterways)

   ii.   the design of the ground including any areas of high risk

   iii.   the presence of large upper tiers or extensive areas of spectator accommodation, their access/egress and the provision of satellite first aid rooms

   iv.   the presence of areas of standing accommodation or temporary demountable stands

   v.   the location of the ground control point, first aid posts, ambulance control point and other key locations under the ground contingency plans and emergency procedures

   vi.   the nature and location of the radio and other communications systems.

b.   Safety management factors
   i.   the safety management structure and lines of communication

   ii.   the ground contingency plans and emergency procedures

   iii.   the training of staff

   iv..   the hazards and risks posed by the event to the spectators

    v.   the anticipated composition and behaviour of the crowd

    vi.   historical data of treatments for injuries and medical conditions including similar events elsewhere

    vii. any requirements of particular sports governing bodies.

18.3 Medical plan

The medical plan should include details of:

a. the medical team command structure and lines of responsibility

b. the ground command and control systems

c. the size, location and number of permanent, temporary or mobile first aid rooms and facilities

d. all medical equipment and materials and their source

e. the role, number and location of ambulances, their capabilities and the crew competencies

f. the duties, number and location of crowd doctors, nurses, paramedics and first aid personnel

g. the communication links to the members of the medical team inside the ground and with other agencies outside the ground

h. procedure for the investigation and management of critical incidents

i. the number and profile of the crowd, with particular reference to the likely presence of older people, young children and those with disabilities

j. the time and duration of the event

k. the procedures for inspecting facilities and equipment

l. the need to respond to particular weather conditions

m. travel times and distances to local accident and emergency hospitals

n. the response to a major incident

o. major incident triage procedures

p. major incident casualty clearing location and procedures

q. procedures for dealing with fatalities

r. the necessary welfare facilities for all medical service personnel.

Particular sports governing bodies may have specific requirements for medical support in order to permit the event to commence or to continue. The medical resources provided for participants should not be regarded as available for spectators and vice versa.

The plan should be reviewed annually or after any significant incident or near miss.

In addition to the medical plan for spectators it is likely that there will be a medical plan for participants and officials. It is not unreasonable to combine the two plans to provide a clear statement of responsibilities.

18.4 First aid room

It is the responsibility of ground management to provide a room or rooms designated for the provision of first aid to spectators. This should be in addition to the sports ground's own medical room for participants.

The first aid room should be provided and equipped in consultation with the local ambulance service NHS trust and representatives of the crowd doctors (see Section 18.8) and the relevant first aid provider. Where a safety certificate is in force the local authority should be consulted.

a. Size

The first aid room should meet the following requirements:

i. The recommended minimum size of the room is 15 square metres. Where the authorised capacity of the ground exceeds 15,000, this size should ideally be increased to at least 25m².

ii. The room should be large enough to contain a couch with adequate privacy screening, with space for people to walk around, and an area for treating sitting casualties. If the authorized capacity of the ground exceeds 15,000 and a room of at least 25m² is provided, an extra couch should be provided.

iii. The room must provide sufficient secure storage space for all the appropriate equipment and materials (see Section 18.5).

b. Fittings and facilities

The first aid room should have the following fittings and facilities:

i. heating, lighting (including emergency lighting), ventilation and appropriate power and auxiliary power supplies

ii. a stainless steel sink plus facilities for hand washing

iii. a supply of hot and cold water, plus drinking water

iv. toilet facilities, which should be accessible to wheelchair users

v. a worktop

vi. a couch or couches as detailed in Section 18.4.a above

vii. telephone lines allowing internal and external communication. The external line should be a direct line; that is, not routed via a switchboard.

c. Design and location

The first aid room's location and design should:

i. be easily accessible to both spectators and the emergency services and their vehicles

ii be clearly signposted throughout the ground, clearly identified, and its location known to all stewards

iii. be designed in such a way as to facilitate easy maintenance in a clean and hygienic condition, free from dust

iv. have a doorway large enough to allow access for a stretcher, ambulance trolley or wheelchair

v. include an area in close proximity where patients, relatives and friends can be seated while waiting.

Consideration should be given to the provision of satellite first aid rooms in sports grounds with, for example, large upper tiers or extensive areas of spectator accommodation.

A suitable site should be identified as a secondary first aid post in the event of the primary first aid post becoming non-operational for any reason.

18.5 Medical and first aid equipment and storage

Suitable arrangements should be provided for the procurement and replacement of the agreed scale of medical and first aid equipment and materials as set out in the medical plan (see Section 18.3).

An indication of equipment typically provided in a first aid room is given in the *Safety of Sports Grounds Specimen General Safety Certificate and Guidance Notes* published by the London District Surveyors' Association (see Bibliography).

Management should ensure that defibrillators are provided at all events. If the management itself does not have defibrillators permanently on site, it should ensure that they are supplied by the medical and/or first aid provider. It is desirable that, where doctors and paramedics are deployed, a manual defibrillator should be provided. Automatic and semi-automatic defibrillators should also be available for suitably trained staff.

Management must provide suitable secure storage for the first aid materials and equipment except any equipment brought in on the event day by the medical provider.

Arrangements should be put in place for the safe disposal of clinical (including sharp items) and non-clinical waste.

18.6 Upkeep and inspection of the first aid room

Ground management is responsible for the upkeep and cleanliness of the first aid room.

As stated in Section 18.14, management should also ensure that the first aid room, equipment and materials are inspected before an event in accordance with the medical plan (see Section 18.3).

All first aid facilities should also be available at any time for inspection by the ground management and, where a safety certificate is in force, by the local authority.

18.7 Provision of competent medical services

Responsibility for ensuring the presence of competent personnel lies with management.

Management should appoint one or more organisations who can supply the number and range of suitably qualified personnel required for the venue and the event.

18.8 Crowd doctor

At an event where the number of spectators is expected to exceed 2,000 (or a higher figure if substantiated within the medical plan and supported by alternative nursing or paramedic cover), at least one crowd doctor, qualified and experienced in pre-hospital immediate care should be present. These doctors' first duty must be to the crowd.

It is likely that the crowd doctor will be drawn from a pool of appropriately trained and qualified individuals. Recommended training for crowd doctors should be the Pre-Hospital Emergency Care Course (PHEC) and the Major Incident Medical Management and Support Course (MIMMS) or equivalent relevant experience.

The whereabouts of the crowd doctor in the ground should be known to all first aid and ambulance staff and to those stationed in the control point, who should be able to make immediate contact with him or her.

The crowd doctor should be at the sports ground prior to spectators being admitted and remain in position until all spectators have left.

The crowd doctor should be aware of:

a. the location and staffing arrangements of the first aid room and details of the ambulance cover

b. the local emergency plans for dealing with major incidents and how these relate to contingency plans for the ground (see Chapter 3).

Table 18.1 Ambulance provision according to anticipated attendance

Anticipated attendance	Minimum paramedic ambulance provision	Statutory ambulance officer	Statutory ambulance authority vehicles
5,000 to 25,000	1	1	–
25,000 to 45,000	1	1	1 major incident equipment vehicle 1 control unit
45,000 or more	2	1	1 major incident equipment vehicle 1 control unit

Notes to Table 18.1

The paramedic ambulance(s) may be supplied by a statutory ambulance authority or a competent private source. In many cases the medical plan will provide for the attendance and define the role of additional ambulances supplied by the medical provider (see Section 18.7).

For anticipated attendances over 5000 a statutory ambulance officer will be required except where this can be justified under the medical plan.

For anticipated attendances of over 25,000, the major incident equipment vehicle and control unit may not be required where this can be justified under the medical plan.

18.9 Ambulance provision

Management should make arrangements for the provision of at least one fully equipped ambulance staffed at paramedic level (see *Table 18.1*) at all events with an anticipated attendance of 5,000 or more (or a higher figure if substantiated within the medical plan and supported by alternative cover).

While the requirements for every event should be examined on an individual basis, *Table 18.1* provides a general guide for ambulance provision which, in most cases, should be considered reasonable:

The ambulance(s) should be at the sports ground prior to spectators being admitted. Its role during the event should be clearly defined in the medical plan.

The medical plan should ensure that where the paramedic level ambulance has been provided for command and co-ordination purposes another ambulance is available for patient care. An ambulance is not required for command and co-ordination when the personnel exercising these functions are deployed in a multi-agency control point with appropriate communications.

The ambulances required by the medical plan may be supplied by the statutory ambulance service, a competent private medical provider or the voluntary sector.

18.10 Numbers of first aiders

As stated in the Glossary, a suitably trained first aider is one who holds the standard certificate of first aid issued to people working as 'First Aiders' under the Health and Safety (First Aid) Regulations 1981.

The provision of first aiders should meet the following minimum requirements:

a. No event should have fewer than two first aiders.

b. At all-seated grounds the ratio should be one first aider per 1,000 up to 10,000 spectators, and thereafter one per 2,000 (of the number of spectators anticipated for the event).

   Where there is reason to believe that spectators will stand in seated areas in large numbers, the number of first aiders in the area concerned should be increased in line in accordance with c. below.

c. At sports grounds with seated and standing accommodation there should be at least one first aider per 1,000 up to 20,000 spectators, and thereafter one per 2,000 (of the number of spectators anticipated for the event)

d. Factors other than crowd numbers (for example, weather, type of event should also be considered (See Section 18.2).

18.11 Role of first aiders

First aiders should:

a. have the maturity, character and temperament to carry out the duties required of them

b. have no other duties or responsibilities

c. should be able to understand and communicate verbal and written instructions in English

d. be in post at the ground prior to spectators being admitted

e. be briefed prior to deployment as to their roles and responsibilities as well as emergency and evacuation procedures

f. be deployed in spectator areas in appropriate numbers to provide care when spectators are admitted and remain deployed in spectator areas throughout the event

g. remain in position until all spectators have left the ground.

18.12 Communication

A system should be in place to allow reliable radio communication on a single channel between a control point and all members of the medical services (see Section 16.2).

Where necessary, provision should be made for a representative of the local ambulance service NHS Trust, the medical provider and/or crowd doctor to have access to the control point, and to be provided with, working facilities and appropriate communications there.

18.13 Major incident plan

As stated in Sections 3.17 and 3.18, ground contingency plans (and the medical plan) must be compatible with the emergency, or major incident plan (see Section 3.20) prepared by the local emergency services. The drafting of the major incident plan within the sports ground medical plan should reflect current Department of Health guidelines (see Bibliography).

The major incident plan should identify areas for dealing with multiple casualties and identify access and egress routes and a rendezvous point, for emergency service vehicles.

Consultation should therefore take place between ground management, the police, fire and ambulance services, and the local authority, in order to produce an agreed plan of action for all foreseeable incidents.

All first aid and medical staff likely to be on duty should be briefed on their role in the major incident plan, preferably before they undertake event-day duties. A copy should be kept in the first aid room.

In the event of a major incident, all medical, ambulance and first aid staff will come under the command of the senior ambulance service NHS trust officer.

18.14 Inspections and records

a. Before the start of the event

Management should ensure that:

  i. sufficient qualified medical, nursing, paramedic and first aid staff are present, and at their posts

  ii. they are properly briefed

  iii. first aid equipment and materials are maintained at the required level

  iv. appropriate medical and ambulance provision is in place.

b. During and after the event

Management should ensure that:

  i. first aiders remain in position until stood down by the safety officer

  ii. management, ambulance officers, first aiders and the crowd doctor should participate in a de-briefing, with comments and any follow-up actions being recorded by management

  iii. a record is kept of the numbers and posts of all ambulance personnel and first aiders in attendance at the event, plus the name of the crowd doctor

  iv. a record is kept of all first aid or medical diagnosis and treatment provided during the event (while preserving medical confidentiality), showing the onward destination of casualties; that is, whether they remained at the event, returned home, went to hospital or to their own family doctor

  v. records are kept readily available for inspection, where appropriate, by the relevant authorities (while preserving medical confidentiality).

19: Media provision

19.1 Management responsibility

Management is responsible for ensuring that media activities do not interfere with or negate the normal safety operation of the ground, and do not hamper the safety, comfort or viewing standards of spectators.

Media companies must provide management with risk assessment method statements and the design calculations for their installations. In addition management should ensure that all media provision, whether permanent or temporary, is included within its own site-specific risk assessment (see Sections 3.3.e, 15.3 and 18.2).

Guidance on the safety implications of broadcasting sports events is available from the Health and Safety Executive (see Bibliography).

19.2 Pre-event planning and briefing

Management should ensure that all arrangements for media coverage are agreed with the companies concerned in good time before the event, and that the safety officer is able to prepare pre-event briefings accordingly.

Where appropriate, any temporary arrangements may also need to be discussed and, where a safety certificate is in force, agreed with, the local authority, at a pre-determined period before the event.

Pre-event planning and briefings should include proposed arrangements for any associated pre-match, half-time or mid-event entertainment. Details of these should be recorded. If appropriate, safety personnel should also be assigned to the role of liaison with the media personnel, and for monitoring the media provision during the event.

If any media provision results in restricted views for any areas of spectator accommodation, tickets for those areas should not be sold, and access to them not permitted for spectators during the event.

Media personnel unfamiliar with emergency procedures at the ground and the relevant requirements and conditions of any safety certificate, should be fully briefed and informed by the safety officer.

19.3 Pre-event inspections

In particular, the management should consider the following:

a. Vehicles should not be parked in such a manner as to obstruct ingress and egress to the ground by spectators or emergency vehicles.

b. Cables should not run along or across gangways, or passageways, or otherwise obstruct the movement of spectators. Where laid in front of pitch perimeter exits, cables should be buried or installed in a cable duct. The use of rubber matting is not recommended.

c. Camera gantries should be securely constructed and should not obscure the view of spectators.

d. Where cameras overhang gantries located above spectator areas, protective measures, such as netting, should guard against falling objects.

e. Where cameras or camera gantries are located in spectator areas, or where sightlines are restricted as a result of their location, capacities should be reduced accordingly. As stated in Section 19.2, management should also ensure that tickets for the affected areas are not sold.

f. The precautions listed above apply also to loudspeaker systems and other media installations; for example, video screens, stages or studios.

g. The output from loudspeaker systems should not drown out police and stewards' radios, or the public address system. Provision should be made for an override switch (normally in the control point), so that the loudspeaker output can be interrupted if necessary.

h. Temporary advertising boards or hoardings should be constructed safely and not obscure spectators' views, nor obstruct access gates or openings in pitch perimeter barriers.

i. Temporary scaffolding, for example for cameras or temporary television studios, should be installed in accordance with the recommendations made by the Institution of Structural Engineers (see Section 14.2 and Bibliography).

j. Temporary barriers protecting media installations should accord with the recommended loadings given in *Table 11.1*.

19.4 Roving media personnel

Management should make provision for the positioning of photographers, camera operators and any other roving media personnel, so as to ensure that the sightlines of spectators are not restricted more than momentarily.

Stewards should be instructed to move any media personnel whose activities create obstructions to either spectators' views or to the safety management operation.

19.5 Identification

All media personnel, and in particular all roving media personnel, should be clearly identified, but in such a way that their clothing cannot be confused with that of the stewards or other safety personnel.

19.6 New construction

It is recommended that the design of sports grounds and stands takes into full consideration the requirements of the media; for example, for the concealed routing of television and radio cabling, and for the avoidance of viewing restrictions when planning camera positions, advertising hoardings and any temporary installations.

20: Alternative events at sports grounds

20.1 Introduction

The increased use of grounds for events other than the specific sport or sports for which they are designed, requires management to consider a number of issues. This should be done well in advance, in consultation with the emergency services and, where a safety certificate is in force, with the local authority.

In all cases, it is stressed that the provision of safe accommodation for spectators and the maintenance of safety standards remains the responsibility of ground management. As part of the planning process for an alternative event, the capacity of the sports ground will need to be reassessed taking account of all of the chapters within the *Guide*.

As stated in Section 3.3.e, management must conduct site-specific risk assessments for all events including any ancillary activities. This includes any alternative use of a sports ground and should take account of any temporary accommodation or facility. The risk assessment must include fire safety (see Section 15.3) and medical provision (see Section 18.2) and consideration of the potential for dynamic crowd loading (see Section 5.5).

Where an event is being staged by an outside organisation, close liaison will be needed between that organisation and the ground management to agree who is responsible for specific safety duties and to ensure that each party understands its responsibilities. The agreement should also be recorded in a written statement.

If doubts arise as to the suitability of the ground itself – its layout or structures – or to the management's ability to adapt its safety management operation to different circumstances, professional advice should be sought and the event should not take place unless the doubts can be adequately addressed in a fully documented process.

It should be noted that this chapter applies not only to the staging of such events as concerts or mass gatherings, but also to the staging of sports other than the sport or sports for which the ground was designed. This might include such events as a boxing match staged at a football ground, or a rugby match staged at an athletics stadium.

Additional advice is also available in *The event safety guide*, issued by the Health and Safety Executive (see Bibliography).

Further guidance on the use of temporary demountable structures can be found in Chapter 14.

20.2 Viewing standards

Management should be aware that where sports grounds are used for alternative events viewing standards may need to be reassessed, particularly if the point of focus is:

a. a single part of the sports ground, for example a stage at one end of the ground rather than a whole field of play or

b. raised above ground level, thereby reducing the amount of stretching and straining necessary to view the event.

In addition video screens are sometimes provided to compensate for any restriction to the view.

20.3 Provision for spectator accommodation

Where the required provision for spectator accommodation is likely to differ from the standard arrangements for the ground, management should ensure that the safety of spectators is not compromised. In particular, management should consider the following:

a. If spectators are to be allowed to view the event from the pitch or area of activity, the total number allowed should take into account the ingress or egress capacity of the entrances and exits available around the pitch or area, and the arrangements made for emergency evacuation, using the methodology set out in Chapter 2. It is important to ensure that any 'access all areas' tickets issued are taken in account in assessing capacities.

b. If spectators are to stand on the pitch or area of activity, suitable arrangements for their safety should be provided. This will include the provision of firm underfoot conditions, barrier protection where necessary (for example, around temporary structures), and effective stewarding and monitoring. *The event safety guide* advises that generally 0.5m² of available floor space per person be used for outdoor music events.

    Front of stage barriers are normally required for events such as concerts. The front of stage barrier is usually temporary and assembled on site from prefabricated elements. Reference should be made to *Temporary Demountable Structures – Guidance on Procurement, Design and Use* published by the Institution of Structural Engineers (see Bibliography) and the relevant British Standard.

c. If there is to be a free movement of spectators between the stands or terraces and the pitch or area of activity, all entry points should be controlled and the numbers monitored.

d. Areas of fixed viewing accommodation from which the event cannot be safely or comfortably viewed in full, owing to the position of temporary structures – such as stages, temporary demountable stands, advertising hoardings or camera platforms – should, wherever possible, be taken out of use and, in any case, discounted from any capacity calculation. Management should ensure that such arrangements do not preclude the attendance of disabled spectators.

20.4 Profile of likely spectators or audience

Different sports and events attract different groups of spectators. Some may attract more women, young children, disabled or elderly people than is the norm for the core sport or sports staged at the ground. Provision for their safety and welfare should therefore be considered in advance. Contingency plans for the ground might also have to be adapted accordingly.

In particular, the following considerations should be addressed:

a. Many of the spectators attending the event might be unfamiliar with the layout of the ground, thus requiring extra signs and stewarding at key points.

b. The response of many spectators to instructions, controls and emergency evacuation procedures might be slower than is the norm for the regular audience.

c.   Toilet and catering arrangements might have to be adapted. If temporary facilities are brought in, their siting and service arrangements should not block any circulation routes, particularly those required for egress or emergency evacuation.

20.5   Briefing of event personnel

Many events will involve the participation of personnel – including technical staff, visiting and contract stewards, officials, media personnel and even participants – who are unfamiliar with the ground and its safety management arrangements. Ground management should therefore ensure that such persons are suitably briefed and familiarised in advance.

Pre-event agreements should make absolutely clear to all concerned the chain of command, and the division of responsibilities.

20.6   Staging of concerts

Before considering the staging of a concert at a sports ground, management should seek guidance from competent persons of the appropriate experience.

Particular concerns to be addressed are as follows:

a.   **The suitability of spectator accommodation**
      It is stressed that not all areas of a ground may be suitable for safely accommodating audiences at a concert.

      Before an area of spectator accommodation is used, whether it is permanent or temporary, an evaluation of the structure must take into account the dynamic loading likely to result from the movements of a concert audience (see Sections 5.5 and 14.6).

b.   **The suitability of systems**
      Conditions during a concert will differ greatly from those experienced during a routine event at the sports ground. Management should thus ensure that all systems will function under such conditions. For example, radio communications might be more difficult owing to the high noise levels.

      Provision should also be made for any imported sound system to be interrupted by safety announcements made from the central control point.

c.   **Keeping gangways clear**
      Particular care may need to be taken to ensure that spectators do not sit or stand in gangways in order to gain an improved view.

d.   **Lighting**
      At certain types of events reduced lighting levels form part of the performance, in order to place greater emphasis on the stage. Care may therefore need to be taken in order to ensure that the safety of spectators is not prejudiced.

20.7   Firework displays

Any firework display should be arranged and located in such a way that spectators and surrounding residents are not at risk, and that there is no threat to structures at the ground or to surrounding industrial or commercial premises (particularly those where petroleum products may be stored).

Management should also ensure that the smoke from any fireworks will disperse and not become concentrated under stand roofs.

Similar precautions should be made if fireworks or flares form a part of any other event to be staged.

Any specific activities which include pyrotechnic displays must be included in the fire risk assessment (see Section 15.3).

20.8 Designing for alternative uses

For new construction: the design of a new sports ground, or section of a ground, should take reasonable account of all likely uses of the ground, with particular emphasis on:

a. The arrangements for emergency evacuation (particularly from and to the area of activity).

b. The design of seated areas. As stated in Section 12.13, if it is intended to stage events for which a greater level of accessibility and comfort will be required – such as concerts or mass gatherings – the dimensions of seats depths should be increased. Extra comfort levels for the actual seats might also be considered in particular areas.

c. Circulation routes should be designed in such a way that, if necessary, a free movement of people can be safely managed for particular events. This will require the installation of flexible dividing structures.

d. To avoid congestion in concourses, the design of toilets should be flexible to cater for differing ratios of males and females.

20.9 Ancillary activities

Many events include ancillary activities such as parachute jumps, fairs, inflatables, bands, dancers and pyrotechnics as pre and post-event entertainment. The potential benefits and problems associated with such activities should be the subject of a site-specific risk assessment in addition to any general risk assessment undertaken by the supplier of the activity.

Annex A: Assessment of capacity – worked examples

Introduction

This Annex includes six worked examples of how to apply the guidance on capacity calculations to different types of standing accommodation. The method of calculation is explained more specifically in Chapter 2 and Diagrams 2.1 and 2.2. Reference should also be made to Chapters 11 and 13 and to section 10.6 (concerning rates of passage).

The examples are as follows:

Worked example 1

A terraced standing area with a continuous crush barrier configuration and conforming to the relevant recommendations of the *Guide* (as described in Section 11.8 and Diagram 11.3).

Worked example 2

A terraced area with a non-continuous barrier configuration (see Section 11.9).

Worked example 3

A terraced area with a non-continuous barrier configuration, with barriers which do not conform to the spacing or loadings specified in Table 11.2.

Worked example 4

A terraced area with crush barriers along the front only.

Worked example 5

A level standing area (see Section 13.19).

Worked example 6

The viewing enclosures at a racecourse, including the lawn and covered terraced stands.

Worked Example 1

A terrace with a continuous crush barrier configuration

Example 1, illustrated in Fig.E.1b, concerns a terraced standing area incorporating all the main recommendations of the *Guide*. The terrace measures 21m from front to back (not including lateral gangways at the front and rear) and is 74m wide.

It is enclosed on three sides and entered from the rear via 12 turnstiles and two 3.6m wide stairways. The rear lateral gangway is also 3.6m wide. From the rear spectators move down five radial gangways each 1.2m wide. The front lateral gangway is 2.4m wide.

Normal egress is via the two stairways and from either side of the front lateral gangway. There are five pitch perimeter gates each 1.2m wide, for forward evacuation in an emergency.

All crush barriers have been tested to a horizontal imposed load of 5.0kN/m length.

The crush barriers are continuous between each radial gangway, each row being spaced 3m apart.

The gangways are 14m apart.

The gradient of the terrace is 25° and 'C' values range between 120mm at the front to 90mm at the rear.

The terrace has a roof that protects the full terrace and there are no restricted views.

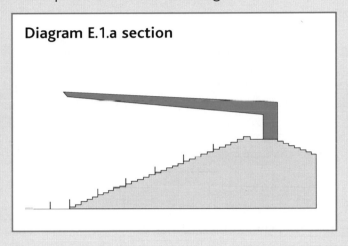

Diagram E.1.a section

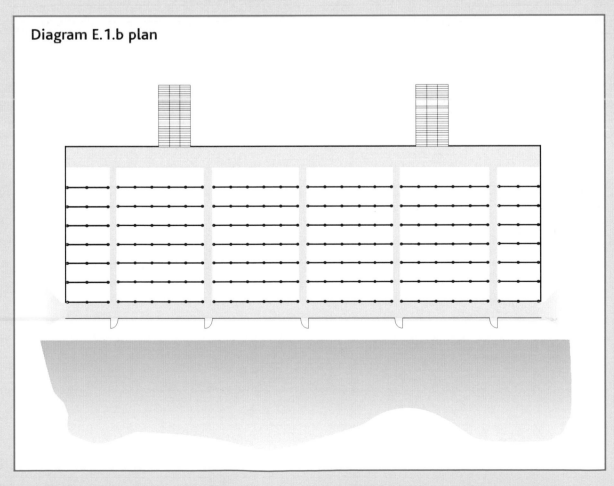

Diagram E.1.b plan

Step 1: available viewing area

Areas available behind barriers
There are four sections of terracing 14m wide, plus two end sections 6m wide.

The total length of barrier provision = (14x4) + (6x2) = 68m.

There are seven rows of barriers each spaced 3m apart (within the recommended maximum of 3.1m for a 25° terrace – as per Table 11.2).

The total depth of the viewing area is therefore 7 x 3 = 21m.

The viewing area is therefore 21 x 68 = $1428m^2$.

Gangway provision
No further calculation is necessary as there are designated gangways that have been taken into account in deriving the viewing area.

The total available viewing area is therefore $1428m^2$.

Step 2: appropriate density

Physical condition
The terrace's physical condition is of a high standard. There are no sightline problems.

Therefore (P) is assessed as 1.0.

Safety management
The club's safety management is generally of a high standard. There are no problems with crowd dispersal or behaviour but at times of high capacity stewards have been unable to keep the gangways clear. As a consequence of discussions within the safety advisory group and the local authority the (S) factor has been set at 0.8. It has been acknowledged that this will increase if the club is able to maintain clear gangways at this figure. If not, a further reduction in the (S) factor will have to be considered.

Therefore (S) is assessed as 0.8.

Appropriate density
The appropriate density is therefore 0.8 x 47 = 37.6 per $10m^2$.

Step 3: holding capacity

The available viewing area = $1428m^2$.

The appropriate density = 37.6 per $10m^2$.

The holding capacity is therefore

$$\frac{1428}{10} \times 37.6 = \textbf{5369}.$$

Step 4: entry capacity

There are 12 turnstiles serving the terrace. Each has been observed to allow a rate of ingress of 660 persons/hour. The rate is also the maximum permissible for purposes of this calculation.

The entry capacity of the terrace is therefore 12 x 660 = **7920**.

Step 5: exit capacity

There are two stairways 3.6m wide at the rear of the terrace and a 2.4m wide exit at each end of the front lateral gangway. Experience indicates that the population of the terrace is predominantly young adult males and observations show that the maximum rates of passage are appropriate, namely 66 persons/metre width/minute for the stairs and 82 persons/metre width/minute for the level walkways.

The normal egress time for the terrace is set at eight minutes.

The exit capacity is therefore
(2 x 3.6 x 66 x 8) + (2 x 2.4 x 82 x 8) = **6950**

Step 6: emergency evacuation capacity

A fire assessment of the stand identified a high risk industrial premises to the rear, which could impact on the normal egress routes and therefore it was deemed that a six minute emergency evacuation time was appropriate. In addition to the normal exits it was deemed acceptable to allow emergency access onto the activity area through the five gates in the activity area perimeter barrier.

Therefore the total of the exit widths available in an emergency is:

Stairways: 7.2m
Front lateral exits: 4.8m
Pitch perimeter gates: 6m

The **emergency evacuation capacity** is therefore:

(7.2 x 66 x 6) + (4.8 x 82 x 6) + (6 x 82 x 6) = **8165**

(Note: as stated in Section 9.9, while in practice spectators may evacuate onto the pitch or activity area in an emergency, this should not form part of the calculation for the emergency evacuation capacity for newly constructed grounds or sections of grounds).

Step 7: final capacity

The final capacity is the lowest of the figures calculated under steps 3, 4, 5, and 6. In this example the lowest figure is the holding capacity.

The **final capacity** is therefore **5369**.

(Note: in Steps 2 and 3 if the (S) factor had been 1 the applicable density would have been 47 per 10m² which would increase the holding capacity to 6711. A holding capacity of 6711 is lower than the capacities calculated under steps 4, 5 and 6 and would therefore have been the final capacity. The increase demonstrates the added capacity that can be achieved by improving (P) and/or (S) factors).

Example 1: network plan

As stated in Section 10.8.d where there are a number of exit routes and / or a choice of routes for spectators to follow, the system should be analysed in the form of a network. In new construction the analysis assists in determining the appropriate dimensions of the elements of passage and in existing construction in understanding congestion issues.

Figure E.1.c illustrates three basic elements of passage of the terrace illustrated in Fig. E.1.b.

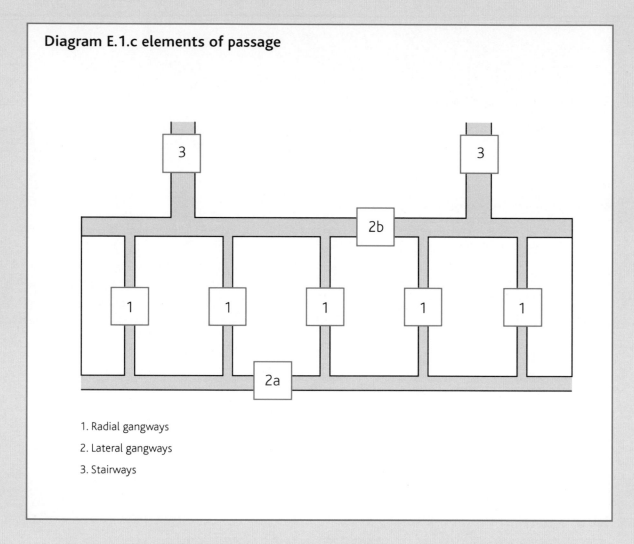

Diagram E.1.c elements of passage

1. Radial gangways
2. Lateral gangways
3. Stairways

The possible spectator flows within each element of passage may be determined from the assumed rates of passage in combination with the available width.

Radial gangways.
The radial gangways are 1.2m wide and the assumed rate of passage is 66 person/m/min.

Each gangway can sustain a free flow of 66 x 1.2 = **79 persons/minute**.

This can occur in both up and down directions.

Lateral gangways.
Gangway 2a is 2.4m wide and the assumed rate of passage is 82 person/m/min.

A free flow of 82 x 2.4 = **196 persons/min** can be sustained.

Gangway 2b is 3.6m wide and the assumed rate of passage is 82 person/m/min.

A free flow of 82 x 3.6 = **295 persons/min** can be sustained.

Stairways

The stairways are 3.6m wide and the assumed rate of passage is 66 person/m/min.

Each stairway can sustain a free flow of 66 x 3.6 = **237 persons/minute**.

Fig.E.1.d illustrates the sustainable free flow capacities of each element of passage.

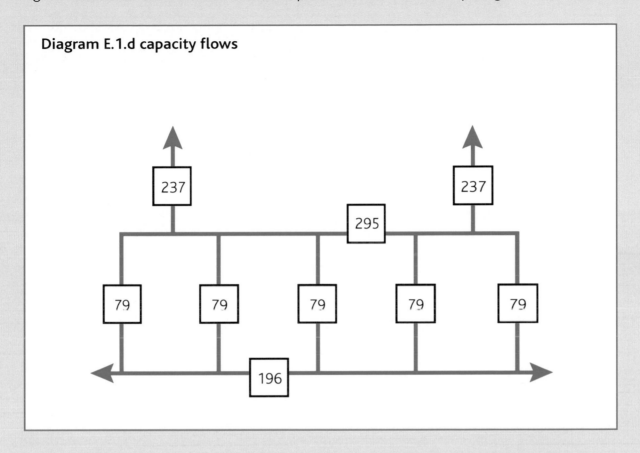

Diagram E.1.d capacity flows

A spectator leaving the terrace will have a choice of direction when entering a radial gangway and also upon reaching either of the lateral gangways. Any analysis needs to be considered in the context of all local circumstances, such as adjoining circulation routes, facilities and patterns of spectator movement. In this instance it is assumed that spectators will seek their shortest exit route.

Hence each lateral gangway will be subjected to a spectator flow of

79 + 79 + (0.5 x 79) = 196 persons/minute.

Whilst the rear gangway can accommodate a greater flow, contraflow could occur on this gangway and the extra width is beneficial. Nevertheless the predicted level of flows into the rear lateral gangway will not promote congestion at the head of either stair.

Worked Example 2

A terrace with non-continuous crush barriers

Example 2, illustrated in Fig.E.2a concerns a terraced standing area. Its overall area (excluding the rear concourse) measures 21m deep by 74m wide. The area is enclosed on two sides and is entered from the north-east corner by a 3.3m wide stair, via six turnstiles. Spectators move from the stair along a rear concourse of the same width, from which they descend onto the terracing.

The terrace is separated from the activity area by a pitch perimeter barrier with four gates of 1.1m width for possible forward evacuation in an emergency. There are no radial or lateral gangways.

Barriers are present in a non-continuous configuration, according to the conditions specified in Section 11.9: that is the alignment of gaps between successive rows of barriers form angles of less than 60°; there are no more than two consecutive gaps in any line of barriers, and these gaps measure at least 1.1m but no more than 1.4m in width.

All barriers are in satisfactory condition having been risk assessed and where necessary tested, in accordance with Sections 11.21 – 11.23, to a horizontal imposed load of 5.0kN/m. Each crush barrier is 4m long. The depth of the spacing between lines of barriers is 3m except for that between line A and line B which is 4m and that from Line F and the rear lateral gangway which is 5m.

Normal egress from the terrace is by a 3.3m wide stairway in the north-east corner and a 2.2m stairway in the north-west corner.

The terrace is not in good condition and has areas of uneven treads. The terrace gradient is 25°. 'C' values range from 80mm at the front to 45mm at the rear. The bases of the floodlight pylons encroach on the viewing area causing restricted views behind each base as illustrated in Fig.E.2.b and Fig.E.2.c. The terrace is not covered and therefore no discount need be made for partial roof cover.

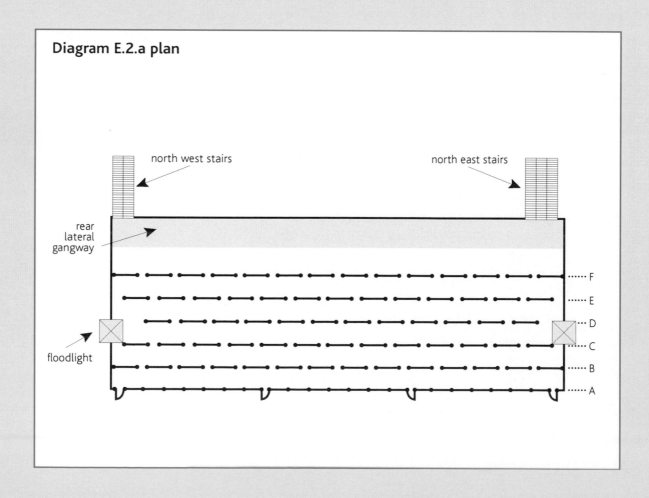

Diagram E.2.a plan

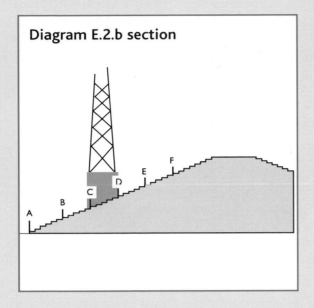

Diagram E.2.b section

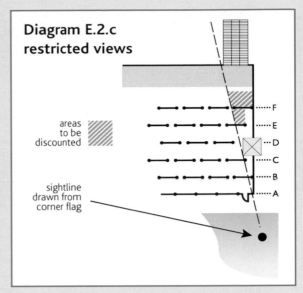

Diagram E.2.c
restricted views

areas
to be
discounted

sightline
drawn from
corner flag

Step 1: available viewing area

Areas available behind barriers

Line A (pitch perimeter barriers):
Length: 74m less 4 exits at 1.1m each = 69.6m.

Depth: The distance between Line A and Line B is 4m however the permitted distance between lines of 5kN/m barriers on a 25° gradient terrace is 3.1m.

The available viewing area provided by Line A is therefore 69.6 x 3.1 = 215.7m².

Line B:
Length: 14 barriers each of 4m length = 56m
Depth: 3m between lines B and C which is within the permitted 3.1m.

The available viewing area provided by Line B is therefore 56 x 3 = 168m².

Line C:
Length: 13 barriers each of 4m length = 52m.
Depth: 3m between lines C and D which is within the permitted 3.1m.

The available viewing area provided by Line C is therefore 52 x 3 = 156m².

Line D:
Length: 12 barriers each of 4m length = 48m.
Depth: 3m between lines D and E which is within the permitted 3.1m.

The available viewing area provided by Line B is therefore 48 x 3 = 144m².

Line E:
Barrier provision on Line E is identical to that for Line C however a deduction in available viewing area is necessary due to the restricted viewing created by the floodlight towers. The required deduction is illustrated in Fig.E.2.c. Each of these areas measure 6.75m².

Deduction = 2 x 6.75m² = 13.5m².

The available viewing area provided by Line E is therefore 156 – 13.5 = 142.5m².

Line F
Length: 14 barriers each of 4m length = 56m.

Depth: The distance between Line F and the edge of the rear lateral gangway is 5m however the permitted distance behind a line of 5kN/m barriers on a 25° gradient terrace is 3.1m.

A deduction due the restricted view is again necessary.

The floodlight towers cause a restricted viewing area behind each end barrier of 14m².

The available viewing area provided by Line F is therefore (56 x 3.1) – (2 x 14) = 145.6m².

The total available viewing area as derived from the barrier layout is therefore:

215.7 + 168 + 156 + 144 + 142.5 + 145.6 = **971.8m²**.

Required gangway provision

The *Guide* recommends radial gangways no greater than 24m apart for areas of standing accommodation. This terrace has no designated radial gangways. Therefore an area that would be taken by radial gangways needs to be deducted.

(Note that the gangways shown in Fig.E.2.d and their position are notional and are illustrated for the purposes of calculation only.)

Area of notional gangways

The minimum width for gangways is 1.1m.

A terrace 74m wide would require 4 gangways.

Therefore the area to be deducted for notional gangways is:

$4 \times 1.1 \times (21 - 2.8) = 80.1m^2$.

The notional gangway provision needs to be deducted from the previously calculated available viewing area

$971.8 - 80.1 = 891.7m^2$.

The available viewing area is therefore 891.7m²

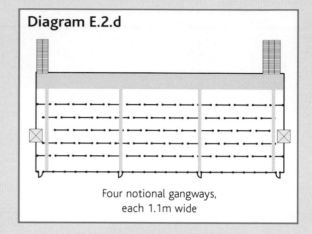

Diagram E.2.d

Four notional gangways,
each 1.1m wide

Step 2: appropriate density

Physical condition

The terrace has areas of uneven treads caused by settlement, plus other areas where the surface is beginning to crumble. The sports ground is used for association and rugby football and poor sightlines will encourage individuals constantly to adjust their position.

After observation and analysis of spectator movements the applicable (P) factor is assessed at 0.5.

Safety management

The stewarding is reasonable but the location of the ingress point onto the terrace is observed to create an uneven distribution of the spectators biased towards the point of ingress.

The applicable (S) factor is assessed to be 0.7.

Appropriate density

The lower value of (P) and (S) is 0.5.

The appropriate density is therefore
$0.5 \times 47 = $ **23.5 per 10m².**

Step 3: the holding capacity

The available viewing area is 891.7m².

The appropriate density is 23.5.

The holding capacity is therefore

$\dfrac{891.7}{10} \times 23.5 = $ **2095.**

Step 4: entry capacity

There are six turnstiles each with a measured flow rate of 690. For the purpose of calculating entry capacity a maximum value of 660 persons/hour per turnstile should be used.

The entry capacity is therefore 6 x 660 = **3960.**

Step 5: exit capacity

Experience indicates that the population of the terrace is predominantly young adult males and observations show that the maximum rate of passage on each stair is appropriate, that is 66 persons/metre width/minute.

The normal egress time for the terrace is set at eight minutes.

The exit capacity is therefore (3.3 + 2.2) x 66 x 8 = **2904.**

Step 6: emergency evacuation capacity

The terrace is non-combustible and the condition and management of the exit routes are good. The maximum allowable evacuation

time of eight minutes is deemed applicable. The emergency evacuation capacity will therefore not be less than the exit capacity.

Step 7: final capacity

The final capacity is the lowest of the figures calculated under steps 3, 4, 5 and 6. In this example the lowest figure is the holding capacity.

The final capacity of the terrace is 2095.

Worked Example 3

A terrace with non-continuous crush barriers not conforming to Table 11.2

Example 3 concerns a terraced standing area of the same plan dimensions as worked examples 1 and 2 (21m deep x 74m wide). There are fewer crush barriers the spacing of which does not meet the requirements of Table 11.2. The barriers are not identical and the levels of loading that each line of barriers has been designed to safely resist differ. Following the annual risk assessment a number of barriers were tested. Two failed in the positions illustrated in Fig.E.3.a.

The failed barriers are to be removed. Until they are replaced they do not contribute to the available viewing area.

The terrace is used to view non-league football matches. The available viewing area is illustrated in Fig.E.3.a as the shaded areas behind each barrier.

The terrace gradient is 20°.

There are three lines of barriers.

Line A is provided by the pitch perimeter wall which is 74m in length and includes four gates that can provide forward emergency evacuation. Each gate is 1.1m wide. The perimeter wall has been tested and shown to satisfy a 5kN/m length loading requirement.

Line B comprises of 5 sound barriers that have been tested and shown to satisfy a 3.4kN/m length loading requirement. The two failed barriers in Line B are discounted for calculation purposes.

Line C comprises of 6 crush barriers that have been tested and shown to satisfy a 5kN/m length loading requirement.

As may be observed from Fig.E.3.a and from cross reference with Table 11.2 the distance between Lines A and B and the distance between Line B and C both exceed the permitted maximum. The distance between Line C and the rear perimeter barrier is within the permitted maximum.

The terrace is uncovered. The surface of the terrace is in reasonably good order with some areas of crumbling concrete due to poor maintenance. There are no restricted views.

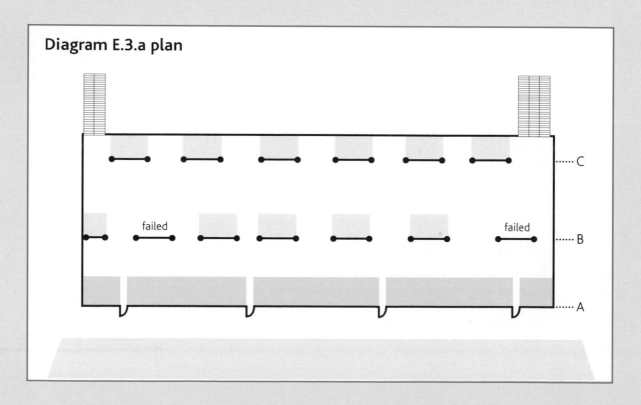

Diagram E.3.a plan

Step 1: available viewing area

Areas available behind barriers

Line A (pitch perimeter wall):
Length: 74m less 4 exits at 1.1m each = 69.6m.

Depth: The distance between Line A and Line B is 6m. However the permitted distance between lines of 5kN/m barriers on a 20° gradient terrace is 3.4m.

The available viewing area provided by Line A is therefore 69.6 x 3.4 = 236.6m².

Line B:
Length: 4 barriers each of 6m length + 1 barrier of 3m length = 24 + 3 = 27m.

Depth: The distance between line B and C is 7m. However, the permitted depth behind a 3.4kN/m barrier on a terrace with a gradient of 20° is 2.3m.

The available viewing area provided by Line B is therefore 27 x 2.3 = 62.1m².

Line C:
Length: 6 barriers each of 6m length = 36m.

Depth: 3m between line C and the edge of the rear lateral gangway which is within the permitted depth of 3.4m behind a 5kN/m barrier on a terrace with a gradient of 20°.

The available viewing area provided by Line C is therefore 36 x 3 = 108m².

The total available viewing area is therefore 236.6 + 62.1 + 108 = 406.7m².

Step 2: appropriate density

Physical condition
The terracing is in reasonable condition but poor maintenance has led to crumbling concrete in some areas. The sightlines are poor. The (P) factor is therefore assessed as 0.8.

Safety management
The excessive spacing between barriers requires particular care in dispersing crowds. This does not happen, leading to surging. The (S) factor is therefore assessed as 0.5.

Appropriate density
The lower value of (P) or (S) is 0.5.

The **appropriate density** is therefore
0.5 x 47 = **23.5 per 10m²**

Step 3: holding capacity

The available viewing area is 406.7 m².
The appropriate density is 23.5.

The holding capacity is therefore

$$\frac{406.7}{10} \times 23.5 = \mathbf{955.}$$

Replacing or strengthening the failed barriers to a loading of 3.4kN/m would increase the holding capacity as follows:

Line B now = 39m (27 + 2 x 6m barriers).

Available viewing area is now 39 x 2.3 = 89.7.

Total available viewing area is now 434.3 m².

In addition, concern over crowd dispersal is reduced and the (S) factor increased to 0.75.

Appropriate density now = 0.75 x 47 = 35.25.

Therefore the holding capacity =

$$\frac{A}{10} \times D = \frac{434.3}{10} \times 35.25 = 1,530$$

Therefore, by replacing or strengthening the two failed barriers, the holding capacity would increase from 955 to 1,530.

Worked Example 4

A standing area with front barriers only

Example 4 shows a terraced standing area at a non-league football ground which has crush barriers along the front only. There are no other crush barriers. The front barriers have been tested to 5.0kN/m length. There are four exit gates for emergency evacuation onto the pitch and no gangways.

The overall area measures 8m deep by 74m wide. The terrace gradient is 20°. The terrace is uncovered and therefore no discount need be made for partial roof cover. The surface of the terracing is in good order, with steps conforming to the dimensions in Chapter 10. There are no restricted views.

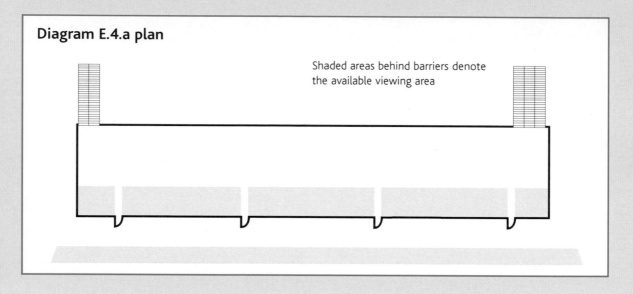

Diagram E.4.a plan

Shaded areas behind barriers denote the available viewing area

Step one: available viewing area

Length: 74m less 4 exits at 1.1m each = 69.6m.

Depth: confined to the permitted distance behind the front barriers, which, for barriers tested to a horizontal imposed load of 5kN/m length on a gradient of 20°, is 3.4m.

The available viewing area is therefore 69.6 x 3.4 = 236.6m²

Step two: appropriate density

Physical condition
The physical condition is of a high standard. There are no sightline problems or concerns over the size of terrace. Therefore (P) is assessed as 1.0.

Safety management
The safety management is good. However, it is important to ensure that concentrations of

spectators are not allowed to gather along the front barrier. Therefore (S) is assessed as 0.9.

The appropriate density is therefore 0.9 x 47 = 42.3 per 10m².

Step three: holding capacity

The available viewing area = 236.6 m².

The appropriate density = 42.3 per 10 m².

The holding capacity is therefore

$$\frac{236.6}{10} \times 42.3 = \textbf{1,000.}$$

Worked Example 5

A level standing area

Level standing areas, with or without a front crush barrier, pose inherent problems, particularly because spectators lining the front of the area restrict the viewing of those spectators immediately behind. This is particularly true where the point of focus (see Section 13.19) is at ground level.

Experience has shown that a concentration of four persons deep is the maximum for safe viewing from such level areas.

Section 2.8.g explains that for level standing areas the available viewing area should not exceed a depth of 1.5m from the front barrier. Based on a level standing area 74m wide the available viewing area will be 1.5 x 74 = 111m².

As in all such calculations, careful consideration should also be given to the assessment of the (P) and (S) factors. For example, if observation identifies crowds of more than four deep forming, consideration should be given to reducing the (S) factor for the purpose of calculation.

Worked Example 6

Viewing accommodation at a racecourse

Establishing the capacity of a sports ground is fundamental to the provision of spectator safety. The nature of the activity coupled with the overall quality of spectator accommodation means that the capacity calculation with respect to a given racecourse is not straightforward. The spectator body at a racecourse will traditionally leave the viewing accommodation between the races to collect winnings, to place bets, to view horses in the parade ring and visit refreshment facilities. Establishing the total capacity will require appropriate site specific risk assessments. However the dominant factor in determining the total capacity calculation is the capacity of the viewing accommodation.

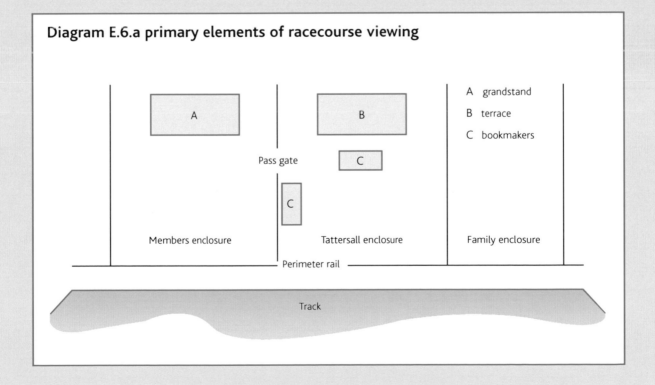

Diagram E.6.a primary elements of racecourse viewing

A   grandstand
B   terrace
C   bookmakers

A

B

Pass gate

C

C

Members enclosure   Tattersall enclosure   Family enclosure

Perimeter rail

Track

Fig.E.6.a is a schematic representation of the primary viewing accommodation to be found at a race course.

The Tattersall enclosure has a covered terrace [B] and a front viewing slope known as a 'lawn'. The Members' enclosure has a stand [A] that combines standing and seated accommodation as described in Section 13.20 and is only accessible by purchase of a more expensive ticket or badge. The Family enclosure consists essentially of a grassed picnic area. There are gates in the fences that separate the enclosures offering transfers to and from adjacent enclosures. Bookmakers' pitches may sit astride the fences serving both enclosures.

Race meetings are staged on 21 days per year, at 18 of these crowd numbers have been shown to be relatively low in the Tattersall Enclosure. On three days per year; the course stages a 'Festival' meeting when crowd numbers are much higher. Capacity calculations are therefore necessary to cater for these high attendance days and to alert management to any special requirements such as the need to have a ticketing limit and the provision of extra covered space.

Capacity calculations are necessary for each element of an enclosure.

Some ticket holders will almost certainly remain in the area behind the stand and watch the races on TV screens. Monitoring of these areas during meetings enables the numbers remaining in this area to be determined and taken into account in calculating the overall capacity of the race course. The maximum viewing numbers in the stands and on the lawns will probably occur once at each meeting during the feature race.

Tattersall enclosure

Entry to the Tattersall enclosure is via two separate gates into the zone at the rear of the stand, one gate leading direct from the highway and one from the car park. Accommodated within this zone and adjacent to the rear of stand there are toilets, food outlets, a bar, Tote counters and other such facilities used by the spectators in between races. Although there is a free movement of spectators between the covered terrace and the lawn, the holding capacity of each should be assessed separately.

Capacity of covered terrace

Figure E.6.b illustrates the covered terrace which has the overall dimensions of 36m x 8m. The tread depth is 400mm and the riser height 140mm.

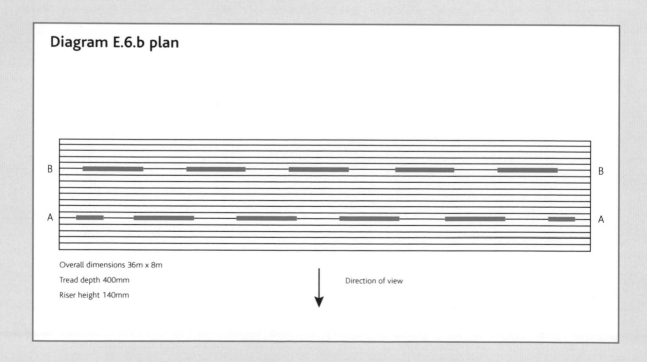

Diagram E.6.b plan

B   B

A   A

Overall dimensions 36m x 8m

Tread depth 400mm   Direction of view

Riser height 140mm

The barrier line AA has four barriers symmetrically positioned on the terrace; each barrier is 4m in length and the barriers are 3m apart. The two shorter 2.5m barriers are positioned 1.5m from the perimeter boundary wall. These barriers protect the people standing on the steps between the lawn and the barrier line AA.

The action at racecourses follows a predictable route which does not require spectators constantly to readjust their position to view the event. Strategically placed large video screens may also be provided to assist the viewing of the whole race. These features coupled with the relatively low crowd densities found on such viewing terraces minimise the potential of surging within the crowd. The spectators in forward rows of the terrace are free to step down onto the lawn if, for any reason, the spectators on the steps in front of the lower row of barriers should stumble forward. A site specific risk assessment taking account of these factors has enabled management to demonstrate that positioning barriers at the front of the terrace is unnecessary.

The barrier line BB has five barriers symmetrically positioned on the terrace; each barrier is 4m in length and the barriers are 3m apart.

All barriers have been designed for 5kN/m. The total barrier length is 41m.

Step 1: available viewing area

The available viewing area is the plan area of the terrace and is therefore

36 x 8 = 288m².

Step 2: appropriate density

Where the distance between the rows of barriers does not conflict with Table 11.2 the appropriate density for a race course terrace may be derived from the ratio of the barrier provision in place as compared with the total length of barrier provision that would be necessary if the terrace was required to accommodate the maximum permitted density of 47.

A continuous barrier system is a requirement if ground management wish to have a spectator density of 47 persons per 10m² on the terrace. In this instance two rows of barriers having a design loading of 5kN/m with radial gangways 24m apart would be required. The continuous barrier system would possess a total length of 60m.

The layout of viewing terraces at racecourses is required to meet the dual needs of providing safe viewing accommodation during the event and also allow quick egress at the end of the race and similarly quick ingress before the start

of the next race. It is for this reason that many racecourses favour a staggered barrier layout.

The applicable density for the terrace derives from the ratio of the barrier provision on the terrace compared to the provision that would allow for 47 persons per 10m². The applicable density is therefore

$$\frac{41}{60} \times 47 = 32 \text{ persons per } 10\text{m}^2.$$

If the distance between rows exceeds the maximum in Table 11.2 the maximum permitted density would have to be reduced from 47. For example if the distance between barrier line AA and barrier line BB was 4.4m as opposed to the maximum 3.4m given in Table 11.2 the maximum density for the area between those barriers would be

$$\frac{3.4}{4.4} \times 47 = 36 \text{ persons per } 10\text{m}^2.$$

Step 2: appropriate density (cont.)

and the applicable density for the area between barrier line AA and barrier line BB would be

$\dfrac{21}{30}$ x 36 = 25 persons per 10m².

Physical condition

The terrace's physical condition is of a high standard. There are no sightline problems.

Therefore (P) is assessed as 1.0.

Safety management

The racecourse's safety management is of a high standard and there are no problems with crowd dispersal or behaviour. The stewarding arrangements in place ensure that the terrace does not become overcrowded and therefore (S) is assessed as 1.0.

The appropriate density for the terrace is therefore 32 persons per 10m².

Step 3: holding capacity

The available viewing area is 288m².

The appropriate density is 32 per 10m².

The holding capacity is therefore

$\dfrac{288}{10}$ x 32 = **922.**

Step 4: entry capacity

The area behind the foremost barriers (line AA) allows for 691 persons.

The foremost barrier spacing provides an access width of 15m. The entry capacity of this element is therefore not an issue.

Step 5: exit capacity

Data obtained from observations of spectator movements on the racecourse indicates that the appropriate rate of egress of racecourse spectators from stairs or steppings (terraces) to be 45 persons/m/minute. The aforementioned

barrier spacing enables the terrace to clear in approximately one minute should spectators choose to do so and the exit capacity is therefore not an issue.

Step 6: terrace capacity

The **capacity of the terrace** derives from the holding capacity and is therefore 922 persons.

Capacity of the lawn

The turfed lawn of the Tattersall enclosure

measures 75m wide by 40m deep. The gradient of the slope is constant and does not exceed 5°.

Step 7: Viewing area of the lawn

The area of the lawn is 3000m².

The bookmakers pitches occupy 300m².

The viewing area is therefore

3000 – 300 = 2700m².

Step 8: Appropriate density

Spectators will congregate more densely along the rails at trackside. An increase in population density at trackside in comparison with that adopted elsewhere on the lawn is recognised in the capacity calculation.

The density adopted on the lawn needs to allow for good circulation and importantly not impede rapid response of medical personnel should they be called upon at anytime during a meeting. The provision of video screens encourages a uniform distribution in the spectator body which includes small children and disabled persons using mobility vehicles.

A trackside density of 40 persons per 10m² is considered appropriate.

Elsewhere on the lawn a density of 20 persons per 10m² has been agreed with the certifying authority as appropriate in this instance.

The racecourse's safety management is of a high standard and there are no problems with crowd dispersal or behaviour. The stewarding arrangements in place ensure that the terrace does not become overcrowded and therefore the (S) factor has been assessed as 1.0.

Step 9: Capacity of the lawn

There is a 75m run of rail and assuming that three rows deep create a standing depth of 1.111m this represents an area of 83m².

The remaining viewing area of the lawn is 2700 – 83 = 2617m².

Adopting a track side density of 40 persons per 10m² and 20 persons per 10m² elsewhere means that the capacity of the lawn is

$$\frac{(2617 \times 20) + (83 \times 40)}{10} = \textbf{5566 persons.}$$

Step 10: Capacity of the viewing accommodation of Tattersall's enclosure

The capacity of the viewing accommodation is given by combining the capacity of the covered terrace and the lawn.

Capacity of Tattersall's enclosure
= 922 + 5566 = **6488 persons.**

Step 11: Exit capacity from the viewing accommodation

There are two wide thoroughfares on either side of the covered terrace. Each could provide a clearway of 12m.

In the event of an emergency there are stewarded gates in the track barriers that allow the spectator body to evacuate the Tattersall enclosure by crossing the race track. The extent of the clearways on either side of the terrace will therefore be dictated by the proportion of the spectator body that moves backwards and forwards during consecutive races.

Experience indicates that 30% of the spectator body within the Tattersall enclosure seek to move between the viewing accommodation of the enclosure and the area to the rear of the enclosure and vice versa between consecutive races. It is considered that a total of 10 minutes is considered a reasonable interval to accommodate these movements. A rate of passage of 60 persons/metre width/minute has been observed. The clearway width that needs to be actively maintained is therefore

$$\frac{0.3 \times 6488}{5 \times 60} = 6.5m$$

Members' enclosure

The calculation of the capacity of the Members' enclosure would proceed in a similar manner to that adopted for the Tattersalls enclosure.

The capacity of any seated accommodation is straightforward but a greater proportion of those seated would be expected to move from their seats between consecutive races.

It is important to note that in the calculations for Tattersall enclosure rates of passage **lower** than the maximum have been adopted for spectator movements on both level routes and stairways. The same rates of passage would be applicable in like elements of the Members' enclosure.

Family enclosure

There are limited facilities in this enclosure which has no terracing or seated accommodation. The lawns are considered as a picnic area and a spectator density of 10 person per 10m² would be considered appropriate.

Annex B: Glossary

Barrier	Any element of a sports ground, permanent or temporary, intended to prevent people from falling, and to retain, stop or guide people. Types of barriers used at sports grounds are further defined in Section 11.1.
Circulation	Free movement of spectators within a sports ground.
Combustible	Able to burn.
Competent	A person shall be regarded as occupationally competent where he or she has sufficient training and experience to meet the national occupational standards relevant to the tasks within their identified role. This includes knowing the limits of personal knowledge, skills and experience.
Concourse	A circulation area providing direct access to and from spectator accommodation, via stairways, ramps, vomitories, or level passageways, and serving as a milling area for spectators for the purposes of refreshment and entertainment. It may also provide direct access to toilet facilities.
Contingency plan	A contingency plan is prepared by the ground management setting out the action to be taken in response to incidents occurring at the venue which might prejudice public safety or disrupt normal operations (for example, the loss of power to CCTV or PA systems).
Control point	A designated room or area within the sports ground from which the safety management structure is controlled and operated. Also known as an 'event control' 'match control', or 'stadium control' room.
Crowd doctor	A qualified medical practitioner, registered with the General Medical Council, who has received training in pre-hospital (emergency) care and major incident management or has equivalent relevant experience.
Crush barrier	A barrier which protects spectators from crushing, positioned in areas of standing accommodation.
Datum	The finished level of the floor, seat row, terrace, ramp, landing, pitch line of stairs, or, in the case of barriers behind seats, the seat level.
Emergency plan	An emergency plan is prepared and owned by the emergency services for dealing with a major incident at the venue or in the vicinity (for example, an explosion, toxic release or large fire). Also known as an emergency procedure plan, or major incident plan.
Exit	A stairway, gangway, passageway, ramp, gateway, door, and all other means of passage used to leave the sports ground and its accommodation.

Exit system	A set of different types of exits, linked to form a means of passage of spectators.
Fire resistance	Ability of a component of a building to resist fire for a stated period of time, when subjected to an appropriate test in accordance with the current relevant British Standard.
First aider	A person who holds the standard certificate of first aid issued to people working as first aiders under the Health and Safety (First Aid) Regulations 1981.
Flammable	Able to burn with a flame.
Guard	See Barrier.
Handrail	A rail normally grasped by hand for guidance or support.
Horizontal imposed load	The load assumed to be produced by the intended use (usually of a barrier).
Key point telephone system	An independent emergency telephone system located at strategic points around the sports ground.
Landing	A level surface at the head, foot, or between flights of stairways, or ramps.
Lateral gangway	Channel for the passage of spectators through viewing accommodation running parallel with terrace steps or seat rows.
Local authority	As defined by the Safety of Sports Grounds Act 1975.
Occupationally competent	See Competent.
Operations manual	A manual which sets out the way a sports ground operates on a daily basis. It should include but not be limited to the stewarding plan, medical plan, planned preventative maintenance schedule, fire risk assessment, event day procedures, contingency plans, capacity calculations, site plans and details of safety equipment.
(P) factor	The term used for the assessment of the physical condition of an area of viewing accommodation.
Paramedic	Is a person who holds a current state registration by the Health Professional Council (HPC).
Pitch perimeter barrier	A barrier which separates spectators from the pitch or area of activity.
Pitch perimeter fence	A barrier higher than 1.1m, which separates spectators from the playing area or area of activity.
Place of reasonable safety	A place within a building or structure where, for a limited period of time, people will have some protection from the effects of fire and smoke. This place, usually a corridor or stairway, will normally have a minimum of 30 minutes fire resistance and allow people to continue their escape to a place of safety.
Place of safety	A place, away from the building, in which people are at no immediate danger from the effects of fire.

Radial gangway	Channel for the passage of spectators through viewing accommodation, running with the slope between terrace steps or seat rows. For the purposes of design and assessment, the criteria applying to radial gangways may be different from those pertaining to stairways.
Ramp	An inclined surface linking two areas at different elevations.
Rate of passage	The number of persons per metre width per minute passing through an element of an exit system.
Refuge	A place of reasonable safety in which a disabled person and others who may need assistance may rest or wait for assistance before reaching a place of safety. It should lead directly to a fire-resisting escape route.
Risk assessment	See Section 3.3.e.
Robustness	The capability of a structure to withstand some misuse and to tolerate accidental damage without catastrophic consequences.
(S) factor	The term used for the assessment of the safety management of an area of viewing accommodation.
Safety certificate	A certificate, issued by the local authority under either the Safety of Sports Grounds Act 1975 or the Fire Safety and safety of Places of Sport Act 1987, which contains such terms and conditions as the local authority considers necessary or expedient to secure reasonable safety at the sports ground when it is in use for the specified activity or activities.
Side gangway	Channel for the forward passage of spectators between an end row of seats and a protective barrier at the edge of a structure.
Sightline	The ability of a spectator to see a predetermined point of focus (such as the nearest touchline or outside lane of a running track) over the top of the head of the spectators sitting immediately in front.
Spectator accommodation	The area of a ground or structure in the ground provided for the use of spectators, including all circulation areas, concourses and the viewing accommodation.
Spectator gallery	A gallery, usually attached to a hospitality area, from which spectators can view the event.
Sports ground	Any place where sports or other competitive activities take place in the open air and where accommodation has been provided for spectators, consisting of artificial structures or of natural structures artificially modified for the purpose.
Stadium	A sports ground where a spectator will normally watch the event from a single point, for example at football and rugby matches, in contrast to those where spectators are likely to be ambulatory, such as at horse racing and golf.
Stairway	That part of a structure which is not a radial gangway but which comprises of at least one flight of steps, including the landings at the head and foot of steps and any landing in between flights.
Stand	A structure providing viewing accommodation for spectators.

Temporary demountable structure	Any structure erected on a temporary basis at a sports ground, including stands, standing terraces, hospitality areas and media installations.
Terrace	An area of steps providing standing accommodation for spectators.
Viewing slope	A non-stepped, sloping area providing standing accommodation for spectators.
Viewing standard	The quality of view available to spectators, consisting of three elements: the sightlines, the presence of any restrictions to viewing, and the distance between the spectator and the pitch or area of activity.
Vomitory	An access route built into the gradient of a stand which directly links spectator accommodation to concourses, and/or routes for ingress, egress or emergency evacuation.

Annex C: Bibliography and further references

1.1 **Safety of Sports Grounds Act 1975**

Fire Safety and the Safety of Places of Sport Act 1987

Health and Safety at Work etc. Act 1974

All available from: The Stationery Office (TSO)
PO Box 29, St Crispins, Duke Street, Norwich NR3 1GN
Tel: 0870 600 5522 Fax: 0870 600 5533
email: book.orders@tso.co.uk
online ordering: www.tso.co.uk/bookshop
Available online at: www.opsi.gov.uk

Safety Certification
Football Licensing Authority, 2001
Available from: FLA, 27 Harcourt House, 19 Cavendish Square, London W1G 0PL
Tel 020 7491 7191
email: fla@flaweb.org.uk   www.flaweb.org.uk

Sports Grounds Safety Certification in Scotland
Scottish Executive
web site: www.scotland.gov.uk/Topics/Sport/SafetyIssues

1.2 **Safety of Sports Grounds Act 1975**
op.cit. Section 1.1

1.3 **Safety of Sports Grounds Act 1975**
op.cit. Section 1.1

3.3 **Safety Certification**
op.cit. Section 1.1

Civil Contingencies Act 2004
Available from: TSO, op.cit. Section 1.1

Five Steps to Risk Assessment
Health and Safety Executive IND(G)163, 2006
Available from HSE Books, PO Box 1999, Sudbury, Suffolk CO10 2WA
Tel: 01787 881165   www.hsebooks.com

Fire Safety Risk Assessment – Large Places of Assembly
Department for Communities and Local Government ISBN: 978-1-85112-821-1, 2006
Available from: Department for Communities and Local Government (DCLG) Publications,
PO Box 236, Wetherby LS23 7NB.
Tel: 0870 1226 236
email: communities@twoten.com
www.firesafetyguides.communities.gov.uk

Practical Fire Safety Guidance for Places of Entertainment and Assembly
Scottish Executive ISBN:978-0-7559-7029-2, 2007
Available from: Scottish Executive
St Andrew's House, Edinburgh, EH1 3DG
email: FireScotlandAct@scotland.gsi.gov.uk
Available online from: www.infoscotland.com/firelaw

3.5   **Essentials of Health and Safety at Work**
Health and Safety Executive ISBN: 9780717661794, 2006

Health and Safety Regulation
Health and Safety Executive HSC 13, 2003

Management of Health and Safety at Work
Health and Safety Executive ISBN: 0717624889, 2000

Successful Health and Safety Management
Health and Safety Executive ISBN: 0717612767, 1997
All available from: HSE Books, op.cit. Section 3.3

3.6   **Regulatory Reform (Fire Safety) Order 2005**
The Fire (Scotland) Act 2005
The Fire Safety (Scotland) Regulations 2006
All available from: TSO, op.cit. Section 1.1

Fire Safety Risk Assessment – Large Places of Assembly
op.cit. Section 3.3

Practical Fire Safety Guidance for Places of Entertainment and Assembly
op.cit. Section 3.3

3.7   **Disability Discrimination Act 2005**
Available from: TSO, op.cit. Section 1.1

3.9   **Guidance Notes for Drawing up a Statement of Safety Policy for Spectators at Football Grounds**
Football Licensing Authority, 1995
Available from: FLA, op.cit. Section 1.1

An introduction to health and safety
Health and Safety Executive IND(G)259, 2003
Available from: HSE Books, op.cit Section 3.3

3.17   **Contingency Planning**
Football Licensing Authority, 2002
Available from: FLA, op. cit. Section 1.1

3.19   **Counter Terrorism Protective Security Advice for Stadia and Arenas –**
National Counter Terrorism Security Office (NaCTSO)
Download from: www.mi5.gov.uk
Email: nsacenquiries@nsac.gsi.gov.uk

3.31   **Sporting Events Control of Alcohol Act 1985**
Criminal Law (Consolidation) (Scotland) Act 1995
Licensing Act 2003
All available from: TSO, op.cit. Section 1.1

4.4   **Private Security Industry Act 2001**
        Violent Crime Reduction Act 2006
        Both available from: TSO, op.cit. Section 1.1

        Get Licensed
        Security Industry Authority, 2007

        Security at Events
        Security Industry Authority, 2007
        Both available from: Security Industry Authority, PO Box 1293, Liverpool L69 1AX
        Tel: 0844 892 1025   Web site: www.the-sia.org.uk

5.4   **The Construction (Design and Management) Regulations 2007**
        Available from: TSO, op. cit. Section 1.1

5.5   **Dynamic Performance Requirements for Permanent Grandstands Subject to**
        Crowd Action
        Institution of Structural Engineers, 2001

        Dynamic Testing of Grandstands and Seating Decks
        Institution of Structural Engineers, 2002

        Temporary Demountable Structures – Guidance on Procurement, Design and Use
        Institution of Structural Engineers, 2007

        Dynamic performance requirements for permanent grandstands subject to crowd
        action – Recommendations for management, design and assessment.
        Institution of Structural Engineers (*Available shortly*)
        All available from: ISE, 11 Upper Belgrave Street, London SW1X 8BH
        Tel: 020 7235 4535   www.istructe.org

5.6   **Safety of Sports Grounds No 6 – Guide to Safety at Sports Grounds During**
        Construction
        London District Surveyors Association, 1999
        Available from: LDSA Publications: PO Box 266
        Bromley, Kent BR2 9ZN
        Tel: 07834 814721
        Email: ldsapublications@ntlworld.com
        www.londonbuildingcontrol.org.uk

5.14   **Appraisal of Existing Structures**
        Institution of Structural Engineers, new edition in preparation
        Available from: ISE, op. cit. Section 5.5

6.1   **Sports Grounds and Stadia Guide No. 1 – *Accessible Stadia***
        Football Stadia Improvement Fund and Football Licensing Authority
        ISBN: 0954629302, 2003
        Available from: FLA, op. cit. Section 1.1

        Fire Safety Risk Assessment – Means of Escape for Disabled People
        (Supplementary Guide)
        Department for Communities and Local Government ISBN: 978 1 85112 873 7, 2007
        Available from: DCLG Publications, op.cit. Section 3.3

6.3 **Sports Grounds and Stadia Guide No. 3 –** *Concourses*
Football Licensing Authority 2006 ISBN: 0954629310
Available from: FLA, op.cit. Section 1.1

6.5 **Safer surfaces to walk on – reducing the risk of slipping (C652)**
Construction Industry Research Information Association C652 ISBN: 0 86017 652 5, 2006
Available from: CIRIA, Classic House, 174-180 Old Street, London EC1V 9BP
Tel: 0207 549 3300
Email:enquiries@ciria.org   www.ciriabooks.com

8.1 **Vertical circulation**
For further design considerations refer to:
Building Regulation Approved Document M Access to and Use of Buildings
Department for Communities and Local Government ISBN: 978 1 85946 211 9, 2006
Available from: www.planningportal.gov.uk/approveddocuments

BS 8300: 2001 Design of buildings and their approaches to meet the needs of disabled people – Code of Practice
Available from: BSI, 389 Chiswick High Road, London W4 4AL
Tel: 020 8996 9001
Available online at: www.bsi-global.co.uk

Sports Grounds and Stadia Guide No.1 – *Accessible Stadia*
op.cit. Section 6.1

8.3 op.cit. Section 6.5

8.11 op.cit. Section 6.5

8.12 **Passenger lifts**
For further design considerations refer to guidance documents listed under Section 8.1 above

9.1 op.cit. Section 6.3

9.7 op.cit. Section 6.5

10.6 **BS EN 13200-1:2003: Spectator facilities – Part 1: Layout criteria for spectator viewing area – Specification**
Available from: BSI, op.cit. Section 8.1

10.12 **BS EN 5588-8:1999: Fire precautions in the design, construction and use of buildings – Part 8: Code of practice for means of escape for disabled people**
Available from: BSI, op.cit. Section 8.1

Sports Grounds and Stadia Guide No. 1 – *Accessible Stadia*
op.cit. Section 6.1

Fire Safety Risk Assessment Supplementary Guide – Means of Escape for Disabled People
op.cit. Section 6.1

11.1 **BS EN 13200-3:2005: Spectator facilities – Part 3: Separating elements – Requirements**
Available from: BSI, op.cit. Section 8.1

11.18   **Stadia crash barriers alert**
Standing Committee on Structural Safety (SCOSS), February 2001
Available from: SCOSS, 11 Upper Belgrave Street, London SW1X 8BH
Tel: 0207 235 4535
Email: scoss@istructe.org.uk   www.scoss.org.uk

12.1   **BS EN 13200-1:2003: Spectator facilities – Part 1: Layout criteria for spectator viewing area – Specification**
op. cit. Section 10.6

Sports Grounds and Stadia Guide No. 1 – *Accessible Stadia*
op. cit. Section 6.1

12.3   op.cit. Section 10.6

12.4   op. cit. Section 6.1

12.8   op.cit. Section 6.5

12.13   op.cit. Section 10.6

12.17   **BS EN 13200:2006-4: Spectator facilities – Part 4: Seats – Product characteristics**
Available from: BSI, op.cit. Section 8.1

12.20   **Standing in Seated Areas at Football Grounds**
op.cit Section 1.1

Stadia: A Design and Development Guide
ISBN: 0750645342

BS EN 13200-1:2003: Spectator facilities – Part 1: Layout criteria for spectator viewing area – Specification
op.cit. Section 10.6

13.8   op.cit. Section 6.5

13.11   op.cit. Section 10.6

13.22   op.cit. Section 6.1

14.2   **Temporary Demountable Structures – Guidance on Procurement, Design and Use**
op.cit. Section 5.5

BS EN 13200-6:2006: Spectator facilities – Part 6: Demountable (temporary) stands
Available from: BSI, op.cit. Section 8.1

14.7   **BS EN 13200-5:2006: Spectator facilities – Part 5: Telescopic stands**
Available from: BSI, op.cit. Section 8.1

15.1   **Regulatory Reform (Fire Safety) Order 2005**
op.cit. Section 3.6

The Fire (Scotland) Act 2005
op.cit. Section 3.6

The Fire Safety (Scotland) Regulations 2006
op.cit. Section 3.6

Fire Safety Risk Assessment – Large Places of Assembly
op.cit. Section 3.3

Practical Fire Safety Guidance for Places of Entertainment and Assembly
op.cit. Section 3.3

15.10   **Safety of Sports Grounds No 3 – Guide to Control over Concessionaire Facilities and Other Services at Sports Grounds**
London District Surveyors Association, 1996
Available from: LDSA Publications, op.cit. Section 5.6

The keeping and use of LPG in vehicles: mobile catering units
Health and Safety Executive / Local Authorities Enforcement Liaison Committee (HELA)
Available from: HSE Books, op.cit. Section 3.3

15.17   **Emergency evacuation of spectators with disabilities**
For further design considerations refer to guidance documents listed under Sections 8.1 and 10.12 above

16.8   **Sports Grounds and Stadia Guide No.2 – *Control Rooms***
Football Licensing Authority ISBN: 0954629329, 2005
Available from: FLA, op.cit. Section 1.1

16.11   **Licensed frequencies**
For further advice contact the Office of Communication
Ofcom Licensing Centre: Tel: 020 7981 3131 or 0300 123 1000 or visit the licensing area on the website: www.ofcom.org.uk

16.16   **Guidance Notes for the Procurement of CCTV for Public Safety at Football Grounds**
Home Office Police Scientific Development Branch publication No. 9/01

Digital Imaging Procedure
Home Office Police Scientific Development Branch publication No. 58/07

Both available from: Home Office Police Scientific Development Branch
Langhurst House, Langhurstwood Road, Horsham, West Sussex, RH12 4WX
Downloadable from www.scienceandresearch.homeoffice.gov.uk/hosdb/publications

16.19   op.cit. Section 16.16

16.28   **Health and Safety at Work etc. Act 1974**
op.cit. Section 1.1

Health and Safety (Safety Signs and Signals) Regulations 1996
Available from: TSO, op.cit. Section 1.1

Signpost to The Health and Safety (Safety Signs and Signals) Regulations 1996
Health and Safety Executive IND(G) 184, 1996
Available from: HSE Books, op.cit. Section 3.3

16.29   op.cit. Section 6.1

17.1   **Safety of Sports Grounds No 4 – Guide to Electrical and Mechanical Services in Sports Grounds**
London District Surveyors Association, 1996
Available from: LDSA Publications, op.cit. Section 5.6

17.6   **Guidance Note 3 to BS 7671 (IEE Wiring Regulations): Inspection and Testing**
Institution of Electrical Engineers (IEE) ISBN: 0852969910, 2002
Available from: Institution of Engineering and Technology (IET)
Michael Faraday House, Six Hills Way, Stevenage SG1 2AY
Tel: 01438 313311

17.10 **Code for Lighting**
Chartered Institute of Building Services Engineers ISBN: 0750656379
Available from: CIBSE, Delta House, 222 Balham High Road, London SW12 9BS
Tel 020 8675 5211   Web site: www.cibse.org

17.13 op.cit. Section 17.10

17.14 **Lifting Operations and Lifting Regulations 1998**
Available from: TSO, op.cit. Section 1.1

17.15 **The Gas Safety (Installation and Use) Regulations 1994**
The Pipework Safety Regulations 1996
Both available from: TSO, op.cit. Section 1.1

18.5 **Safety of Sports Grounds No 1 – Specimen General Safety Certificate and Guidance Notes**
London District Surveyors' Association, 2004
Available from: LDSA Publications, op.cit. Section 5.6

18.13 **NHS Emergency Planning Guidance**
Department of Health, 2005
www.dh.gov.uk/en/Policyandguidance/emergencyplanning/index.htm

19.1 **Safety in broadcasting sports events**
Health and Safety Executive ETIS 1, 1996
Available from: HSE Books, op.cit. Section 3.3

19.3 op.cit. Section 5.5

20.1 **The Event Safety Guide**
Health and Safety Executive ISBN: 0 7176 2453 6, 1999
Available from: HSE Books, op.cit. Section 3.3

20.3 op.cit. Section 5.5

Annex D: Summary of new guidance

This section briefly summarises or highlights some of the key areas in which this fifth edition of the *Guide* differs from the previous edition. The list is not comprehensive and in all cases reference should be made to the full text of the *Guide*.

General issues

Greater emphasis is given to the responsibility of management to undertake its own risk assessments.

The safety of spectators with disabilities should not be considered in isolation. Therefore the material from the chapter "Spectator accommodation – disabilities" in the previous edition has been integrated into the relevant subject chapters.

Chapter 1. How to use this *Guide*

New chapter: emphasises how to use and apply the *Guide* (replaces the Introduction from the previous edition).

Chapter 2. Calculating the safe capacity of a sports ground

(P) and (S) factors: risk assessments must be undertaken by management and taken into account when assessing the (P) and (S) factors. These should be reassessed annually or where there is a significant change to the structure, event or personnel.

New guidance: determining the expected occupation levels of all areas including open land to which the public have access, for instance at horse racing and golf events.

Chapter 3. Management – responsibility and planning for safety

Risk assessments: required for all events including ancillary activities. .

New guidance: on safety officer appointment, training and deputising, on steward numbers, on counter-terrorism and on pre-event activities.

Chapter 4. Management – stewarding

Standards and training: new guidance is provided on the training and qualifications of stewards.

Security personnel and contract or agency stewards: new sections have been included.

Chapter 5. Management – structures, installations and components

Structural appraisal: new guidance on methods to be used.

Chapter 6. Circulation – general

Spectators with disabilities: acknowledgement of the dispersal of disabled spectators throughout a sports ground including upper levels.

Chapter 7. Circulation – Ingress

Admission policies: new guidance on the impact of electronic entry card systems.

Chapter 8. Circulation – stairways and ramps

Stair risers, height and number: for new construction, a maximum number of risers of 12 and a maximum riser height of 170mm to accord with Building Regulations.

Passenger lifts and escalators: new guidance

Chapter 9. Circulation – concourses and vomitories

Concourses: new guidance on capacities and the prevention of overcrowding.

Chapter 10. Circulation – egress and emergency evacuation

Rate of passage: new recommendations to accord with the British Standard.

Management of evacuation of spectators with disabilities: new guidance to reflect the inclusive nature of new sports grounds.

Chapter 11. Barriers

Barrier loadings: a new recommendation for escalators.

Barrier heights: clarification that reduced barrier heights in front of fixed seating are for seated spectators only.

Temporary barriers: temporary barriers should be of the same height and strength as any permanent barrier in a similar position.

Barrier test regime: the risk assessment should determine the period at which all barriers are tested.

Chapter 12. Spectator accommodation – seating

Provision of seated accommodation: now includes accessible viewing areas for spectators with all kinds of disabilities.

Seating row depth: for new construction, recommended new minimum of 800mm.

Standing in seated areas: advice on how to respond to safety issues.

Chapter 13. Spectator accommodation – standing

Crush barriers: confirmation that, to achieve the highest permitted capacity levels for a standing area, a continuous crush barrier must be provided.

Level standing accommodation: advice on level standing areas and differing sightline requirements, for example at horse racing or concerts.

Standing accommodation and disabled spectators: advice that standing areas should be accessible to all spectators.

Chapter 14. Spectator accommodation – temporary demountable structures

References: to newly published guidance and standards on demountable and telescopic stands.

Chapter 15. Fire safety

Fire risk assessment: mandatory requirement under new fire legislation.

Places of safety: definition of places of safety and places of reasonable safety aligned with new legislation.

New guidance: on emergency evacuation of spectators with disabilities and staff awareness and training.

Chapter 16. Communications

Control points: guidance on a secondary control point.

Chapter 17. Electrical and mechanical services

Planned preventative maintenance schedule: may be relevant when assessing the (S) factor.

Chapter 18. Medical and first aid provision for spectators

New guidance: on risk assessment and medical plan, equipment and storage, provision of competent medical services personnel, ambulance provision, numbers of first aiders.

Chapter 19. Media provision

Risk assessments: must be supplied by media companies to management and management should ensure that all media provision is included within a site specific risk assessment.

Chapter 20. Alternative events at sports grounds

New emphasis: as part of the planning process for an alternative event, the capacity of the sports ground will need to be reassessed taking account of all of the chapters within the *Guide*.

Index